ISBN 978-1-5283-7897-0
PIBN 10121785

THE

WORKS

OF

WILLIAM E. CHANNING, D. D.

SIXTH COMPLETE EDITION,

WITH

AN INTRODUCTION.

VOL. II.

BOSTON:

JAMES MUNROE AND COMPANY.

1846.

mg 19343

CONTENTS OF VOL. II.

SLAVERY.

1*

SLAVERY.

INTRODUCTION.

THE first question to be proposed by a rational being is, not what is profitable, but what is Right. Duty must be primary, prominent, most conspicuous among the objects of human thought and pursuit. If we cast it down from its supremacy, if we inquire first for our interests, and then for our duties, we shall certainly err. We can never see the right clearly and fully, but by making it our first concern. No judgment can be just or wise, but that which is built on the conviction of the paramount worth and importance of duty. This is the fundamental truth, the supreme law of reason; and the mind which does not start from this, in its inquiries into human affairs, is doomed to great, perhaps fatal error.

The right is the supreme good, and includes all other goods. In seeking and adhering to it, we secure our true and only happiness. All prosperity, not founded on it, is built on sand. If human affairs are controlled, as we believe, by Almighty Rectitude and Impartial Goodness, then to hope for happiness from wrong-doing

is as insane as to seek health and prosperity by rebell-
ing against the laws of nature, by sowing our seed on
the ocean, or making poison our common food. There
is but one unfailing good; and that is, fidelity to the
Everlasting Law written on the heart, and re-written
and republished in God's Word.

Whoever places this faith in the everlasting law of
rectitude must, of course, regard the question of slavery
first and chiefly as a moral question. All other considerations will weigh little with him, compared with its
moral character and moral influences. The following
remarks, therefore, are designed to aid the reader in
forming a just moral judgment of slavery. Great truths,
inalienable rights, everlasting duties, these will form the
chief subjects of this discussion. There are times when
the assertion of great·principles is the best service a
man can render society. The present is a moment of
bewildering excitement, when men's minds are stormed
and darkened by strong passions and fierce conflicts;
and also a moment of absorbing worldliness, when the
moral law is made to bow to expediency, and its high
and strict requirements are denied, or dismissed as metaphysical abstractions or impracticable theories. At such
a season, to utter great principles without passion, and
in the spirit of unfeigned and universal good-will, and
to engrave them deeply and durably on men's minds, is
to do more for the world, than to open mines of wealth,
or to frame the most successful schemes of policy.

Of late our country has been convulsed by the question of slavery; and the people, in proportion as they
have felt vehemently, have thought superficially, or hardly thought at all; and we see the results in a singular
want of well-defined principles, in a strange vagueness

and inconsistency of opinion, and in the proneness to excess which belongs to unsettled minds. The multitude have been called, now to contemplate the horrors of slavery, and now to shudder at the ruin and bloodshed which must follow emancipation. The word Massacre has resounded through the land, striking terror into strong as well as tender hearts, and awakening indignation against whatever may seem to threaten such a consummation. The consequence is, that not a few dread all discussion of the subject, and, if not reconciled to the continuance of slavery, at least believe that they have no duty to perform, no testimony to bear, no influence to exert, no sentiments to cherish and spread, in relation to this evil. What is still worse, opinions either favoring or extenuating it are heard with little or no disapprobation. Concessions are made to it, which would once have shocked the community ; whilst to assail it is pronounced unwise and perilous. No stronger reason for a calm exposition of its true character can be given, than this very state of the public mind. A community can suffer no greater calamity than the loss of its principles. Lofty and pure sentiment is the life and hope of a people. There was never such an obligation to discuss slavery as at this moment, when recent events have done much to unsettle and obscure men's minds in regard to it. This result is to be ascribed in part to the injudicious vehemence of those who have taken into their hands the cause of the slave. Such ought to remember, that to espouse a good cause is not enough. We must maintain it in a spirit answering to its dignity. Let no man touch the great interests of humanity, who does not strive to sanctify himself for the work by cleansing his heart of all wrath and uncharitableness, who cannot hope that he is in a measure baptized into the spirit of universal love. Even sympathy with the injured and oppressed may do harm, by being partial, exclusive, and bitterly indignant. How far the declension of the spirit of freedom is to be ascribed to the cause now suggested, I do not say. The effect is plain, and whoever sees and laments the evil should strive to arrest it.

Slavery ought to be discussed. We ought to think, feel, speak, and write about it. But whatever we do in regard to it should be done with a deep feeling of responsibility, and so done as not to put in jeopardy the peace of the Slave-holding States. On this point public opinion has not been and cannot be too strongly pronounced. Slavery, indeed, from its very nature, must be a ground of alarm wherever it exists. Slavery and security can by no device be joined together. But we may not, must not, by rashness and passion increase the peril. To instigate the slave to insurrection is a crime, for which no rebuke and no punishment can be too severe. This would be to involve slave and master in common ruin. It is not enough to say, that the Constitution is violated by any action endangering the slave-holding portion of our country. A higher law than the Constitution forbids this unholy interference. Were our national union dissolved, we ought to reprobate, as sternly as we now do, the slightest manifestation of a disposition to stir up a servile war. Still more, were the Free and the Slave-holding States not only separated, but engaged in the fiercest hostilities, the former would deserve the abhorrence of the world and the indignation of Heaven, were they to resort to insurrection and massacre as means of victory. Better were it for us to bare our own breasts to the knife of the slave, than to arm him with it against his master.

It is not by personal, direct action on the mind of the slave that we can do him good. Our concern is with the free. With the free we are to plead his cause. And this is peculiarly our duty, because we have bound ourselves to resist his own efforts for his emancipation. We suffer him to do nothing for himself. The more, then, should be done for him. Our physical power is pledged against him in case of revolt. Then our moral power should be exerted for his relief. His weakness, which we increase, gives him a claim to the only aid we can afford, to our moral sympathy, to the free and faithful exposition of his wrongs. As men, as Christians, as citizens, we have duties to the slave, as well as to every other member of the community. On this point we have no liberty. The eternal law binds us to take the side of the injured; and this law is peculiarly obligatory when we forbid him to lift an arm in his own defence.

Let it not be said we can do nothing for the slave. We can do much. We have a power mightier than armies, the power of truth, of principle, of virtue, of right, of religion, of love. We have a power, which is growing with every advance of civilization, before which the slave-trade has fallen, which is mitigating the sternest despotisms, which is spreading education through all ranks of society, which is bearing Christianity to the ends of the earth, which carries in itself the pledge of destruction to every institution which debases humanity. Who can measure the power of Christian philanthropy, of enlightened goodness, pouring itself forth in prayers and persuasions, from the press and

pulpit, from the lips and hearts of devoted men, and
more and more binding together the wise and good in
the cause of their race? All other powers may fail.
This must triumph. It is leagued with God's omnipotence. It is God himself acting in the hearts of his
children. It has an ally in every conscience, in every
human breast, in the wrong-doer himself. This spirit
has but begun its work on earth. It is breathing itself
more and more through literature, education, institutions, and opinion. Slavery cannot stand before it.
Great moral principles, pure and generous sentiments,
cannot be confined to this or that spot. They cannot
be shut out by territorial lines, or local legislation.
They are divine inspirations, and partake of the omni-
presence of their Author. The deliberate, solemn conviction of good men through the world, that slavery is
a grievous wrong to human nature, will make itself felt.
To increase this moral power is every man's duty. To
embody and express this great truth is in every man's
power ; and thus every man can do something to break
the chain of the slave.

There are not a few persons, who, from vulgar modes
of thinking, cannot be interested in this subject. Because the slave is a degraded being, they think slavery
a low topic, and wonder how it can excite the attention
and sympathy of those who can discuss or feel for any
thing else. Now the truth is, that slavery, regarded
only in a philosophical light, is a theme worthy of the
highest minds. It involves the gravest questions about
human nature and society. It carries us into the problems which have exercised for ages the highest understandings. It calls us to inquire into the foundation,
nature, and extent of human rights, into the distinction

between a person and a thing, into the true relations of man to man, into the obligations of the community to each of its members, into the ground and laws of property, and, above all, into the true dignity and indestructible claims of a moral being. I venture to say, there is no subject, now agitated by the community, which can compare in philosophical dignity with slavery; and yet to multitudes the question falls under the same contempt with the slave himself. To many, a writer seems to lower himself who touches it. The falsely refined, who want intellectual force to grasp it, pronounce it unworthy of their notice.

But this subject has more than philosophical dignity. It has an important bearing on character. Our interest in it is one test by which our comprehension of the distinctive spirit of Christianity must be judged. Christianity is the manifestation and inculcation of Universal Love. The great teaching of Christianity is, that we must recognise and respect human nature in all its forms in the poorest, most ignorant, most fallen. We must look beneath " the flesh," to " the spirit." The spiritual principle in man is what entitles him to our brotherly regard. To be just to 'this is the great injunction of our religion. To overlook this, on account of condition or color, is to violate the great Christian law. We have reason to think that it is one design of God, in appointing the vast diversities of human condition, to put to the test, and to bring out most distinctly, the principle of spiritual love. It is wisely ordered, that human nature is not set before us in a few forms of beauty, magnificence, and outward glory. To be dazzled and attracted by these would be no sign of reverence for what is interior and spiritual in human nature. To lead us to discern and love this, we are brought into connection with fellow-creatures whose outward circumstances are repulsive. To recognise our own spiritual nature and God's image in these humble forms, to recognise as brethren those who want all outward distinctions, is the chief way in which we are to manifest the spirit of Him who came to raise the fallen and to save the lost. We see, then, the moral importance of the question of slavery. According to our decision of it, we determine our comprehension of the Christian law. He who cannot see a brother, a child of God, a man possessing all the rights of humanity, under a skin darker than his own, wants the vision of a Christian. He worships the Outward. The spirit is not yet revealed to him. To look unmoved on the degradation and wrongs of a fellow-creature, because burned by a fiercer sun, proves us strangers to justice and love, in those universal forms which characterize Christianity. The greatest of all distinctions, the only enduring one, is moral goodness, virtue, religion. Outward distinctions cannot add to the dignity of this. The wealth of worlds is " not sufficient for a burnt-offering " on its altar. A being capable of this is invested by God with solemn claims on his fellow-creatures. To exclude millions of such beings from our sympathy, because of outward disadvantages, proves, that in whatever else we surpass them, we are not their superiors in Christian virtue.

The spirit of Christianity, I have said, is distinguished by Universality. It is universal justice. It respects all the rights of all beings. It suffers no being, however obscure, to be wronged, without condemning the wrong-doer. Impartial, uncompromising, fearless, it screens no favorites, is dazzled by no power, spreads its shield over the weakest, summons the mightiest to its bar, and speaks to the conscience in tones under which the mightiest have quailed. It is also universal love, comprehending those that are near and those that are far off, the high and the low, the rich and poor, descending to the fallen, and especially binding itself to those in whom human nature is trampled under foot. Such is the spirit of Christianity; and nothing but the illumination of this spirit can prepare us to pass judgment on slavery.

These remarks are intended to show the spirit in which slavery ought to be approached, and the point of view from which it will be regarded in the present discussion. My plan may be briefly sketched.

1. I shall show that man cannot be justly held and used as Property.

2. I shall show that man has sacred rights, the gifts of God, and inseparable from human nature, of which slavery is the infraction.

3. I shall offer some explanations, to prevent misapplication of these principles.

4. I shall unfold the evils of slavery.

5. I shall consider the argument which the Scriptures are thought to furnish in favor of slavery.

6. I shall offer some remarks on the means of removing it.

7. I shall offer some remarks on abolitionism.

8. I shall conclude with a few reflections on the duties belonging to the times.

In the first two sections, I propose to show that slavery is a great wrong, but I do not intend to pass sen-

tence on the character of the slave-holder. These two
subjects are distinct. Men are not always to be interpreted by their acts or institutions. The same acts
in different circumstances admit, and even require, very
different constructions. I offer this remark that the
subject may be approached without prejudice or personal reference. The single object is to settle great
principles. Their bearing on individuals will be a subject of distinct consideration.

CHAPTER I.

PROPERTY.

THE slave-holder claims the slave as his Property. The very idea of a slave is, that he belongs to another, that he is bound to live and labor for another, to be another's instrument, and to make another's will his habitual law, however adverse to his own. Another owns him, and, of course, has a right to his time and strength, a right to the fruits of his labor, a right to task him without his consent, and to determine the kind and duration of his toil, a right to confine him to any bounds, a right to extort the required work by stripes, a right, in a word, to use him as a tool, without contract, against his will, and in denial of his right to dispose of himself, or to use his power for his own good. " A slave," says the Louisiana code, " is in the power of the master to whom he belongs. The master may sell him, dispose of his person, his industry, his labor; he can do nothing, possess nothing, nor acquire any thing, but which must belong to his master." " Slaves shall be deemed, taken, reputed, and adjudged," say the South-Carolina laws, "to be chattels personal in the hands of their masters, and possessions to all intents and purposes whatsoever." Such is slavery, a claim to man as property.

Now this claim of property in a human being is alto-

2*

gether false, groundless. No such right of man in man can exist. A human being cannot be justly owned. To hold and treat him as property is to inflict a great wrong, to incur the guilt of oppression.

This position there is a difficulty in maintaining, on account of its exceeding obviousness. It is too plain for proof. To defend it is like trying to confirm a self-evident truth. To find arguments is not easy, because an argument is something clearer than the proposition to be sustained. The man who, on hearing the claim to property in man, does not see and feel distinctly that it is a cruel usurpation, is hardly to be reached by reasoning, for it is hard to find any plainer principles than what he begins with denying. I will endeavour, however, to illustrate the truth which I have stated.

1. It is plain, that, if one man may be held as property, then every other man may be so held. If there be nothing in human nature, in our common nature, which excludes and forbids the conversion of him who possesses it into an article of property ; if the right of the free to liberty is founded, not on their essential attributes as rational and moral beings, but on certain adventitious, accidental circumstances, into which they have been thrown ; then every human being, by a change of circumstances, may justly be held and treated by another as property. If one man may be rightfully reduced to slavery, then there is not a human being on whom the same chain may not be imposed. Now let every reader ask himself this plain question: Could I, can I, be rightfully seized, and made an article of property ; be made a passive instrument of another's will and pleasure ; be subjected to another's irresponsible

power; be subjected to stripes at another's will; be denied the control and use of my own limbs and faculties for my own good? Does any man, so questioned, doubt, waver, look about him for an answer? Is not the reply given immediately, intuitively, by his whole inward being? Does not an unhesitating, unerring conviction spring up in my breast, that no other man can acquire such a right in myself? Do we not repel, indignantly and with horror, the thought of being reduced to the condition of tools and chattels to a fellow-creature? Is there any moral truth more deeply rooted in us, than that such a degradation would be an infinite wrong? And, if this impression be a delusion, on what single moral conviction can we rely? This deep assurance, that we cannot be rightfully made another's property, does not rest on the hue of our skins, or the place of our birth, or our strength, or wealth. These things do not enter our thoughts. The consciousness of indestructible rights is a part of our moral being. The consciousness of our humanity involves the persuasion, that we cannot be owned as a tree or a brute. As men, we cannot justly be made slaves. Then no man can be rightfully enslaved. In casting the yoke from ourselves as an unspeakable wrong, we condemn ourselves as wrong-doers and oppressors in laying it on any who share our nature. —It is not necessary to inquire whether a man, by extreme guilt, may not forfeit the rights of his nature, and be justly punished with slavery. On this point crude notions prevail. But the discussion would be foreign to the present subject. We are now not speaking of criminals. We speak of innocent men, who have given us no hold on them by guilt; and our own consciousness is a proof that such cannot rightfully be seized as property by a fellow-creature.

2. A man cannot be seized and held as property, because he has Rights. What these rights are, whether few or many, or whether all men have the same, are questions for future discussion. All that is assumed now is, that every human being has *some* rights. This truth cannot be denied, but by denying to a portion of the race that moral nature which is the sure and only foundation of rights. This truth has never, I believe, been disputed. It is even recognised in the very codes of slave legislation, which, while they strip a man of liberty, affirm his right to life, and threaten his murderer with punishment. Now, I say, a being having rights cannot justly be made property; for this claim over him virtually annuls all his rights. It strips him of all power to assert them. It makes it a crime to assert them. The very essence of slavery is, to put a man defenceless into the hands of another. The right claimed by the master, to task, to force, to imprison, to whip, and to punish the slave, at discretion, and especially to prevent the least resistance to his will, is a virtual denial and subversion of all the rights of the victim of his power. The two cannot stand together. Can we doubt which of them ought to fall ?

3. Another argument against property is to be found in the Essential Equality of men. I know that this doctrine, so venerable in the eyes of our fathers, has lately been denied. Verbal logicians, have told us that men are "born equal" only in the sense of being equally born. They have asked whether all are equally tall,

strong, or beautiful ; or whether nature, Procrustes-like, reduces all her children to one standard of intellect and virtue. By such arguments it is attempted to set aside the principle of equality, on which the soundest moralists have reared the structure of social duty ; and in these ways the old foundations of despotic power, which our fathers in their simplicity thought they had subverted, are laid again by their sons.

It is freely granted, that there are innumerable diversities among men ; but be it remembered, they are ordained to bind men together, and not to subdue one to the other ; ordained to give means and occasions of mutual aid, and to carry forward each and all, so that the good of all is equally intended in this distribution of various gifts. Be it also remembered, that these diversities among men are as nothing in comparison with the attributes in which they agree ; and it is this which constitutes their essential equality. All men have the same rational nature and the same power of conscience, and all are equally made for indefinite improvement of these divine faculties, and for the happiness to be found in their virtuous use. Who, that comprehends these gifts, does not see that the diversities of the race vanish before them ? Let it be added, that the natural advantages, which distinguish one man from another, are so bestowed as to counterbalance one another, and bestowed without regard to rank or condition in life. Whoever surpasses in one endowment is inferior in others. Even genius, the greatest gift, is found in union with strange infirmities, and often places its possessors below ordinary men in the conduct of life. Great learning is often put to shame by the mother-wit and keen good sense of uneducated men. Nature, indeed, pays

no heed to birth or condition in bestowing her favors.
The noblest spirits sometimes grow up in the obscurest spheres. Thus equal are men ; and among these
equals, who can substantiate his claim to make others his
property, his tools, the mere instruments of his private
interest and gratification ? Let this claim begin, and
where will it stop ? If one may assert it, why not all ?
Among these partakers of the same rational and moral
nature, who can make good a right over others, which
others may not establish over himself ? Does he insist
on superior strength of body or mind ? Who of us has
no superior in one or the other of these endowments ?
Is it sure that the slave or the slave's child may not
surpass his master in intellectual energy, or in moral
worth ? Has nature conferred distinctions, which tell
us plainly who shall be owners and who be owned ?
Who of us can unblushingly lift his head and say, that
God has written " Master " there ? or who can show
the word " Slave " engraven on his brother's brow ?
The equality of nature makes slavery a wrong. Nature's seal is affixed to no instrument by which property
in a single human being is conveyed.

4. That a human being cannot be justly held and
used as property, is apparent from the very nature of
property. Property is an exclusive right. It shuts out
all claim but that of the possessor. What one man
owns, cannot belong to another. What, then, is the
consequence of holding a human being as property ?
Plainly this. He can have no right to himself. His
limbs are, in truth, not morally his own. He has not a
right to his own strength. It belongs to another. His
will, intellect, and muscles, all the powers of body and

mind which are exercised in labor, he is bound to regard as another's. Now, if there be property in any
thing, it is that of a man in his own person, mind, and
strength. All other rights are weak, unmeaning, compared with this, and, in denying this, all right is denied.
It is true, that an individual may forfeit by crime his
right to the use of his limbs, perhaps to his limbs, and
even to life. But the very idea of forfeiture implies,
that the right was originally possessed. It is true, that
a man may by contract give to another a limited right
to his strength. But he gives only because he possesses
it, and gives it for considerations which he deems beneficial to himself; and the right conferred ceases at once
on violation of the conditions on which it was bestowed.
To deny the right of a human being to himself, to his
own limbs and faculties, to his energy of body and mind,
is an absurdity too gross to be confuted by any thing
but a simple statement. Yet this absurdity is involved
in the idea of his belonging to another.

5. We have a plain recognition of the principle now
laid down, in the universal indignation excited towards
a man who makes another his slave. Our laws know
no higher crime than that of reducing a man to slavery.
To steal or to buy an African on his own shores, is
piracy. In this act the greatest wrong is inflicted, the
most sacred right violated. But if a human being cannot without infinite injustice be seized as property, then
he cannot without equal wrong be held and used as
such. The wrong in the first seizure lies in the desti-
nation of a human being to future bondage, to the criminal use of him as a chattel or brute. Can that very use,
which makes the original seizure an enormous wrong,

become gradually innocent? If the slave receive injury without measure at the first moment of the outrage,
is he less injured by being held fast the second or the
third? Does the duration of wrong, the increase of it
by continuance, convert it into right? It is true, in
many cases, that length of possession is considered as
giving a right, where the goods were acquired by unlawful means. But in these cases, the goods were such
as might justly be appropriated to individual use. They
were intended by the Creator to be owned. They fulfil
their purpose by passing into the hands of an exclusive
possessor. It is essential to rightful property in a thing,
that the thing from its nature may be rightfully appropriated. If it cannot originally be made one's own without crime, it certainly cannot be continued as such without guilt. Now the ground, on which the seizure of the
African on his own shore is condemned, is, that he is a
man, who has by his nature a right to be free. Ought
not, then, the same condemnation to light on the continuance of his yoke? Still more. Whence is it, that
length of possession is considered by the laws as conferring a right? I answer, from the difficulty of determining the original proprietor, and from the apprehension of unsettling all property by carrying back inquiry
beyond a certain time. Suppose, however, an article
of property to be of such a nature that it could bear the
name of the true original owner stamped on it in bright
and indelible characters. In this case, the whole ground,
on which length of possession bars other claims, would
fail. The proprietor would not be concealed, or rendered doubtful by the lapse of time. Would not he,
who should receive such an article from a robber or a
succession of robbers, be involved in their guilt? Now

the true owner of a human being is made manifest to all. It is Himself. No brand on the slave was ever so conspicuous as the mark of property which God has set on him. God, in making him a rational and moral being, has put a glorious stamp on him, which all the slave legislation and slave-markets of worlds cannot efface. Hence, no right accrues to the master from the length of the wrong which has been done to the slave.

6. Another argument against the right of property in man, may be drawn from a very obvious principle of moral science. It is a plain truth, universally received, that every right supposes or involves a corresponding obligation. If, then, a man has a right to another's person or powers, the latter is under obligation to give himself up as a chattel to the former. This is his duty. He is bound to be a slave; and bound not merely by the Christian law, which enjoins submission to injury, not merely by prudential considerations, or by the claims of public order and peace; but bound because another has a right of ownership, has a moral claim to him, so that he would be guilty of dishonesty, of robbery, in withdrawing himself from this other's service. It is his duty to work for his master, though all compulsion were withdrawn; and in deserting him he would commit the crime of taking away another man's property, as truly as if he were to carry off his owner's purse. Now do we not instantly feel, can we help feeling, that this is false? Is the slave thus morally bound? When the African was first brought to these shores, would he have violated a solemn obligation by slipping his chain, and flying back to his native home? Would he not have been bound to seize the precious opportunity of escape?

Is the slave under a moral obligation to confine himself, his wife, and children, to a spot where their union in a moment may be forcibly dissolved? Ought he not, if he can, to place himself and his family under the guardianship of equal laws? Should we blame him for leav-. ing his yoke? Do we not feel, that, in the same condition, a sense of duty would quicken our flying steps? Where, then, is the obligation which would necessarily be imposed, if the right existed which the master claims? The absence of obligation proves the want of the right. The claim is groundless. It is a cruel wrong.

7. I come now to what is to my own mind the great argument against seizing and using a man as property. He cannot be property in the sight of God and justice, because he is a Rational, Moral, Immortal Being; because created in God's image, and therefore in the highest sense his child; because created to unfold godlike faculties, and to govern himself by a Divine Law written on his heart, and republished in God's Word. His whole nature forbids that he should be seized as property. From his very nature it follows, that so to seize him is to offer an insult to his Maker, and to inflict aggravated social wrong. Into every human being God has breathed an immortal spirit, more precious than the whole outward creation. No earthly or celestial language can exaggerate the worth of a human being. No matter how obscure his condition. Thought, Reason, Conscience, the capacity of Virtue, the capacity of Christian Love, an immortal Destiny, an intimate moral connection with God, — here are attributes of our common humanity which reduce to insignificance all outward distinctions, and make every human being un-

speakably dear to his Maker. No matter how ignorant
he may be. The capacity of Improvement allies him
to the morè instructed of his race, and places within
his reach the knowledge and happiness of higher worlds.
Every human being has in him the germ of the greatest
idea in the universe, the idea of God; and to unfold
this is the end of his existence. Every human being
has in his breast the elements of that Divine, Everlasting Law, which the highest orders of the creation obey:
He has the idea of Duty; and to unfold, revere, obey
this, is the very purpose for which life was given.
Every human being has the idea of what is meant by
that word, Truth; that is, he sees, however dimly, the
great object of Divine and created intelligence, and is
capable of ever-enlarging perceptions of truth. Every
human being has affections, which may be purified and
expanded into a Sublime Love. He has, too, the idea
of Happiness, and a thirst for it which cannot be appeased. Such is our nature. Wherever we see a
man, we see the possessor of these great capacities.
Did God make such a being to be owned as a tree or
a brute? How plainly was he made to exercise, unfold, improve his highest powers, made for a moral,
spiritual good! and how is he wronged, and his Creator opposed, when he is forced and broken into a tool
to another's physical enjoyment!

Such a being was plainly made for an End in Him
self. He is a Person, not a Thing. He is an End,
not a mere Instrument or Means. He was made for
his own virtue and happiness. Is this end reconcilable
with his being held and used as a chattel? The sacrifice of such a being to another's will, to another's
present, outward, ill-comprehended good, is the greatest

violence which can be offered to any creature of God. It is to degrade him from his rank in the universé, to make him a means, not an end, to cast him out from God's spiritual family into the brutal herd.

Such a being was plainly made to obey a Law within Himself. This is the essence of a moral being. He possesses, as a part of his nature, and the most essential part, a sense of Duty, which he is to reverence and follow, in opposition to all pleasure or pain, to all interfering human wills. The great purpose of all good education and discipline is, to make a man Master of Himself, to excite him to act from a principle in his own mind, to lead him to propose his own perfection as his supreme law and end. And is this highest purpose of man's nature to be reconciled with entire subjection to a foreign will, to an outward, overwhelming force, which is satisfied with nothing but complete submission ?

The end of such a being as we have described, is, manifestly, Improvement. Now it is the fundamental law of our nature, that all our powers are to improve by free exertion. Action is the indispensable condition of progress to the intellect, conscience, and heart. Is it not plain, then, that a human being cannot, without wrong, be owned by another, who claims, as proprietor, the right to repress the powers of his slaves, to withhold from them the means of developement, to keep them within the limits which are necessary to contentment in chains, to shut out every ray of light and every generous sentiment, which may interfere with entire subjection to his will ?

No man, who seriously considers what human nature is, and what it was made for, can think of setting up a claim to a fellow-creature. What ! own a spiritual being a being made to know and adore God, and who is to outlive the sun and stars! What! chain to our lowest uses a being made for truth and virtue! convert into a brute instrument that intelligent nature, on which the idea of Duty has dawned, and which is a nobler type of God than all outward creation! Should we not deem it a wrong which no punishment could expiate, were one of our children seized as property, and driven by the whip to toil? And shall God's child, dearer to him than an only son to a human parent, be thus degraded? Every thing else may be owned in the universe; but a moral, rational being cannot be property. Suns and stars may be owned, but not the lowest spirit. Touch any thing but this. Lay not your hand on God's rational offspring. The whole spiritual world cries out, Forbear! The highest intelligences recognise their own nature, their own rights, in the humblest human being. By that priceless, immortal spirit which dwells in him, by that likeness of God which he wears, tread him not in the dust, confound him not with the brute.

We have thus seen, that a human being cannot rightfully be held and used as property. No legislation, not that of all countries or worlds, could make him so. Let this be laid down, as a first, fundamental truth. Let us hold it fast, as a most sacred, precious truth. Let us hold it fast against all customs, all laws, all rank, wealth, and power. Let it be armed with the whole authority of the civilized and Christian world.

I have taken it for granted that no reader would be so wanting in moral discrimination and moral feeling, as to urge, that men may rightfully be seized and held as property, because various governments have so ordained. What! is human legislation the measure of right? Are God's laws to be repealed by man's? Can government do no wrong? To what a mournful extent is the history of human governments a record of wrongs! How much does the progress of civilization consist in the substitution of just and humane, for barbarous and oppressive laws! The individual, indeed, is never authorized to oppose physical force to unrighteous ordinances of government, as long as the community choose to sustain them. But criminal legislation ought to be freely and earnestly exposed. Injustice is never so terrible, and never so corrupting, as when armed with the sanctions of law. The authority of government, instead of being a reason for silence under wrongs, is a reason for protesting against wrong with the undivided energy of argument, entreaty, and solemn admonition.

CHAPTER II.

——

RIGHTS.

I now proceed to the second division of the subject. I am to show, that man has sacred Rights, the gifts of God, and inseparable from human nature, which are violated by slavery. Some important principles, which belong to this head, were necessarily anticipated under the preceding ; but they need a fuller exposition. The whole subject of Rights needs to be reconsidered. Speculations and reasonings about it have lately been given to the public, not only false, but dangerous to freedom, and there is a strong tendency to injurious views. Rights are made to depend on circumstances, so that pretences may easily be made or created for violating them successively, till none shall remain. Human rights have been represented as so modified and circumscribed by men's entrance into the social state, that only the shadows of them are left. They have been spoken of as absorbed in the public good ; so that a man may be innocently enslaved, if the public good shall so require. To meet fully all these errors, for such I hold them, a larger work than the present is required. The nature of man, his relations to the state, the limits of civil government, the elements of the public good, and the degree to which the individual must be surrendered to this good, these are the topics which the present subject involves. I cannot enter into them particularly, but shall lay down what seem to me the great and true principles in regard to them. I shall show, that man has rights from his very nature,. not the gifts of society, but of God; that they are not surrendered on entering the social state; that they must not be taken away under the plea of public good; that the Individual is never to be sacrificed to the Community; that the idea of Rights is to prevail above all the interests of the state.

Man has rights by nature. The disposition of some to deride abstract rights, as if all rights were uncertain, mutable, and conceded by society, shows a lamentable ignorance of human nature. Whoever understands this must see in it an immovable foundation of rights. These are gifts of the Creator, bound up indissolubly with our moral constitution. In the order of things, they precede society, lie at its foundation, constitute man's capacity for it, and are the great objects of social institutions. The consciousness of rights is not a creation of human art, a conventional sentiment, but essential to and inseparable from the human soul.

Man's rights belong to him as a Moral Being, as capable of perceiving moral distinctions, as a subject of moral obligation. As soon as he becomes conscious of Duty, a kindred consciousness springs up, that he has a Right to do what the sense of duty enjoins, and that no foreign will or power can obstruct his moral action without crime. He feels, that the sense of duty was given to him as a Law, that it makes him responsible for himself, that to exercise, unfold, and obey it is the end of his being, and that he has a right to exercise and obey it without hindrance or opposition. A consciousness of dignity, however obscure, belongs also to this divine principle ; and, though he may want words to do justice to his thoughts, he feels that he has that within him which makes him essentially equal to all around him.

The sense of duty is the fountain of human rights. In other words, the same inward principle, which teaches the former, bears witness to the latter. Duties and Rights must stand or fall together. It has been too common to oppose them to one another ; but they are indissolubly joined together. That same inward principle, which teaches a man what he is bound to do to others, teaches equally, and at the same instant, what others are bound to do to *him*. That same voice, which forbids him to injure a single fellow-creature, forbids every fellow-creature to do *him* harm. His conscience, in revealing the moral law, does not reveal a law for himself only, but speaks as a Universal Legislator. He has an intuitive conviction, that the obligations of this divine code press on others as truly as on himself. That principle, which teaches him that he sustains the relation of brotherhood to all human beings, teaches him that this relation is reciprocal, that it gives indestructible claims, as well as imposes solemn duties, and that what he owes to the members of this vast family, they owe to him in return. Thus the moral nature involves rights. These enter into its very essence. They are taught by the very voice which enjoins duty. Accordingly there is no deeper principle in human nature, than the consciousness of rights. So profound, so ineradicable is this sentiment, that the oppressions of ages have nowhere wholly stifled it.

Having shown the foundation of human rights in hu-

man nature, it may be asked what they are.   Perhaps
they do not admit very accurate definition, any more than
human duties ; for the Spiritual cannot be weighed and
measured like the Material.   Perhaps a minute criticism
may find fault with the most guarded exposition of
them ; but they may easily be stated in language which
the unsophisticated mind will recognise as the truth.
Volumes could not do justice to them ; and yet, perhaps they may be comprehended in one sentence.   They
may all be comprised in the right, which belongs to
every rational being, to exercise his powers for the promotion of his own and others' Happiness and Virtue.
These are the great purposes of his existence.   For
these his powers were given, and to these he is bound to
devote them.   He is bound to make himself and others
better and happier, according to his ability.   His ability
for this work is a sacred trust from God, the greatest of
all trusts.   He must answer for the waste or abuse of it.
He consequently suffers an unspeakable wrong, when
stripped of it by others, or forbidden to employ it for
the ends for which it is given ; when the powers, which
God has given for such generous uses, are impaired or
destroyed by others, or the means for their action and
growth are forcibly withheld.   As every human being is
bound to employ his faculties for his own and others'
good, there is an obligation on each to leave all free
for the accomplishment of this end; and whoever respects this obligation, whoever uses his own, without
invading others' powers, or obstructing others' duties,
has a sacred, indefeasible right to be unassailed, unob-
structed, unharmed by all with whom he may be connected.   Here is the grand, all-comprehending right of
human nature.   Every man should revere it, should

assert it for himself and for all, and should bear solemn testimony against every infraction of it, by whomsoever made or endured.

Having considered the great fundamental right of human nature, particular rights may easily be deduced. Every man has a right to exercise and invigorate his intellect or the power of knowledge, for knowledge is the essential condition of successful effort for every good ; and whoever obstructs or quenches the intellectual life in another, inflicts a grievous and irreparable wrong. Every man has a right to inquire into his duty, and to conform himself to what he learns of it. Every man has a right to use the means, given by God and sanctioned by virtue, for bettering his condition. He has a right to be respected according to his moral worth ; a right to be regarded as a member of the community to which he belongs, and to be protected by impartial laws ; and a right to be exempted from coercion, stripes, and punishment, as long as he respects the rights of others. He has a right to an equivalent for his labor. He has a right to sustain domestic relations, to discharge their duties, and to enjoy the happiness which flows from fidelity in these and other domestic relations. Such are a few of human rights ; and if so, what a grievous wrong is slavery !

Perhaps nothing has done more to impair the sense of the reality and sacredness of human rights, and to sanction oppression, than loose ideas as to the change made in man's natural rights by his entrance into civil society. It is commonly said, that men part with a portion of these by becoming a community, a body politic ; that government consists of powers surrendered by the individual ; and it is said, " If certain rights and powers may be surrendered, why not others ? why not all ? what limit is to be set ? The good of the community, to which a part is given up, may demand the whole ; and in this good, all private rights are merged." This is the logic of despotism. We are grieved that it finds its way into republics, and that it sets down the great principles of freedom as abstractions and metaphysical theories, good enough for the cloister, but too refined for practical and real life.

Human rights, however, are not to be so reasoned away. They belong, as we have seen, to man as a moral being, and nothing can divest him of them but the destruction of his nature. They are not to be given up to society as a prey. On the contrary, the great end of civil society is to secure them. The great end of government is to repress *all wrong*. Its highest function is to protect the weak against the powerful, so that the obscurest human being may enjoy his rights in peace. Strange that an institution, built on the idea of Rights, should be used to unsettle this idea, to confuse our moral perceptions, to sanctify wrongs as means of general good !

It is said, that, in forming civil society, the individual surrenders a part of his rights. It would be more proper to say, that he adopts new modes of securing them. He consents, for example, to desist from self-defence, that he and all may be more effectually defended oy the public force. He consents to submit his cause to an umpire or tribunal, that justice may be more impartially awarded, and that he and all may more certainly receive their due. He consents to part with a portion of his property in taxation, that his own and others' property may be the more secure. He submits to certain restraints, that he and others may enjoy more enduring freedom. He expects an equivalent for what he relinquishes, and insists on it as his right. He is wronged by partial laws, which compel him to contribute to the state beyond his proportion, his ability, and the measure of benefits which he receives. How absurd is it to suppose, that, by consenting to be protected by the state, and by yielding it the means, he surrenders the very rights which were the objects of his accession to the social compact!

The authority of the state to impose laws on its members I cheerfully allow; but this has limits, which are found to be more and more narrow in proportion to the progress of moral science. The state is equally restrained with individuals by the Moral Law. For example, it may not, must not, on any account, put an innocent man to death, or require of him a dishonorable or criminal service. It may demand allegiance, but only on the ground of the protection it affords. It may levy taxes, but only because it takes all property and all interests under its shield. It may pass laws, but only impartial ones, framed for the whole, and not for the few. It must not seize, by a special act, the property of the humblest individual, without making him an equivalent. It must regard every man, over whom it extends its authority, as a vital part of itself, as entitled to its care and to its provisions for liberty and happiness. If, in an emergency, its safety, which is the interest of each and all, may demand the imposition of peculiar restraints on one or many, it is bound to limit these restrictions to the precise point which its safety prescribes, to remove the necessity of them as far and as fast as possible, to compensate by peculiar protection such as it deprives of the ordinary means of protecting themselves, and, in general, to respect and provide for liberty in the very acts which for a time restrain it. The idea of Rights should be fundamental and supreme in civil institutions. Government becomes a nuisance and scourge, in proportion as it sacrifices these to the many or the few. Government, I repeat it, is equally bound with the individual by the Moral Law. The ideas of Justice and Rectitude, of what is due to man from his fellow-creatures, of the claims of every moral being, are far deeper and more primitive than Civil Polity. Government, far from originating them, owes to them its strength. Right is older than human law. Law ought to be its voice. It should be built on, and should correspond to, the principle of justice in the human breast, and its weakness is owing to nothing more than to its clashing with our indestructible moral convictions.

That government is most perfect, in which Policy is most entirely subjected to Justice, or in which the supreme and constant aim is to secure the rights of every human being. This is the beautiful idea of a free government, and no government is free but in proportion as it realizes this. Liberty must not be confounded with popular institutions. A representative government may be as despotic as an absolute monarchy. In as far as it tramples on the rights, whether of many or one, it is a despotism. The sovereign power, whether wielded by a single hand or several hands, by a king or a congress, which spoils one human being of the immunities and privileges bestowed on him by God, is so far a tyranny. The great argument in favor of representative institutions is, that a people's rights are safest in

their own hands, and should never be surrendered to an
irresponsible power. Rights, Rights, lie at the foundation of a popular government ; and when this betrays
them, the wrong is more aggravated than when they are
crushed by despotism.

Still the question will be asked, "Is not the General
Good the supreme law of the state ? Are not all restraints on the individual just, which this demands?
When the rights of the individual clash with this, must
they not yield? Do they not, indeed, cease to be
rights ? Must not every thing give place to the General Good?" I have started this question in various
forms, because I deem it worthy of particular exami-
nation. Public and private morality, the freedom and
safety of our national institutions, are greatly concerned
in settling the claims of the " General Good." In
monarchies, the Divine Right of kings swallowed up
all others. In republics, the General Good threatens
the same evil. It is a shelter for the abuses and usurpations of government, for the profligacies of statesmen,
for the vices of parties, for the wrongs of slavery. In
considering this subject, I take the hazard of repeating
principles already laid down ; but this will be justified
by the importance of reaching and determining the truth.
Is the General Good, then, the supreme law, to which
every thing must bow ?

This question may be settled at once by proposing
another. Suppose the public good to require, that a
number of the members of a state, no matter how few,
should perjure themselves, or should disclaim their faith
in God and virtue. Would their right to follow conscience and God be annulled? Would they be bound
to sin ? Suppose a conqueror to menace a state with

ruin, unless its members should insult their parents, and stain themselves with crimes at which nature revolts. Must the public good prevail over purity and our holiest affections ? Do we not all feel that there are higher goods than even the safety of the state ? that there is a higher law than that of mightiest empires ? that the idea of Rectitude is deeper in human nature than that of private or public interest ? and that this is to bear sway over all private and public acts ?

The supreme law of a state is not its safety, its power, its prosperity, its affluence, the flourishing state of agriculture, commerce, and the arts. These objects, constituting what is commonly called the Public Good, are indeed proposed, and ought to be proposed, in the constitution and administration of states. But there is a higher law, even Virtue, Rectitude, the voice of Conscience, the Will of God. Justice is a greater good than property, not greater in degree, but in kind. Universal benevolence is infinitely superior to prosperity. Religion, the love of God, is worth incomparably more than all his outward gifts. A community, to secure or aggrandize itself, must never forsake the Right, the Holy, the Just.

Moral Good, Rectitude in all its branches, is the Supreme Good ; by which I do not intend, that it is the surest means to the security and prosperity of the state. Such, indeed, it is, but this is too low a view. It must not be looked upon as a Means, an Instrument. It is the Supreme End, and states are bound to subject to it all their legislation, be the apparent loss of prosperity ever so great. National wealth is not the End. It derives all its worth from national virtue. If accumulated by rapacity, conquest, or any degrading means, or if concentrated in the hands of the few, whom it strengthens to crush the many, it is a curse. National wealth is a blessing, only when it springs from and represents the intelligence and virtue of the community ; when it is a fruit and expression of good habits, of respect for the rights of all, of impartial and beneficent legislation ; when it gives impulse to the higher faculties, and occasion and incitement to justice and beneficence. No greater calamity can befall a people than to prosper by crime. No success can be a compensation for the wound inflicted on a nation's mind by renouncing Right as its Supreme Law.

Let a people exalt Prosperity above Rectitude, and a more dangerous end cannot be proposed. Public Prosperity, General Good, regarded by itself, or apart from the moral law, is something vague, unsettled, and uncertain, and will infallibly be so construed by the selfish and grasping as to secure their own aggrandizement. It may be made to wear a thousand forms, according to men's interests and passions. This is illustrated by every day's history. Not a party springs up, which does not sanctify all its projects for monopolizing power by the plea of General Good. Not a measure, however ruinous, can be proposed, which cannot be shown to favor one or another national interest. The truth is, that, in the uncertainty of human affairs, an uncertainty growing out of the infinite and very subtile causes which are acting on communities, the consequences of no measure can be foretold with certainty. The best concerted schemes of policy often fail ; whilst a rash and profligate administration may, by unexpected concurrences of events, seem to advance a nation's glory. In regard to the means of national prosperity,

4 *

the wisest are weak judges. For example, the present
rapid growth of this country, carrying, as it does, vast
multitudes beyond the institutions of religion and education, may be working ruin, whilst the people exult in
it as a pledge of greatness. We are too short-sighted
to find our law in outward interests. To states, as to
individuals, Rectitude is the Supreme Law. It was
never designed that the public good, as disjoined from
this, as distinct from justice and reverence for all rights,
should be comprehended and made our end. Statesmen
work in the dark, until the idea of Right towers above
expediency or wealth. Woe to that people which would
found its prosperity in wrong! It is time that the low
maxims of policy, which have ruled for ages, should fall.
It is time that public interest should no longer hallow
injustice, and fortify government in making the weak
their prey.

In this discussion, I have used the phrase, Public or
General Good, in its common acceptation, as signify-
ing the safety and prosperity of a state. Why can it
not be used in a larger sense? Why can it not be made
to comprehend inward and moral, as well as outward
good? And why cannot the former be understood to
be incomparably the most important element of the public weal? Then, indeed, I should assent to the proposition, that the General Good is the Supreme Law.
So construed, it would support the great truths which
I have maintained. It would condemn the infliction of
wrong on the humblest individual, as a national calamity.
It would plead with us to extend to every individual the
means of improving his character and lot.

If the remarks under this head be just, it will follow,
that the good of the Individual is more important than

the outward prosperity of the State. The former is not vague and unsettled, like the latter, and it belongs to a higher order of interests. It consists in the free exertion and expansion of the individual's powers, especially of his higher faculties ; in the energy of his intellect, conscience, and good affections ; in sound judgment ; in the acquisition of truth ; in laboring honestly for himself and his family ; in loving his Creator, and subjecting his own will to the Divine ; in loving his fellow-creatures, and making cheerful sacrifices to their happiness ; in friendship ; in sensibility to the beautiful, whether in nature or art ; in loyalty to his principles ; in moral courage ; in self-respect ; in understanding and asserting his rights ; and in the Christian hope of immortality. Such is the good of the Individual ; a more sacred, exalted, enduring interest, than any accessions of wealth or power to the State. Let it not be sacrificed to these. He should find, in his connexion with the community, aids to the accomplishment of these purposes of his being, and not be chained and subdued by it to the inferior interests of any fellow-creature.

In all ages the Individual has, in one form or another, been trodden in the dust. In monarchies and aristocracies, he has been sacrificed to One or to the Few ; who, regarding government as an heirloom in their families, and thinking of the people as made only to live and die for their glory, have not dreamed that the sovereign power was designed to shield every man, without exception, from wrong. In the ancient Republics, the Glory of the State, especially Conquest, was the end to which the individual was expected to offer himself a victim, and in promoting which, no cruelty was to be declined, no human right revered. He was merged in a great whole, called the Commonwealth, to which his whole nature was to be immolated. It was the glory of the American people, that, in their Declaration of Independence, they took the ground of the indestructible rights of every human being. They declared all men to be essentially equal, and each born to be free. They did not, like the Greek or Roman, assert for themselves a liberty, which they burned to wrest from other states. They spoke in the name of humanity, as the representatives of the rights of the feeblest, as well as mightiest of their race. They published universal, everlasting principles, which are to work out the deliverance of every human being. Such was their glory. Let not the idea of Rights be erased from their children's minds by false ideas of public good. Let not the sacredness of Individual Man be forgotten in the feverish pursuit of property. It is more important that the Individual should respect himself, and be respected by others, than that the wealth of both worlds should be accumulated on our shores. National wealth is not the end of society. It may exist where large classes are depressed and wronged. It may undermine a nation's spirit, institutions, and independence. It can have no value and no sure foundation, until the supremacy of the Rights of the Individual is the first article of a nation's faith, and until reverence for them becomes the spirit of public men.

Perhaps it will be replied to all which has now been said, that there is an argument from experience, which invalidates the doctrines of this section. It may be said, that human rights, notwithstanding what has been said of their sacredness, do and must yield to the exigencies of real life; that there is often a stern necessity in human affairs to which they bow. I may be asked, whether, in the history of nations, circumstances do not occur, in which the rigor of the principles now laid down must be relaxed; whether, in seasons of imminent peril to the state, private rights must not give way. I may be asked, whether the establishment of martial law and a dictator has not sometimes been justified and demanded by public danger; and whether, of course, the rights and liberties of the individual are not held at the discretion of the state. I admit, in reply, that extreme cases may occur, in which the exercise of rights and freedom may be suspended; but suspended only for their ultimate and permanent security. At such times, when the frantic fury of the many, or the usurpations of the few, interrupt the administration of law, and menace property and life, society, threatened with ruin, puts forth instinctively spasmodic efforts for its own preservation. It flies to an irresponsible dictator for its protection. But in these cases, the great idea of Rights predominates amidst their apparent subversion. A power above all laws is conferred, only that the empire of law may be restored. Despotic restraints are imposed, only that liberty may be rescued from ruin. All rights are involved in the safety of the state; and hence, in the cases referred to, the safety of the state becomes the supreme law. The individual is bound for a time to forego his freedom, for the salvation of institutions, without which liberty is but a name. To argue from such sacrifices, that he may be permanently made a slave, is as great an insult to reason as to humanity. It may be added, that sacrifices, which may be demanded for the safety, are not due from the individual to the prosperity

of the state. The great end of civil society is to secure
rights, not accumulate wealth; and to merge the former
in the latter is to turn political union into degradation
and a scourge. The community is bound to take the
rights of each and all under its guardianship. It must
substantiate its claim to universal obedience by redeem-
ing its pledge of universal protection. It must immolate
no man to the prosperity of the rest. Its laws should
be made for all, its tribunals opened to all. It cannot
without guilt abandon any of its members to private
oppression, to irresponsible power.

We have thus established the reality and sacredness
of human rights; and that slavery is an infraction of
these, is too plain to need any labored proof. Slavery
violates, not one, but all; and violates them, not inci-
dentally, but necessarily, systematically, from its very
nature. In starting with the assumption, that the slave
is property, it sweeps away every defence of human
rights, and lays them in the dust. Were it necessary, I
might enumerate them, and show how all fall before this
terrible usurpation; but a few remarks will suffice.

Slavery strips man of the fundamental right to inquire
into, consult, and seek his own happiness. His powers
belong to another, and for another they must be used.
He must form no plans, engage in no enterprises, for
bettering his condition. Whatever be his capacities,
however equal to great improvements of his lot, he is
chained 'for life, by another's will, to the same unvaried
toil. He is forbidden to do, for himself or others, the
work for which God stamped him with his own image,
and endowed him with his own best gifts. — Again,
the slave is stripped of the right to acquire property

Being himself owned, his earnings belong to another. He can possess nothing but by favor. That right, on which the developement of men's powers so much depends, the right to make accumulations, to gain exclusive possessions by honest industry, is withheld. " The slave can acquire nothing," says one of the slave codes, " but what must belong to his master ; " and however this definition, which moves the indignation of the free, may be mitigated by favor, the spirit of it enters into the very essence of slavery. — Again, the slave is stripped of his right to his wife and children. They belong to another, and may be torn from him, one and all, at any moment, at his master's pleasure. — Again, the slave is stripped of the right to the culture of his rational powers. He is in some cases deprived by law of instruction, which is placed within his reach by the improvements of society and the philanthropy of the age. He is not allowed to toil, that his children may enjoy a better education than himself. The most sacred right of human nature, that of developing his best faculties, is denied. Even should it be granted, it would be conceded as a favor, and might at any moment be withheld by the capricious will of another. — Again, the slave is deprived of the right of self-defence. No injury from a white man is he suffered to repel, nor can he seek redress from the laws of his country. If accumulated insult and wrong provoke him to the slightest retaliation, this effort for self-protection, allowed and commended to others, is a crime, for which he must pay a fearful penalty. — Again, the slave is stripped of the right to be exempted from all harm, except for wrong-doing. He is subjected to the lash by those, whom he has never consented to serve, and whose claim to him as property we have seen to be a usurpation ; and this power of punishment, which, if justly claimed, should be exercised with a fearful care, is often delegated to men in whose hands there is a moral certainty of its abuse.

I will add but one more example of the violation of human rights by slavery. The slave virtually suffers the wrong of robbery, though with utter unconsciousness on the part of those who inflict it. It may, indeed, be generally thought, that, as he is suffered to own nothing, he cannot fall, at least, under this kind of violence. But it is not true that he owns nothing. Whatever he may be denied by man, he holds from nature the most valuable property, and that from which all other is derived, I mean his strength. His labor is his own, by the gift of that God, who nerved his arm, and gave him intelligence and conscience to direct the use of it to his own and others' happiness. No possession is so precious as a man's force of body and mind. The exertion of this in labor is the great foundation and source of property in outward things. The worth of articles of traffic is measured by the labor expended in their production. To the great mass of men, in all countries, their strength or labor is their whole fortune. To seize on this would be to rob them of their all. In truth, no robbery is so great, as that to which the slave is habitually subjected. To take by force a man's whole estate, the fruit of years of toil, would, by universal consent, be denounced as a great wrong ; but what is this, compared with seizing the man himself, and appropriating to our use the limbs, faculties, strength, and labor, by which all property is won and held fast ? The right of property in outward things is as nothing, compared with our right to ourselves. Were the slave-holder stripped of his fortune, he would count the violence slight, compared with what he would suffer, were his person seized and devoted as a chattel to another's use. Let it not be said, that the slave receives an equivalent, that he is fed and clothed, and is not, therefore, robbed. Suppose another to wrest from us a valued possession, and to pay us his own price. Should we not think ourselves robbed ? Would not the laws pronounce the invader a robber ? Is it consistent with the right of property, that a man should determine the equivalent for what he takes from his neighbour ? Especially is it to be hoped, that the equivalent due to the laborer will be scrupulously weighed, when he himself is held as property, and all his earnings are declared to be his master's. So great an infraction of human right is slavery !

In reply to these remarks, it may be said, that the theory and practice of slavery differ ; that the rights of the slave are not as wantonly sported with as the claims of the master might lead us to infer ; that some of his possessions are sacred ; that not a few slave-holders refuse to divorce husband and wife, to sever parent and child ; and that, in many cases, the power of punishment is used so reluctantly, as to encourage insolence and insubordination. All this I have no disposition to deny. Indeed, it must be so. It is not in human nature to wink wholly out of sight the rights of a fellow-creature. Degrade him as we may, we cannot altogether forget his claims. In every slave-country, there are, undoubtedly, masters, who desire and purpose to respect these, to the full extent which the nature of the relation will allow. Still, human rights are denied. They lie wholly at another's mercy ; and we must have studied history in vain, if we need be told that they will be continually the prey of this absolute power. — The evils, involved in and flowing from the denial and infraction of the rights of the slave, will form the subject of a subsequent chapter.

CHAPTER III.

EXPLANATIONS.

I have endeavoured to show, in the preceding sections, that slavery is a violation of sacred rights, the infliction of a great wrong. And here a question arises. It may be asked, whether, by this language, I intend to fasten on the slave-holder the charge of peculiar guilt. On this point, great explicitness is a duty. Sympathy with the slave has often degenerated into injustice towards the master. I wish, then, to be understood, that, in ranking slavery among the greatest wrongs, I speak of the injury endured by the slave, and not of the character of the master. These are distinct points. The former does not determine the latter. The wrong is the same to the slave, from whatever motive or spirit it may be inflicted. But this motive or spirit determines wholly the character of him who inflicts it. Because a great injury is done to another, it does not follow, that he who does it is a depraved man; for he may do it unconsciously, and, still more, may do it in the belief that he confers a good. We have learned little of moral science and of human nature, if we do not know, that guilt is to be measured, not by the outward act, but by unfaithfulness to conscience; and that the consciences of men are often darkened by education, and other inauspicious influences. All men have partial consciences, or want comprehension of some duties. All partake, in a measure, of the errors of the community in which they live. Some are betrayed into moral mistakes by the very force with which conscience acts in regard to some particular duty. As the intellect, in grasping one truth, often loses its hold of others, and, by giving itself up to one idea, falls into exaggeration ; so the moral sense, in seizing on a particular exercise of philanthropy, forgets other duties, and will even violate many important precepts, in its passionate eagerness to carry one to perfection. Innumerable illustrations may be given of the liableness of men to moral error. The practice, which strikes one man with horror, may seem to another, who was born and brought up in the midst of it, not only innocent, but meritorious. We must judge others, not by our light, but by their own. We must take their place, and consider what allowance we in their position might justly expect. Our ancestors at the North were concerned in the slave-trade. Some of us can recollect individuals of the colored race, who were torn from Africa, and grew old under our parental roofs. Our ancestors committed a deed now branded as piracy. Were they, therefore, the offscouring of the earth ? Were not some of them among the best of their times. The administration of religion, in almost all past ages, has been a violation of the sacred rights of conscience. How many sects have persecuted and shed blood ! Were their members, therefore, monsters of depravity ? The history of our race is made up of wrongs, many of which were committed without a suspicion of their true character, and many from an urgent sense of duty. A man, born among slaves, accustomed to this relation from his birth, taught its necessity by venerated parents, associating it with all whom he reveres, and too familiar with its evils to see and feel their magnitude, can hardly be expected to look on slavery as it appears to more impartial and distant observers. Let it not be said, that, when new light is offered him, he is criminal in rejecting it. Are we all willing to receive new light? Can we wonder that such a man should be slow to be convinced of the criminality of an abuse sanctioned by prescription, and which has so interwoven itself with all the habits, employments, and economy of life, that he can hardly conceive of the existence of society without this all-pervading element? May he not be true to his convictions of duty in other relations, though he grievously err in this? If, indeed, through cupidity and selfishness, he stifle the monitions of conscience, warp his judgment, and repel the light, he incurs great guilt. If he want virtue to resolve on doing right, though at the loss of every slave, he incurs great guilt. But who of us can look into his heart? To whom are the secret workings there revealed?

Still more. There are masters, who have thrown off the natural prejudices of their position, who see slavery as it is, and who hold the slave chiefly, if not wholly, from disinterested considerations; and these deserve great praise. They deplore and abhor the institution; but believing that partial emancipation, in the present condition of society, would bring unmixed evil on bond and free, they think themselves bound to continue the relation, until it shall be dissolved by comprehensive and systematic measures of the state. There are many of them who would shudder as much as we at reducing a freeman to bondage, but who are appalled by what

5*

seem to them the perils and difficulties of liberating multitudes, born and brought up to that condition.
There are many, who, nominally holding the slave as
property, still hold him for his own good, and for the
public order, and would blush to retain him on other
grounds.   Are such men to be set down among the
unprincipled ?   Am I told, that by these remarks I ex-
tenuate slavery ?   I reply, slavery is still a heavy yoke,
and strips man of his dearest rights, be the master's
character what it may.   Slavery is not less a curse,
because long use may have blinded most, who support
it, to its evils.   Its influence is still blighting, though
conscientiously upheld.   Absolute monarchy is still a
scourge, though among despots there have been good
men.   It is possible to abhor and oppose bad institutions, and yet to abstain from indiscriminate condemnation of those who cling to them, and even to see in
their ranks greater virtue than in ourselves.   It is true,
and ought to be cheerfully acknowledged, that in the
Slave-holding States may be found some of the greatest names of our history, and, what is still more important, bright examples of private virtue and Christian
love.

There is, however, there must be, in slave-holding
communities, a large class, which cannot be too severely
condemned.   There are many, we fear, very many,
who hold their fellow-creatures in bondage from selfish,
base motives.   They hold the slave for gain, whether
justly or unjustly, they neither ask nor care.   They cling
to him as property, and have no faith in the principles
which will diminish a man's wealth.   They hold him,
not for his own good, or the safety of the state, but with
precisely the same views, with which they hold a labor-

mg horse, that is, for the profit which they can wring from him. They will not hear a word of his wrongs; for, wronged or not, they will not let him go. He is their property, and they mean not to be poor for righteousness' sake. Such a class there undoubtedly is among slave-holders; how large, their own consciences must determine. We are sure of it; for, under such circumstances, human nature will and must come to this mournful result. Now, to men of this spirit, the explanations we have made do in no degree apply. Such men ought to tremble before the rebukes of outraged humanity and indignant virtue. Slavery upheld for gain, is a great crime. He, who has nothing to urge against emancipation, but that it will make him poorer, is bound to Immediate Emancipation. He has no excuse for wresting from his brethren their rights. The plea of benefit to the slave and the state avails him nothing. He extorts, by the lash, that labor to which he has no claim, through a base selfishness. Every morsel of food, thus forced from the injured, ought to be bitterer than gall. His gold is cankered. The sweat of the slave taints the luxuries for which it streams. Better were it for the selfish wrong-doer, of whom I speak, to live as the slave, to clothe himself in the slave's raiment, to eat the slave's coarse food, to till his fields with his own hands, than to pamper himself by day, and pillow his head on down at night, at the cost of a wantonly injured fellow-creature. No fellow-creature can be so injured without taking terrible vengeance. He is terribly avenged even now. The blight which falls on the soul of the wrong-doer, the desolation of his moral nature, is a more terrible calamity than he inflicts. In deadening his moral feelings, he dies to the proper happiness of

a man.   In hardening his heart against his fellow-
creatures, he sears it to all true joy.   In shutting his
ear against the voice of justice, he shuts out all the harmonies of the universe, and turns the voice of God
within him into rebuke.   He may prosper, indeed, and
hold faster the slave by whom he prospers; but he riv-
ets heavier and more ignominious chains on his own soul
than he lays on others. No punishment is so terrible
as prosperous guilt.   No fiend, exhausting on us all his
power of torture, is so fearful as an oppressed fellow-
creature.   The cry of the oppressed, unheard on earth,
is heard in heaven.   God is just, and if justice reign,
then the unjust must terribly suffer.   Then no being
can profit by evil-doing.   Then all the laws of the universe are ordinances against guilt.   Then every enjoyment gained by wrong-doing will be turned into a curse.
No laws of nature are so irrepealable as that law which
binds guilt and misery.   God is just.   Then all the
defences, which the oppressor rears against the couse-
quences of wrong-doing, are vain, as vain as would be
his strivings to arrest by his single arm the ocean or
whirlwind.   He may disarm the slave.   Can he disarm
that slave's Creator ?   He can crush the spirit of insurrection in a fellow-being.   Can he crush the awful
spirit of justice and retribution in the Almighty ?   He
can still the murmur of discontent in his victim.   Can
he silence that voice which speaks in thunder, and is to
break the sleep of the grave ?   Can he always still the
reproving, avenging voice in his own breast ?

   I know it will be said, " You would make us poor."
Be poor, then, and thank God for your honest poverty.
Better be poor than unjust.   Better beg than steal.
Better live in an alms-house, better die, than trample on

a fellow-creature and reduce him to a brute, for selfish gratification. What! Have we yet to learn, that "it profits us nothing to gain the whole world, and lose our souls"?

Let it not be replied, in scorn, that we of the North, notorious for love of money, and given to selfish calculation, are not the people to call others to resign their wealth. I have no desire to shield the North; though I might say, with truth, that a community, more generally controlled by the principles of morality and religion, cannot be found. We have, without doubt, a great multitude, who, were they slave-holders, would sooner die than relax their iron grasp, than yield their property in men to justice and the commands of God. We have those who would fight against abolition, if by this measure the profit of their intercourse with the South should be materially impaired. The present excitement among us is, in part, the working of mercenary principles. But because the North joins hands with the South, shall iniquity go unpunished or unrebuked? Can the league of the wicked, the revolt of worlds, repeal the everlasting law of heaven and earth? Has God's throne fallen before Mammon's? Must duty find no voice, no organ, because corruption is universally diffused? Is not this a fresh motive to solemn warning, that, everywhere, Northward and Southward, the rights of human beings are held so cheap, in comparison with worldly gain?

CHAPTER IV.

THE EVILS OF SLAVERY.

The subject of this section is painful and repulsive.
We must not, however, turn away from the contemplation of human sufferings and guilt.   Evil is permitted by
the Creator, that we should strive against it, in faith,
and hope, and charity.   We must never quail before it
because of its extent and duration, never feel as if its
power were greater than that of goodness.   It is meant
to call forth deep sympathy with human nature, and
unwearied sacrifices for human redemption.   One great
part of the mission of every man on earth is to contend
with evil in some of its forms ; and there are some evils
so dependent on opinion, that every man, in judging
and reproving them faithfully, does something towards
their removal.   Let us not, then, shrink from the contemplation of human sufferings.   Even sympathy, if
we have nothing more to offer, is a tribute acceptable
to the Universal Father. — On this topic, exaggeration
should be conscientiously shunned ; and, at the same
time, humanity requires that the whole truth should be
honestly spoken.

In treating of the evils of slavery, I, of course, speak
of its general, not universal effects, of its natural tendencies, not unfailing results.   There are the same

natural differences among the bond as the free, and there is a great diversity in the circumstances in which they are placed. The house-slave, selected for ability and faithfulness, placed amidst the habits, accommodations, and improvements of civilized life, admitted to a degree of confidence and familiarity, and requiting these privileges with attachment, is almost necessarily more enlightened and respectable than the field-slave, who is confined to monotonous toils, and to the society and influences of beings as degraded as himself. The mechanics in this class are sensibly benefited by occupations which give a higher action to the mind. Among the bond, as the free, will be found those to whom nature seems partial, and who are carried almost instinctively towards what is good. I speak of the natural, general influences of slavery. Here, as everywhere else, there are exceptions to the rule, and exceptions which multiply with the moral improvements of the community in which the slave is found. But these do not determine the general character of the institution. It has general tendencies, founded in its very nature, and which predominate vastly wherever it exists. These tendencies it is my present purpose to unfold.

1. The first rank among the evils of slavery must be given to its Moral influence. This is throughout debasing. Common language teaches this. We can say nothing more insulting of another, than that he is slavish. To possess the spirit of a slave is to have sunk to the lowest depths. We can apply to slavery no worse name than its own. Men have always shrunk instinctively from this state, as the most degraded. No punishment, save death, has been more dreaded, and to avoid it death has often been endured.

In expressing the moral influence of slavery, the first and most obvious remark is, that it destroys the proper consciousness and spirit of a Man. The slave, regarded and treated as property, bought and sold like a brute, denied the rights of humanity, unprotected against insult, made a tool, and systematically subdued, that he may be a manageable, useful tool, how can he help regarding himself as fallen below his race? How must his spirit be crushed! How can he respect himself? He becomes bowed to servility. This word, borrowed from his condition, expresses the ruin wrought by slavery within him. The idea, that he was made for his own virtue and happiness, scarcely dawns on his mind. To be an instrument of the physical, material good of another, whose will is his highest law, he is taught to regard as the great purpose of his being. Here lies the evil of slavery. Its whips, imprisonments, and even the horrors of the middle passage from Africa to America, these are not to be named, in comparison with this extinction of the proper consciousness of a human being, with the degradation of a man into a brute.

It may be said, that the slave is used to his yoke; that his sensibilities are blunted; that he receives, without a pang or a thought, the treatment which would sting other men to madness. And to what does this apology amount? It virtually declares, that slavery has done its perfect work, has quenched the spirit of humanity, that the Man is dead within the slave. Is slavery, therefore, no wrong? It is not, however, true, that this work of debasement is ever so effectually done as to extinguish all feeling. Man is too great a creature to be wholly ruined by man. When he seems dead, he only sleeps. There are occasionally some sullen murmurs in the calm of slavery, showing that life still beats in the soul, that the idea of Rights cannot be wholly effaced from the human being.

It would be too painful, and it is not needed, to detail the processes by which the spirit is broken in slavery. I refer to one only, the selling of slaves. The practice of exposing fellow-creatures for sale, of having markets for men as for cattle, of examining the limbs. and muscles of a man and a woman as of a brute, of putting human beings under the hammer of an auctioneer, and delivering them, like any other articles of merchandise, to the highest bidder, all this is such an insult to our common nature, and so infinitely degrading to the poor victim, that it is hard to conceive of its existence, except in a barbarous country.

That slavery should be most unpropitious to the slave as a moral being will be farther apparent, if we consider that his condition is throughout a Wrong, and that consequently it must tend to unsettle all his notions of duty. The violation of his own rights, to which he is inured from birth, must throw confusion over his ideas of all human rights. He cannot comprehend them ; or, if he does, how can he respect them, seeing them, as he does, perpetually trampled on in his own person ? The injury to the character, from living in an atmosphere of wrong, we can all understand. To live in a state of society, of which injustice is the chief and all-pervading element, is too severe a trial for human nature, especially when no means are used to counteract its influence.

Accordingly, the most common distinctions of morality are faintly apprehended by the slave. Respect for property, that fundamental law of civil society, can hardly be instilled into him. His dishonesty is proverbial. Theft from his master passes with him for no crime. A system of force is generally found to drive to fraud. How necessarily will this be the result of a relation in which force is used to extort from a man his labor, his natural property, without any attempt to win his consent! Can we wonder, that the uneducated conscience of the man who is daily wronged should allow him in reprisals to the extent of his power? Thus the primary social virtue, justice, is undermined in the slave.

That the slave should yield himself to intemperance, licentiousness, and, in general, to sensual excess, we must also expect. Doomed to live for the physical indulgences of others, unused to any pleasures but those of sense, stripped of self-respect, and having nothing to gain in life, how can he be expected to govern himself? How naturally, I had almost said necessarily, does he become the creature of sensation, of passion, of the present moment! What aid does the future give him in withstanding desire? That better condition, for which other men postpone the cravings of appetite, never opens before him. The sense of character, the power of opinion, another restraint on the free, can do little or nothing to rescue so abject a class from excess and debasement. In truth, power over himself is the last virtue we should expect in the slave, when we think of him as subjected to absolute power, and made to move passively from the impulse of a foreign will. He is trained to cowardice, and cowardice links itself naturally with low vices. Idleness, to his apprehension, is paradise, for he works without hope of reward. Thus slavery robs him of moral force, and prepares him to fall a prey to appetite and passion.

That the slave finds in his condition little nutriment for the social virtues we shall easily understand, if we consider, that his chief relations are to an absolute master, and to the companions of his degrading bondage; that is, to a being who wrongs him, and to associates whom he cannot honor, whom he sees debased. His dependence on his owner loosens his ties to all other beings. He has no country to love, no family to call his own, no objects of public utility to espouse, no impulse to generous exertion. The relations, dependences, and responsibilities, by which Providence forms the soul to a deep, disinterested love, are almost struck out of his lot. An arbitrary rule, a foreign, irresistible will, taking him out of his own hands, and placing him beyond the natural influences of society, extinguishes in a great degree the sense of what is due to himself, and to the human family around him.

The effects of slavery on the character are so various, that this part of the discussion might be greatly extended; but I will touch only on one topic. Let us turn, for a moment, to the great Motive by which the slave is made to labor. Labor, in one form or another, is appointed by God for man's improvement and happiness, and absorbs the chief part of human life, so that the Motive which excites to it has immense influence on character. It determines very much, whether life shall serve or fail of its end. The man, who works from honorable motives, from domestic affections, from desire of a condition which will open to him greater happiness and usefulness, finds in labor an exercise and invigoration of virtue. The day-laborer, who earns,

with horny hand and the sweat of his face, coarse food
for a wife and children whom he loves, is raised, by this
generous motive, to true dignity ; and, though wanting
the refinements of life, is a nobler being than those who
think themselves absolved by wealth from serving others.   Now the slave's labor brings no dignity, is an exercise of no virtue, but throughout a degradation ; so
that one of God's chief provisions for human improvement becomes a curse.   The motive from which he
acts debases him.   It is the whip.   It is corporal punishment.   It is physical pain inflicted by a fellow-creature.   Undoubtedly labor is mitigated to the slave, as
to all men, by habit.   But this is not the motive.   Take
away the whip, and he would be idle.   His labor brings
no new comforts to wife or child.   The motive which
spurs him is one, by which it is base to be swayed.
Stripes are, indeed, resorted to by civil government,
when no other consideration will deter from crime ; but
he, who is deterred from wrong-doing by the whipping-
post, is among the most fallen of his race.   To work
in sight of the whip, under menace of blows, is to be
exposed to perpetual insult and degrading influences.
Every motion of the limbs, which such a menace urges,
is a wound to the soul.   How hard must it be for a
man, who lives under the lash, to respect himself!
When this motive is substituted for all the nobler ones
which God ordains, is it not almost necessarily death
to the better and higher sentiments of our nature?   It
is the part of a man to despise pain in comparison with
disgrace, to meet it fearlessly in well-doing, to perform
the work of life from other impulses.   It is the part of
a brute to be governed by the whip.   Even the brute
is, seen to act from more generous incitements.   The

horse of a noble breed will not endure the lash. Shall we sink man below the horse ?

Let it not be said, that blows are seldom inflicted. Be it so. We are glad to know it. But this is not the point. The complaint now urged is not of the amount of the pain inflicted, but of its influence on the character, when made the great motive to human labor. It is not the endurance, but the dread of the whip, it´is the substitution of this for natural and honorable motives to action, which we abhor and condemn. It matters not, whether few or many are whipped. A blow given to a single slave is a stripe on the souls of all who see or hear it. It makes all abject, servile. It is not the wound given to the flesh, of which we now complain. Scar the back, and you have done nothing, compared with the wrong done to the soul. You have either stung that soul with infernal passions, with thirst for revenge; or, what perhaps is more discouraging, you have broken and brutalized it. The human spirit has perished under your hands, as far as it can be destroyed `by human force.

I know it is sometimes said, in reply to these remarks, that all men, as well as slaves, act from necessity; that we have masters in hunger and thirst; that no man loves labor for itself; that the pains, which are inflicted on us by the laws of nature, the elements and seasons, are so many lashes driving us to our daily task. Be it so. Still the two cases are essentially different. The necessity laid on us by natural wants is most kindly in its purpose. It is meant to awaken all our faculties, to give full play to body and mind, and thus to give us a new consciousness of the powers derived to us from God. We are, indeed, subjected to a stern nature;

6 *

we are placed amidst warring elements, scorching heat, withering cold, storms, blights, sickness, death. And what is the design? To call forth our powers, to lay on us great duties, to make us nobler beings. We are placed in the midst of a warring nature, not to yield to it, not to be its slaves, but to conquer it, to make it the monument of our skill and strength, to arm ourselves with its elements, its heat, winds, vapors, and mineral treasures, to find, in its painful changes, occasions and incitements to invention, courage, endurance, mutual and endearing dependences, and religious trust. The developement of human nature, in all its powers and affections, is the end of that hard necessity which is laid on us by nature. Is this one and the same thing with the whip laid on the slave? Still more; it is the design of nature, that, by energy, skill, and self-denial, we should so far anticipate our wants, or accumulate supplies, as to be able to diminish the toil of the hands, and to mix with it more intellectual and liberal occupations. Nature does not lay on us an unchangeable task, but one which we may all lighten by honest, self-denying industry. Thus she invites us to throw off her yoke, and to make her our servant. Is this the invitation which the master gives his slaves? Is it his aim to awaken the powers of those on whom he lays his burdens, and to give them increasing mastery over himself? Is it not his aim to curb their wills, break their spirits, and shut them up for ever in the same narrow and degrading work? Oh, let not nature be profaned, let not her parental rule be blasphemed, by comparing with her the slave-holder!

2. Having considered the moral influence of slavery,

I proceed to consider its Intellectual influence, another great topic. God gave us intellectual power, that it should be cultivated ; and a system which degrades it, and can only be upheld by its depression, opposes one of his most benevolent designs. Reason is God's image in man, and the capacity of acquiring truth is among his best aspirations. To call forth the intellect is a principal purpose of the circumstances in which we are placed, of the child's connection with the parent, and of the necessity laid on him in maturer life to provide for himself and others. The education of the intellect is not confined to youth ; but the various experience of later years does vastly more than books and colleges to ripen and invigorate the faculties.

Now the whole lot of the slave is fitted to keep his mind in childhood and bondage. Though living in a land of light, few beams find their way to his benighted understanding. No parent feels the duty of instructing him. No teacher is provided for him, but the Driver, who breaks him, almost in childhood, to the servile tasks which are to fill up his life. No book is opened to his youthful curiosity. As he advances in years, no new excitements supply the place of teachers. He is not cast on himself, made to depend on his own energies. No stirring prizes in life awaken his dormant faculties. Fed and clothed by others like a child, directed in every step, doomed for life to a monotonous round of labor, he lives and dies without a spring to his powers, often brutally unconscious of his spiritual nature. Nor is this all. When benevolence would approach him with instruction, it is repelled. He is not allowed to be taught. The light is jealously barred out. The voice, which would speak to him as a man, is put to silence. He

must not even be enabled to read the Word of God.
His immortal spirit is systematically crushed.

It is said, I know, that the ignorance of the slave is
necessary to the security of the master, and the quiet of
the state ; and this is said truly. Slavery and knowledge cannot live together. To enlighten the slave is to
break his chain. To make him harmless, he must be
kept blind. He cannot be left to read, in an enlightened age, without endangering his master; for what
can he read, which will not give, at least, some hint
of his wrongs ? Should his eye chance to fall on the
"Declaration of Independence," how would the truth
glare on him, that "All men are born free and equal!"
All knowledge furnishes arguments against slavery.
From every subject, light would break forth to reveal
his inalienable and outraged rights. The very exercise
of his intellect would give him the consciousness of
being made for something more than a slave. I agree
to the necessity laid on his master to keep him in darkness. And what stronger argument against slavery can
be conceived ? It compels the master to degrade systematically the mind of the slave ; to war against human
intelligence ; to resist that improvement which is the
end of the Creator. "Woe to him that taketh away
the key of knowledge!" To kill the body is a great
crime. The spirit we cannot kill, but we can bury it
in death-like lethargy ; and is this a light crime in the
sight of its Maker ?

Let it not be said, that almost everywhere the laboring classes are doomed to ignorance, deprived of the
means of instruction. The intellectual advantages of
the laboring freeman, who is intrusted with the care of
himself, raise him far above the slave ; and, accordingly,

superior minds are constantly seen to issue from the less educated classes. Besides, in free communities, philanthropy is not forbidden to labor for the improvement of the ignorant. The obligation of the prosperous and instructed to elevate their less favored brethren is taught, and not taught in vain. Benevolence is making perpetual encroachments on the domain of ignorance and crime. In communities, on the other hand, cursed with slavery, half the population, sometimes more, are given up, intentionally and systematically, to hopeless ignorance. To raise this mass to intelligence and self-government is a crime. The sentence of perpetual degradation is passed on a large portion of the human race. In this view, how great the ill-desert of slavery!

3. I proceed, now, to the Domestic influences of slavery; and here we must look for a dark picture. Slavery virtually dissolves the domestic relations. It ruptures the most sacred ties on earth. It violates home. It lacerates the best affections. The domestic relations precede, and, in our present existence, are worth more than all our other social ties. They give the first throb to the heart, and unseal the deep fountains of its love. Home is the chief school of human virtue. Its responsibilities, joys, sorrows, smiles, tears, hopes, and solicitudes, form the chief interests of human life. Go where a man may, home is the centre to which his heart turns. The thought of his home nerves his arm and lightens his toil. For that his heart yearns, when he is far off. There he garners up his best treasures. God has ordained for all men alike the highest earthly happiness, in providing for all the sanctuary of home. But the slave's home does not merit

the name. To him it is no sanctuary. It is open to
violation, insult, outrage. His children belong to another, are provided for by another, are disposed of by
another. The most precious burden with which the
heart can be charged, the happiness of his child, he
must not bear. He lives not for his family, but for a
stranger. He cannot improve their lot. His wife and
daughter he cannot shield from insult. They may be
torn from him at another's pleasure, sold as beasts of
burden, sent he knows not whither, sent where he cannot reach them, or even interchange inquiries and mes-
sages of love. To the slave marriage has no sanctity.
It may be dissolved in a moment at another's will. His
wife, son, and daughter may be lashed before his eyes,
and not a finger must be lifted in their defence. He
sees the scar of the lash on his wife and child. Thus
the slave's home is desecrated. Thus the tenderest relations, intended by God equally for all, and intended
to be the chief springs of happiness and virtue, are
sported with wantonly and cruelly. What outrage so
great as to enter a man's house, and tear from his side
the beings whom God has bound to him by the holiest
ties ? Every man can make the case his own. Every
mother can bring it home to her own heart.

And let it not be said, that the slave has not the
sensibilities of other men. Nature is too strong even
for slavery to conquer. Even the brute has the yearnings of parental love. But suppose that the conjugal
and parental ties of the slave may be severed without a
pang. What a curse must be slavery, if it can so blight
the heart with more than brutal insensibility, if it can
sink the human mother below the Polar she-bear, which
"howls and dies for her sundered cub!" But it does

not and cannot turn the slave to stone. It leaves, at least, feeling enough to make these domestic wrongs occasions of frequent and deep suffering. Still it must do much to quench the natural affections. Can the wife, who has been brought up under influences most unfriendly to female purity and honor, who is exposed to the whip, who may be torn away at her master's will, and whose support and protection are not committed to a husband's faithfulness, can such a wife, if the name may be given her, be loved and honored as a woman should be? Or can the love, which should bind together man and his offspring, be expected under an institution which subverts, in a great degree, filial dependence and parental authority and care? Slavery withers the affections and happiness of home at their very root, by tainting female purity. Woman, brought up in degradation, placed under another's power and at another's disposal, and never taught to look forward to the happiness of an inviolate, honorable marriage, can hardly possess the feelings and virtues of her sex. A blight falls on her in her early years. Those who have daughters can comprehend her lot. In truth, licentiousness among bond and free is the natural issue of all-polluting slavery. Domestic happiness perishes under its touch, both among bond and free.

How wonderful is it, that, in civilized countries, men can be so steeled by habit as to invade without remorse the peace, purity, and sacred relations of domestic life, as to put asunder those whom God has joined together, as to break up households by processes more painful than death! And this is done for pecuniary profit! What! Can men, having human feeling, grow rich by the desolation of families? We hear of some of the

Southern States enriching themselves by breeding slaves
for sale.   Of all the licensed occupations of society this
is the most detestable.   What!   Grow men like cattle!
Rear human families, like herds of swine, and then
scatter them to the four winds for gain! Among the
imprecations uttered by man on man, is there one more
fearful, more ominous, than the sighing of the mother
bereft of her child by unfeeling cupidity? If blood
cry to God, surely that sigh will be heard in heaven.

Let it not be said, that members of families are often
separated in all conditions of life.   Yes, but separated
under the influence of love.   The husband leaves wife
and children, that he may provide for their support,
and carries them with him in his heart and hopes.   The
sailor, in his lonely night-watch, looks homeward, and
well-known voices come to him amidst the roar of the
waves.   The parent sends away his children, but sends
them to prosper, and to press them again to his heart
with a joy enhanced by separation.   Are such the sep-
arations which slavery makes?   And can he, who has
scattered other families, ask God to bless his own?

4. I proceed to another important view of the evils
of slavery.   Slavery produces and gives license to Cruelty.   By this it is not meant, that cruelty is the universal, habitual, unfailing result.   Thanks to God, Christianity has not entered the world in vain.   Where it has
not cast down, it has mitigated bad institutions.   Slavery in this country differs widely from that of ancient
times, and from that which the Spaniards imposed on
the aboriginals of South America.   There is here an
increasing disposition to multiply the comforts of the
slaves, and in this let us rejoice.   At the same time,

we must remember, that, under the light of the present day, and in a country where Christianity and the rights of men are understood, a diminished severity may contain more guilt than the ferocity of darker ages. Cruelty in its lighter forms is now a greater crime than the atrocious usages of antiquity at which we shudder. " The times of that ignorance God winked at, but *now* he calleth men everywhere to repent." It should also be considered, that the slightest cruelty to the slave is an aggravated wrong, because he is unjustly held in bondage, unjustly held as property. We condemn the man who enforces harshly a righteous claim. What, then, ought we to think of lashing and scarring fellow-creatures, for the purpose of upholding an unrighteous, usurped power, of extorting labor which is not our due ?

I have said, that cruelty is not the habit of the Slave States of this country. Still, that it is frequent we cannot doubt. Reports, which harrow up our souls, come to us from that quarter ; and we know that they must be essentially correct, because it is impossible that a large part, perhaps the majority, of the population of a country can be broken to passive, unlimited submission, without examples of terrible severity.

Let it not be said, as is sometimes done, that cruel deeds are perpetrated everywhere else, as well as in slave-countries. Be it so ; but in all civilized nations unscourged by slavery, a principal object of legislation is to protect every man from cruelty, and to bring every man to punishment, who wantonly tortures or wounds another ; whilst slavery plucks off restraint from the ferocious, or leaves them to satiate their rage with impunity.—Let it not be said, that these barbarities are regarded nowhere with more horror than at the South.

Be it so. They are abhorred, but allowed. The power of individuals to lacerate their fellow-creatures is given to them by the community. The community abhors the abuse, but confers the power which will certainly be abused, and thus strips itself of all defence before the bar of Almighty Justice. It must answer for the crimes which are shielded by its laws. — Let it not be said, that these cruelties are checked by the private interest of the slave-holder. Does regard to private interest save from brutal treatment the draught-horse in our streets? And may not a vast amount of suffering be inflicted, which will not put in peril the life or strength of the slave?

To substantiate the charge of cruelty, I shall not, as I have said, have recourse to current reports, however well established. I am willing to dismiss them all as false. I stand on other ground. Reports may lie, but our daily experience of human nature cannot lie. I summon no witnesses, or rather I appeal to a witness everywhere present, a witness in every heart. Who, that has watched his own heart, or observed others, does not feel that man is not fit to be trusted with absolute, irresponsible power over man? It must be abused. The selfish passions and pride of our nature will as surely abuse it, as the storm will ravage, or the ocean swell and roar under the whirlwind. A being, so ignorant, so headstrong, so passionate, as man, ought not to be trusted with this terrible dominion. He ought not to desire it. He ought to dread it. He ought to cast it from him, as most perilous to himself and others.

Absolute power was not meant for man. There is, indeed, an exception to this rule. There is one case, in which God puts a human being wholly defenceless into another's hands. I refer to the child, who is wholly subjected to the parent's will. But observe how carefully, I might almost say anxiously, God has provided against the abuse of this power. He has raised up for the child in the heart of the parent, a guardian, whom the mightiest on earth cannot resist. He has fitted the parent for this trust, by teaching him to love his offspring better than himself. No eloquence on earth is so subduing as the moaning of the infant when in pain. No reward is sweeter than that infant's smile. We say, God has put the infant into the parent's hands. Might we not more truly say, that he has put the parent into the child's power? That little being sends forth his father to toil, and makes the mother watch over him by day, and fix on him her sleepless eyes by night. No tyrant lays such a yoke. Thus God has fenced and secured from abuse the power of the parent; and yet even the parent has been known, in a moment of passion, to be cruel to his child. Is man, then, to be trusted with absolute power over a fellow-creature, who, instead of being commended by nature to his tenderest love, belongs to a despised race, is regarded as property, is made the passive instrument of his gratification and gain? I ask no documents to prove the abuses of this power, nor do I care what is said to disprove them. Millions may rise up and tell me that the slave suffers little from cruelty. I know too much of human nature, human history, human passion, to believe them. I acquit slave-holders of all peculiar depravity. I judge them by myself. I say, that absolute power always corrupts human nature more or less. I say, that extraordinary, almost miraculous self-control is necessary to secure the slave-holder from provocation and passion;

and is self-control the virtue which, above all others, grows up amidst the possession of irresponsible dominion? Even when the slave-holder honestly acquits himself of cruelty, he may be criminal. His own consciousness is to be distrusted. Having begun with wronging the slave, with wresting from him sacred rights, he may be expected to multiply wrongs, without thought. The degraded state of the slave may induce in the master a mode of treatment essentially inhuman and insulting, but which he never dreams to be cruel. The influence of slavery in indurating the moral feeling and blinding men to wrong, is one of its worst evils.

But suppose the master to be ever so humane. Still, he is not always watching over his slave. He has his pleasures to attend to. He is often absent. His terrible power must be delegated. And to whom is it delegated? To men prepared to govern others, by having learned to govern themselves? To men having a deep interest in the slaves? To wise men, instructed in human nature? To Christians, trained to purity and love? Who does not know, that the office of Overseer is among the last which an enlightened, philanthropic, self-respecting man would choose? Who does not know, how often the overseer pollutes the plantation by his licentiousness, as well as scourges it by his severity? In the hands of such a man, the lash is placed. To such a man is committed the most fearful trust on earth! For his cruelties, the master must answer, as truly as if they were his own. Nor is this all. The master does more than delegate his power to the overseer. How often does he part with it wholly to the slave-dealer! And has be weighed the responsibility of such a transfer? Does he not know, that, in selling his slaves into merciless hands, he is merciless himself, and must give an account to God for every barbarity of which they become the victims ? The notorious cruelty of the slave-dealers, can be no false report, for it belongs to their vocation. These are the men, who throng and defile our Seat of Government, whose slave-markets and slave-dungeons turn to mockery the language of freedom in the halls of Congress, and who make us justly the by-word and the scorn of the nations. Is there no cruelty in putting slaves under the bloody lash of the slave-dealers, to be driven like herds of cattle to distant regions, and there to pass into the hands of strangers, without a pledge of their finding justice or mercy ? · What heart, not seared by custom, would not recoil from such barbarity ?

It has been seen, that I do not ground my argument at all on cases of excessive cruelty. I should attach less importance to these than do most persons, even were they more frequent. They form a very, very small amount of suffering, compared with what is inflicted by abuses of power too minute for notice. Blows, insults, privations, which make no noise, and leave no scar, are incomparably more destructive of happiness than a few brutal violences, which move general indignation. A weak, despised being, having no means of defence or redress, living in a community armed against his rights, regarded as property, and as bound to entire, unresisting compliance with another's will, if not subjected to inflictions of ferocious cruelty, is yet exposed to less striking and shocking forms of cruelty, the amount of which must be a fearful mass of suffering.

But could it be proved, that there are no cruelties in slave-countries, we ought not then to be more recon-

ciled to slavery than we now áre. For what would this
show? That cruelty is not needed. And why not
needed? Because the slave is entirely subdued to his
lot. No man will be wholly unresisting in bondage, but
he who is thoroughly imbued with the spirit of a slave.
If the colored race never need punishment, it is because the feelings of men are dead within them, because
they have no consciousness of rights, because they are
cowards, without respect for themselves, and without
confidence in the sharers of their degraded lot. The
quiet of slavery is like that which the Roman legions
left in ancient Britain, the stillness of death. Why were
the Romans accustomed to work their slaves in chains
by day, and confine them in dungeons by night? Not
because they loved cruelty for its own sake; but because their slaves were stung with a consciousness of
degradation, because they brought from the forests of
Dacia some rude ideas of human dignity, or from civilized countries some experience of social improvements,
which naturally issued in violence and exasperation.
They needed cruelty, for their own wills were not broken to another's, and the spirit of freemen was not wholly gone. The slave *must* meet cruel treatment either
inwardly or outwardly. Either the soul or the body
must receive the blow. Either the flesh must be tortured, or the spirit be struck down. Dreadful alter-
native to which slavery is reduced!

5. I proceed to another view of the evils of slavery.
I refer to its influence on the Master. This topic cannot, perhaps, be so handled as to avoid giving offence;
but without it an imperfect view of the subject would be
given. I will pass over many views. I will say noth-

ing of the tendency of slavery to unsettle the ideas of
Right in the slave-holder, to impair his convictions of
Justice and Benevolence ; or of its tendency to associate
with labor ideas of degradation, and to recommend idleness as an honorable exemption. I will confine myself
to two considerations.

The first is, that slavery, above all other influences,
nourishes the passion for power and its kindred vices.
There is no passion which needs a stronger curb. Men's
worst crimes have sprung from the desire of being masters, of bending others to their yoke. And the natural
tendency of bringing others into subjection to our absolute will, is to quicken into fearful activity the imperious,
haughty, proud, self-seeking propensities of our nature.
Man cannot, without imminent peril to his virtue, own
a fellow-creature, or use the word of absolute command to his brethren. God never delegated this power.
It is a usurpation of the Divine dominion, and its natural influence is to produce a spirit of superiority to Divine as well as to human laws.

Undoubtedly this tendency is in a measure counteracted by the spirit of the age and the genius of Christianity, and in conscientious individuals it may be wholly
overcome ; but we see its fruits in the corruptions of
moral sentiment which prevail among slave-holders. A
quick resentment of whatever is thought to encroach
on personal dignity, a trembling jealousy of reputation,
vehemence of the vindictive passions, and contempt
of all laws, human and divine, in retaliating injury, —
these take rank among the virtues of men whose self-
estimation has been fed by the possession of absolute
power.

Of consequence, the direct tendency of slavery is to

annihilate the control of Christianity. Humility is by
eminence the spirit of Christianity. No vice was so
severely rebuked by our Lord, as the passion for ruling
over others. A deference towards all human beings as
our brethren, a benevolence which disposes us to serve
rather than to reign, to concede our own rather than
to encroach on others' rights, to forgive, not avenge
wrongs, to govern our own spirits, instead of breaking
the spirit of an inferior or foe, — this is Christianity ; a
religion too high and pure to be understood and obeyed
anywhere as it should be, but which meets singular hostility in the habits of mind generated by slavery.

The slave-holder, indeed, values himself on his lofti-
ness of spirit. He has a consciousness of dignity, which
imposes on himself and others. But truth cannot stoop
to this lofty mien. Truth, moral Christian truth, condemns it, and condemns those who bow to it. Self-
respect, founded on a consciousness of our moral nature
and immortal destiny, is, indeed, a noble principle ; but
this sentiment includes, as a part of itself, respect for
all who partake our nature. A consciousness of dignity, founded on the subjection of others to our absolute
will, is inhuman and unjust. It is time that the teachings of Christ were understood. In proportion as a
man acquires a lofty bearing from the habit of command
over wronged and depressed fellow-creatures, so far he
casts away true honor, so far he has fallen in the sight
of God and Virtue.

I approach a more delicate subject, and one on which
I shall not enlarge. To own the persons of others, to
hold females in slavery, is necessarily fatal to the purity
of a people. That unprotected females, stripped by
their degraded condition of woman's self-respect, should

be used to minister to other passions in men than the love of gain, is next to inevitable. Accordingly, in such a community, the reins are given to youthful licentiousness. Youth, everywhere in peril, is in these circumstances urged to vice with a terrible power. And the evil cannot stop at youth. Early licentiousness is fruitful of crime in mature life. How far the obligation to conjugal fidelity, the sacredness of domestic ties, will be revered amidst such habits, such temptations, such facilities to vice, as are involved in slavery, needs no exposition. So sure and terrible is retribution even in this life! Domestic happiness is not blighted in the slave's hut alone. The master's infidelity sheds a blight over his own domestic affections and joys. Home, without purity and constancy, is spoiled of its holiest charm and most blessed influences. I need not say, after the preceding explanations, that this corruption is far from being universal. Still, a slave-country reeks with licentiousness. It is tainted with a deadlier pestilence than the plague.

But the worst is not told. As a consequence of criminal connections, many a master has children born into slavery. Of these, most, I presume, receive protection, perhaps indulgence, during the life of the fathers; but at their death, not a few are left to the chances of a cruel bondage. These cases must have increased, since the difficulties of emancipation have been multiplied. Still more; it is to be feared that there are cases, in which the master puts his own children under the whip of the overseer, or else sells them to undergo the miseries of bondage among strangers. I should rejoice to learn that my impressions on this point are false. If they be true, then our own country, calling

itself enlightened and Christian, is defiled with one of
the greatest enormities on earth.   We send missionaries
to heathen lands.   Among the pollutions of heathenism
I know nothing worse than this.   The heathen, who
feasts on his country's foe, may hold up his head by the
side of the Christian, who sells his child for gain, sells
him to be a slave.   God forbid that I should charge
this crime on a people !   But however rarely it may
occur, it is a fruit of slavery, an exercise of power belonging to slavery, and no laws restrain or punish it.
Such are the evils which spring naturally from the licentiousness generated by slavery.

6. I cannot leave the subject of the evils of slavery,
without saying a word of its Political influence.   Under
this head, I shall not engage in discussions which belong
to the economist.   I shall not repeat, what has been
often proved, that slave-labor is less productive than
free ; nor shall I show, how the ability of a community
to unfold its resources in peace, and to defend itself in
war, must be impaired, by degrading the laboring population to a state, which takes from them motives to toil,
and renders them objects of suspicion or dread.   I wish
only to speak of the influence of slavery on Free Institutions.   This influence, we are gravely told, is favorable, and therefore I am bound to give it a brief notice.
Political liberty is said to find strength and security in
domestic servitude.   Strange mode, indeed, of ensuring
freedom to ourselves, to violate it in the persons of others !   Among the new lights of the age, the most wonderful discovery is, that to spoil others of their rights is
the way to assert the sacredness of our own.

And how is slavery proved to support free institutions? Slave-holding, we are told, infuses an indomitable spirit, and this is a pledge against tyranny. But do we not know that Asia and Africa, slave-holding countries from the earliest date of history, have been paralyzed for ages and robbed of all manly force by despotism? In the feudal ages, the baron, surrounded by his serfs, had undoubtedly enough of a fiery spirit to keep him free, if this were the true defence of freedom; but gradually his pride was curbed, his power broken; a greater tyrant swallowed him up; and the descendants of nobles, who would have died sooner than brooked a master, were turned into courtiers, as pliant as their fathers had been ferocious.

. But " the free states of antiquity," we are told, " had slaves." So had the monarchies of the same periods. With which of these institutions was slavery most congenial? To which did it most probably give support? Besides, it is only by courtesy that we call the ancient republics free. Rome in her best days was an aristocracy; nor were private rights, which it is the chief office of liberty to protect, rendered a whit more secure by the gradual triumphs of the people over patrician power. Slavery was at all periods the curse of Rome. The great mass of her free population, throwing almost every laborious occupation on the slaves, became an idle, licentious rabble; and this unprincipled populace, together with the slaves, furnished ready instruments for every private and public crime. When Clodius prowled the streets of Rome for the murder of Cicero and the best citizens, his train was composed in part of slaves, fit bloodhounds for his nefarious work. The Republic in its proudest days was desolated and convulsed by servile wars. Imperial Rome was over-

whelmed by savage hordes, for this among other reasons,
that her whole peasantry consisted either of slaves, or
of nominal freemen degraded to a servile condition, so
that the legions could be recruited only from tribes of
barbarians whom she had formerly subdued.

But the great argument in favor of the political benefits of slavery, remains to be stated. In plain language
it amounts to this, that slavery excludes the laboring
or poorer classes from the elective franchise, from political power ; and it is the turbulence of these classes
which is supposed to constitute the chief peril of liberty.
But in slave-holding communities, are there no distinctions of condition among the free ? Are none comparatively poor ? Is there no democracy ? Was not Ath-
ens, crowded as she was with slaves, the most turbulent
of democracies ? And further, do not the idleness and
impatience of restraint, into which the free of a slave-
holding community naturally fall, generate an intenser
party-spirit, fiercer political passions, and more desperate instruments of ambition, than can be found among
the laboring classes in a community where slavery is
unknown ? In which of the two great divisions of our
own country are political strifes most likely to be settled
by the sword ? In the Slave-holding States, or the
Free ? The laboring classes, when brought up under
free institutions and equal laws, are not necessarily or
peculiarly disposed to abuse the elective franchise.
Their daily toil, often exhausting, secures them from
habitual political excitement. The most powerful spirits among them are continually rising to a prosperity,
which gives them an interest in public order. There is
also a general diffusion of property, the result of unfettered industry, which forms a general motive to the sup-

port of the laws. It should be added, that the domestic virtues and religious sentiments, which in a Christian country spread through all ranks, and spread more widely among the industrious than the idle, are powerful checks on the passions, strong barriers against civil convulsion. Idleness, rather than toil, makes the turbulent partisan. Whoever knows the state of society in the Free States, can testify, that the love of liberty, pride in our free institutions, and jealousy of rights, are nowhere more active than in those very classes which in a slave-holding country are reduced to servitude. Undoubtedly the jealousies, passions, and prejudices of the laboring portion of the community may work evil, and even ruin to the state; and so may the luxury, the political venality, the gambling spirit of trade, and the cupidity, to be found in other ranks or conditions. If freedom must be denied wherever it will be endangered, then every class in society must be reduced to slavery.

Free institutions rest on two great political virtues, the love of liberty and the love of order. The slave-holder (I mean the slave-holder by choice) is of necessity more or less wanting in both. How plain is it, that no man can love liberty with a true love, who has the heart to wrest it from others! Attachment to freedom does not consist in spurning indignantly a yoke prepared for our own necks; for this is done even by the savage and the beast of prey. It is a moral sentiment, an impartial desire and choice, that others as well as ourselves may be protected from every wrong, may be exempted from every unjust restraint. Slave-holding, when perpetuated selfishly and from choice, is at open war with this generous principle. It is a plain, habitual contempt of human rights, and of course impairs that sense of their sanctity, which is their best protection. It offers, every day and hour, a precedent of usurpation to the ambitious. It creates a caste with despotic powers; and under such guardians is liberty peculiarly secure? It creates a burning zeal for the rights of a privileged class, but not for the Rights of Men. These the voluntary slave-holder casts down by force; and, in the changes of human affairs, the time may not be distant, when he will learn, that force, accustomed to triumph over right, is prone to leap every bound, and to make the proud as well as abject stoop to its sway.

Slavery is also hostile to the love of order, which, in union with the love of liberty, is the great support of free institutions. Slave-holding in a republic tends directly to. lawlessness. It gives the habit of command, not of obedience. The absolute master is not likely to distinguish himself by subjection to the civil power. The substitution of passion and self-will for law, is nowhere so common as in the Slave-holding States. 'In these it is thought honorable to rely on one's own arm, rather than on the magistrate, for the defence of many rights. In some, perhaps many, districts, the chief peace-officer seems to be the weapon worn as part of the common dress; and the multitude seem to be more awed by one another's passions, than by the authority of the state. Such communities have no pledge of stable liberty. Reverence for the laws, as manifestations of the public will, is the very spirit of free institutions. Does this spirit find its best nutriment in the habits and feelings generated by slavery?

Slavery is a strange element to mix up with free institutions. It cannot but endanger them. It is a pattern for every kind of wrong. The slave brings insecurity

on the free. Whoever holds one human being in bondage, invites others to plant the foot on his own neck.
Thanks to God, not one human being can be wronged
with impunity. The liberties of a people ought to tremble, until every man is free. Tremble they will. Their
true foundation is sapped by the legalized degradation
of a single innocent man to slavery. That foundation
is impartial justice, is respect for human nature, is respect for the rights of every human being.

I have endeavoured, in these remarks, to show the
hostility between slavery and free institutions. If, however, I err, if these institutions cannot stand without
slavery for their foundation, then I say, Let them fall.
Then they ought to be buried in perpetual ruins. Then
the name of republicanism ought to become a by-word
and reproach among the nations. Then monarchy, limited as it is in England, is incomparably better and happier than our more popular forms. Then despotism, as
it exists in Prussia, where equal laws are in the main
administered with impartiality, ought to be preferred.
A republican government, bought by the sacrifice of
half or more than half of a people, by stripping them of
their most sacred rights, by degrading them to a brutal
condition, would cost too much. A freedom so tainted
with wrong ought to be our abhorrence. They, who
tell us that slavery is a necessary condition of a republic,
do not justify the former, but pronounce a sentence of
reprobation on the latter. If they speak truth, we are
bound as a people to seek more just and generous institutions, under which the rights of all will be secure.

I have now placed before the reader the chief evils
of slavery. We are told, however, that these are not

without mitigation, that slavery has advantages which do much to counterbalance its wrongs and pains. Not a few are partially reconciled to the institution by the language of confidence in which its benefits are sometimes announced. I shall therefore close this chapter with a very brief consideration of what are thought to be the advantages of slavery.

It is often said, that the slave does less work than the free laborer; he bears a lighter burden than liberty would lay on him. Perhaps this is generally true; yet, when circumstances promise profit to the master from the imposition of excessive labor, the slave is not spared. In the West Indies, the terrible waste of life among the over-worked cultivators, required large supplies from Africa to keep up the failing population. In this country it is probably true, that the slave works less than the free laborer; but it does not therefore follow, that his work is lighter. For what is it that lightens toil? It is Hope; it is Love; it is Strong Motive. That labor is light which we do from the heart, to which a great good quickens us, which is to better our lot. That labor is light which is to comfort, adorn, and cheer our homes, to give instruction to our children, to solace the declining years of a parent, to give to our grateful and generous sentiments the means of exertion. Great effort from great motives is the best definition of a happy life. The easiest labor is a burden to him who has no motive for performing it. How wearisome is the task imposed by another, and wrongfully imposed! The slave cannot easily be made to do a freeman's work; and why? Because he wants a freeman's spirit, because the spring of labor is impaired within him, because he works as a machine, not a free agent. The compulsion, under which he toils for another, takes from labor its sweetness, makes the daily round of life arid and dull, makes escape from toil the chief interest of life.

We are further told, that the slave is freed from all care, that he is sure of future support, that when old he is not dismissed to the poor-house, but fed and sheltered in his own hut. This is true ; but it is also true that nothing can be gained by violating the great laws and essential rights of our nature. The slave, we are told, has no care, his future is provided for. Yet God created him to provide for the future, to take care of his own happiness ; and he cannot be freed from this care without injury to his moral and intellectual life. Why has God given foresight and power over the future, but to be used ? Is it a blessing to a rational creature to be placed in a condition which chains his faculties to the present moment, which leaves nothing before him to rouse the intellect or touch the heart ? Be it also remembered, that the same provision, which relieves the slave from anxiety, cuts him off from hope. The future is not, indeed, haunted by spectres of poverty, nor is it brightened by images of joy. It stretches before him sterile, monotonous, expanding into no refreshing verdure, and sending no cheering whisper of a better lot.

It is true that the free laborer may become a pauper ; and so may the free rich man, both of the North and the South. Still, our capitalists never dream of flying to slavery as a security against the almshouse. Freedom undoubtedly has its perils. It offers nothing to the slothful and dissolute. Among a people left to seek their own good in their own way, some of all classes fail from vice, some from incapacity, some from misfortune. All

classes will furnish members to the body of the poor.
But in this country the number is small, and ought constantly to decrease. The evil, however lamentable, is
not so remediless and spreading as to furnish a motive
for reducing half the population to chains. Benevolence does much to mitigate it. The best minds are
inquiring how it may be prevented, diminished, removed.
It is giving excitement to a philanthropy which creates
out of misfortune new bonds of union between man and
man.

Our slave-holding brethren, who tell us that the condition of the slave is better than that of the free laborer
at the North, talk ignorantly and rashly. They do not,
cannot know, what to us is matter of daily observation,
that from the families of our farmers and mechanics have
sprung our most distinguished men, men who have done
most for science, arts, letters, religion, and freedom ;
and that the noblest spirits among us would have been
lost to their country and mankind, had the laboring class
here been doomed to slavery. They do not know,
what we rejoice to tell them, that this class partakes
largely of the impulse given to the whole community ;
that the means of intellectual improvement are multiplying to the laborious as fast as to the opulent ; that
our most distinguished citizens meet them as brethren,
and communicate to them in public discourses their own
most important acquisitions. Undoubtedly, the Christian, republican spirit is not working, even here, as it
should. The more improved and prosperous classes
have not yet learned, that it is their great mission to elevate morally and intellectually the less advanced classes
of the community ; but the great truth is more and more
recognised, and accordingly a new era may be said to
be opening on society.

It is said, however, that the slave, if not to be compared to the free laborer at the North, is in a happier
condition than the Irish peasantry. Let this be granted.
Let the security of the peasant's domestic relations, let
his church and his school-house, and his faint hope of
a better lot pass for nothing. Because Ireland is suffering from the misgovernment and oppression of ages,
does it follow that a less grinding oppression is a good?
Besides, are not the wrongs of Ireland acknowledged?
Is not British legislation laboring to restore her prosperity? Is it not true, that, whilst the slave's lot admits
no important change, the most enlightened minds are
at work to confer on the Irish peasant the blessings of
education, of equal laws, of new springs to exertion, of
new sources of wealth? Other men, however fallen,
may be lifted up. An immovable weight presses on
the slave.

But still we are told, the slave is gay. He is not
as wretched as our theories teach. After his toil, he
sings, he dances, he gives no signs of an exhausted
frame or gloomy spirit. The slave happy! Why, then,
contend for rights? Why follow with beating hearts
the struggles of the patriot for freedom? Why canonize
the martyr to freedom? The slave happy! Then happiness is to be found in giving up the distinctive attributes of a man; in darkening intellect and conscience;
in quenching generous sentiments; in servility of spirit;
in living under a whip; in having neither property nor
rights; in holding wife and child at another's pleasure;
in toiling without hope; in living without an end! The
slave, indeed, has his pleasures. His animal nature
survives the injury to his rational and moral powers;
and every animal has its enjoyments. The kindness

of Providence allows no human being to be wholly divorced from good.   The lamb frolics ; the dog leaps
for joy ; the bird fills the air with cheerful harmony ;
and the slave spends his holyday in laughter and the
dance.   Thanks to Him who never leaves himself without witness ; who cheers even the desert with spots
of verdure ; and opens a fountain of joys in the most
withered heart !   It is not possible, however, to contemplate the occasional gayety of the slave without some
mixture of painful thought.   He is, gay, because he has
not learned to think ; because he is too fallen to feel
his wrongs ; because he wants just self-respect.   We
are grieved by the gayety of the insane.   There is a
sadness in the gayety of him whose lightness of heart
would be turned to bitterness and indignation, were one
ray of light to awaken in him the spirit of a man.

That there are those among the free, who are more
wretched than slaves, is undoubtedly true ; just as there
is incomparably greater misery among men than among
brutes.   The brute never knows the agony of a human
spirit torn by remorse, or wounded in its love.   But
would we cease to be human, because our capacity for
suffering increases with the elevation of our nature ?   All
blessings may be perverted, and the greatest perverted
most.   Were we to visit a slave-country, undoubtedly
the most miserable human beings would be found among
the free ; for among them the passions have wider sweep,
and the power they possess may be used to their own
ruin.   Liberty is not a necessity of happiness.   It is
only a means of good.   It is a trust which may be
abused.   Are all such trusts to be cast away ?   Are
they not the greatest gifts of Heaven ? .

But the slave, we are told, often manifests affection

to his master, grieves at his departure, and welcomes his return. I will not endeavour to explain this, by saying that the master's absence places the slave under the overseer. Nor will I object, that the slave's propensity to steal from his master, his need of the whip to urge him to toil, and the dread of insurrection which he inspires, are signs of any thing but love. There is, undoubtedly, much more affection in this relation than could be expected. Of all races of men, the African is the mildest and most susceptible of attachment. He loves, where the European would hate. He watches the life of a master, whom the North American Indian, in like circumstances, would stab to the heart. The African is affectionate. Is this a reason for holding him in chains ? We cannot, however, think of this most interesting feature of slavery with unmixed pleasure. It is the curse of slavery, that it can touch nothing which it does not debase. Even love, that sentiment given us by God to be the germ of a divine virtue, becomes in the slave a weakness, almost a degradation. His affections lose much of their beauty and dignity. He ought, indeed, to feel benevolence toward his master ; but to attach himself to a man who keeps him in the dust and denies him the rights of a man ; to be grateful and devoted to one who extorts his toil and debases him into a chattel ; this has a taint of servility, which makes us grieve whilst we admire. However, we would not diminish the attachment of the slave. He is the happier for his generosity. Let him love his master, and let the master win love by kindness. We only say, let not this manifestation of a generous nature in the slave be turned against him. Let it not be made an answer to an exposition of his wrongs. Let it not be used as a weapon for his perpetual degradation.

But the slave, we are told, is taught Religion. This is the most cheering sound which comes to us from the land of bondage. We are rejoiced to learn, that any portion of the slaves are instructed in that truth, which gives inward freedom. They hear at least one voice of deep, genuine love, the voice of Christ; and read in his cross what all other things hide from them, the unutterable worth of their spiritual nature. This portion, however, is small. The greater part are still buried in heathen ignorance. Besides, religion, though a great good, can hardly exert its full power on the slave. Will it not be taught to make him obedient to his master, rather than to raise him to the dignity of a man? Is slavery, which tends so proverbially to debase the mind, the preparation for spiritual truth? Can the slave comprehend the principle of Love, the essential principle of Christianity, when he hears it from the lips of those whose relations to him express injustice and selfishness? But suppose him to receive Christianity in its purity, and to feel all its power. Is this to reconcile us to slavery? Is a being, who can understand the sublimest truth which has ever entered the human mind, who can love and adore God, who can conform himself to the celestial virtue of the Saviour, for whom that Saviour died, to whom heaven is opened, whose repentance now gives joy in heaven, — is such a being to be held as property, driven by force as the brute, and denied the rights of man by a fellow-creature, by a professed disciple of the just and merciful Saviour? Has he a religions nature, and dares any one hold him as a slave?

I have now completed my views of the evils of slavery, and have shown how little they are mitigated by what are thought its advantages. In this whole discussion I have cautiously avoided quoting particular examples of its baneful influences. I have not brought together accounts of horrible cruelty which come to us from the South. I have confined myself to the natural tendencies of slavery, to evils bound up in its very nature, which, as long as man is man, cannot be separated from it. That these evils are unmixed, I do not say. More or less of good may often be found in connexion with them. No institution, be it what it may, can make the life of a human being wholly evil, or cut off every means of improvement. God's benevolence triumphs over all the perverseness and folly of man's devices. He sends a cheering beam into the darkest abode. The slave has his hours of exhilaration. His hut occasionally rings with thoughtless mirth. Among this class, too, there are and must be, occasionally, higher pleasures. God is no respecter of persons; and in some slaves there is a happy nature which no condition can destroy, just as among children we find some whom the worst education cannot spoil. The African is so affectionate, imitative, and docile, that in favorable circumstances he catches much that is good ; and accordingly the influence of a wise and kind master will be seen in the very countenance and bearing of his slaves. Among this degraded people, there are, occasionally, examples of superior intelligence and virtue, showing the groundlessness of the opinion that they are incapable of filling a higher rank than slavery, and showing that human nature is too generous and hardy to be wholly destroyed in the most unpropitious state. We also witness in this class, and very often, a superior physical developement, a grace of form and motion, which almost extorts a

feeling approaching respect. I mean not to affirm, that
slavery excludes all good, for human life cannot long
endure under the privation of every thing happy and improving. I have spoken of its natural tendencies and
results. These are wholly and only evil.

I am aware that it will be replied to the views now
given of slavery, that persons living at a distance from
it cannot comprehend it, that its true character can be
learned only from those who know it practically, and are
familiar with its operations. To this I will not reply,
that I have seen it near at hand. It is sufficient to reply, that men may lose the power of seeing an object
fairly, by being too near as well as by being too remote.
The slave-holder is too familiar with slavery to understand it. To be educated in injustice is almost necessarily to be blinded by it more or less. To exercise
usurped power from birth is the surest way to look upon
it as a right and a good. The slave-holder tells us, that
he only can instruct us about slavery. But suppose
that we wished to learn the true character of despotism;
should we go to the palace, and take the despot as our
teacher ? Should we pay much heed to his assurance,
that he alone could understand the character of absolute
power, and that we in a republic could know nothing of
the condition of men subjected to irresponsible will?
The sad influence of slavery, in darkening the mind
which is perpetually conversant with it, is disclosed to
us in the recent attempts made at the South to represent
this institution as a good. Freemen, who would sooner
die than resign their rights, talk of the happiness of
those from whom every right is wrested. They talk of
the slave as "property," with the same confidence as
if this were the holiest claim. This is one of the mourn-

ful effects of slavery. It darkens the moral sense of the master. And can men, whose position is so unfavorable to just, impartial judgment, expect us to acquiesce in their views?

There is another reply. If the Slave-holding States expect us to admit their views of this institution, they must allow it to be freely discussed among themselves. Of what avail is their testimony in favor of slavery, when not a tongue is allowed to say a word in its condemnation? Of what use is the press, when it can publish only on one side? In large portions of the Slave-holding States, freedom of speech on this subject is at an end. Whoever should publish among them the sentiments respecting slavery, which are universally adopted through the civilized world, would put his life in jeopardy, would probably by flayed or hung. On this great subject, which affects vitally their peace and prosperity, their moral and political interests, no philanthropist, who has come to the truth, can speak his mind. Even the minister of religion, who feels the hostility between slavery and Christianity, dares not speak. His calling might not save him from popular rage. Thus slavery avenges itself. It brings the masters under despotism. It takes away that liberty which a freeman prizes as life, liberty of speech. All this, we are told, is necessary, and so it may be; but an institution imposing such a necessity cannot be a good : and one thing is plain ; the testimony of men placed under such restraints cannot be too cautiously received. We have better sources of knowledge. We have the testimony of ages, and the testimony of the unchangeable principles of human nature. These assure us that slavery is " evil, and evil continually."

I ought not to close this head without acknowledging,
(what I cheerfully do,) that in many cases the kindness
of masters does much for the mitigation of slavery.
Could it be rendered harmless, the efforts of many
would not be spared to make it so. It is evil, not
through any singular corruption in the slave-holder,
but from its own nature, and in spite of all efforts to
make it a good. It is evil, not because it exists on this
or that spot. Were it planted at the North, it might
become a greater curse, more hardening and depraving,
than it now proves under a milder sky. It is not of ₊the
particular form of slavery in this country that I complain.
I am willing to allow that it is here comparatively mild ;
that on many plantations no abuses exist, but such as
are inseparable from its very nature. The mischief lies
in its very nature. "Men do not gather grapes of thorns,
or figs of thistles." An institution so founded in wrong,
so imbued with injustice, cannot be made a good. It
cannot, like other institutions, be perpetuated by being
improved. To improve it, is to prepare the way for its
subversion. Every melioration of the slave's lot is a
step toward freedom. Slavery is thus radically, essentially evil. Every good man should earnestly pray, and
use every virtuous influence, that an institution so blighting to human nature may be brought to an end.

CHAPTER V.

SCRIPTURE.

Attempts are often made to support slavery by the authority of Revelation. " Slavery," it is said, " is allowed in the Old Testament, and not condemned in the New. Paul commands slaves to obey. He commands masters, not to release their slaves, but to treat them justly. .Therefore slavery is right, is sanctified by God's Word." In this age of the world, and amidst the light which has been thrown on the true interpretation of the Scriptures, such reasoning hardly deserves notice. A few words only will be offered in reply.

This reasoning proves too much. If usages, sanctioned in the Old Testament and not forbidden in the New, are right, then our moral code will undergo a sad deterioration. Polygamy was allowed to the Israelites, was the practice of the holiest men, and was common and licensed in the age of the Apostles. But the Apostles nowhere condemn it, nor was the renunciation of it made an essential condition of admission into the Christian church. It is true, that in one passage Christ has condemned it by implication. But is not slavery condemned by stronger implication, in the many passages which make the new religion to consist in serving one another, and in doing to others what we

would that they should do to ourselves? Why may rot
Scripture be used to stock our houses with wives as
well as with slaves?

Again. Paul is said to sanction slavery. Let us now
ask, What was slavery in the age of Paul? It was
the slavery, not so much of black as of white men, not
merely of barbarians, but of Greeks, not merely of the
ignorant and debased, but of the virtuous, educated, and
refined. Piracy and conquest were the chief means of
supplying the slave-market, and they heeded neither
character nor condition. Sometimes the greater part
of the population of a captured city was sold into bondage, sometimes the whole, as in the case of Jerusalem.
Noble and royal families, the rich and great, the learned
and powerful, the philosopher and poet, the wisest and
best men, were condemned to the chain. Such was
ancient slavery. And this, we are told, is allowed and
confirmed by the word of God! Had Napoleon, on
capturing Berlin or Vienna, doomed most or the whole
of their inhabitants to bondage; had he seized on venerable matrons, the mothers of illustrious men, who were
reposing, after virtuous lives, in the bosom of grateful
families; had he seized on the delicate, refined, beautiful young woman, whose education had prepared her
to grace the sphere in which God had placed her, and
over all whose prospects the freshest hopes and most
glowing imaginations of early life were breathed; had he
seized on the minister of religion, the man of science,
the man of genius, the sage, the guides of the world;
had he scattered these through the slave-markets of the
world, and transferred them to the highest bidders at
public auction, the men to be converted into instruments
of slavish toil, the women into instruments of lust, and

both to endure whatever indignities and tortures absolute power can inflict ; we should then have had a picture, in the present age, of slavery as it existed in the time of Paul. Such slavery, we are told, was sanctioned by the Apostle! Such, we are told, he pronounced to be morally right! Had Napoleon sent some cargoes of these victims to these shores, we might have bought them, and degraded the noblest beings to our lowest uses, and might have cited Paul to testify to our innocence! Were an infidel to bring this charge against the Apostle, we should say that he was laboring in his vocation; but that a professed Christian should so insult this sainted philanthropist, this martyr to truth and benevolence, is a sad proof of the power of slavery to blind its supporters to the plainest truth.

Slavery, in the age of the Apostle, had so penetrated society, was so intimately interwoven with it, and the materials of servile war were so abundant, that a religion, preaching freedom to the slave, would have shaken the social fabric to its foundation, and would have armed against itself the whole power of the state. Paul did not then assail the institution. He satisfied himself with spreading principles, which, however slowly, could not but work its destruction. He commanded Philemon to receive his fugitive slave, Onesimus, "not as a slave, but above a slave, as a brother beloved;" and he commanded masters to give to their slaves that which was "*just* and *equal*"; thus asserting for the slave the rights of a Christian and a Man; and how, in his circumstances, he could have done more for the subversion of slavery, I do not see.

Let me offer another remark. The perversion of Scripture to the support of slavery is singularly inexcus-

9 *

able in this country.   Paul not only commanded slaves
to obey their masters.   He delivered these precepts :
" Let every soul be subject unto the higher powers.
For there is no power but of God ; the powers that be
are ordained of God.   Whosoever, therefore, resisteth
the power, resisteth the ordinance of God ; and they
that resist shall receive to themselves damnation."   This
passage was written in the time of Nero.   It teaches
passive obedience to despotism more strongly than any
text teaches the lawfulness of slavery.   Accordingly, it
has been quoted for ages by the supporters of arbitrary
power, and made the stronghold of tyranny.   Did our
fathers acquiesce in the most obvious interpretation of
this text ?   Because the first Christians were taught to
obey despotic rule, did our fathers feel as if Christianity had stripped men of their rights ?   Did they argue, that tyranny was to be excused, because forcible
opposition to it is in most cases wrong ?   Did they argue, that absolute power ceases to be unjust, because,
as a general rule, it is the duty of subjects to obey ?
Did they infer that bad institutions ought to be perpetual, because the subversion of them by force will almost
always inflict greater evil than it removes ?   No ; they
were wiser interpreters of God's Word.   They believed
that despotism was a wrong, notwithstanding the general
obligation upon its subjects to obey ; and that whenever
a whole people should so feel the wrong as to demand
its removal, the time for removing it had fully come.
Such is the school in which we here have been brought
up.   To us, it is no mean proof of the divine original
of Christianity, that it teaches human brotherhood and
favors human rights ; and yet, on the ground of two or
three passages, which admit different constructions, we

make Christianity the minister of slavery, the forger of chains for those whom it came to make free.

It is a plain rule of Scriptural criticism, that particular texts should be interpreted according to the general tenor and spirit of Christianity. And what is the general, the perpetual teaching of Christianity in regard to social duty? "All things whatsoever ye would that men should do to you, do ye even so to them; for this is the law and the prophets." Now does not every man feel, that nothing, nothing, could induce him to consent to be a slave? Does he not feel, that, if reduced to this abject lot, his whole nature, his reason, conscience, affections, would cry out against it as the greatest of calamities and wrongs? Can he pretend, then, that, in holding others in bondage, he does to his neighbour what he would that his neighbour should do to him? Of what avail are a few texts, which were designed for local and temporary use, when urged against the vital, essential spirit, and the plainest precepts of our religion?

I close this section with a few extracts from a recent work of one of our most distinguished writers; not that I think additional arguments necessary, but because the authority of Scripture is more successfully used than any thing else to reconcile good minds to slavery.

"This very course, which the Gospel takes on this subject, seems to have been the only one that could have been taken in order to effect the universal abolition of slavery. The Gospel was designed, not for one race or for one time, but for all races and for all times. It looked, not at the abolition of this form of evil for that age alone, but for its universal abolition. Hence the important object of its author was to gain it a lodgment in every part of the known world; so that, by its universal diffusion among all classes of society, it might quietly and peacefully modify and subdue the evil passions of men ; and thus, without violence, work a revolution in the whole mass of mankind. In this manner alone could its object, a universal moral revolution, have been accomplished. For if it had forbidden the *evil*, instead of subverting the *principle*, if it had proclaimed the unlawfulness of slavery, and taught slaves to *resist* the oppression of their masters, it would instantly have arrayed the two parties in deadly hostility throughout the civilized world ; its announcement would have been the signal of servile war ; and the very name of the Christian religion would have been forgotten amidst the agitations of universal bloodshed. The fact, under these circumstances, that the Gospel does not forbid slavery, affords no reason to suppose that it does not mean to prohibit it ; much less does it afford ground for belief that Jesus Christ intended *to authorize it.*

" It is important to remember, that two grounds of moral obligation are distinctly recognised in the Gospel. The first is our duty to man as man ; that is, on the ground of the relation which men sustain to each other ; the second is our duty to man as a creature of God ; that is, on the ground of the relation which we all sustain to God. — Now it is to be observed, that it is precisely upon this latter ground that the slave is commanded to obey his master. It is never urged, like the duty of obedience to parents, *because it is right*, but because the cultivation of meekness and forbearance under injury will be well-pleasing unto God. — The manner in which the duty of servants or slaves is inculcated, therefore, affords no ground for the assertion, that the Gospel authorizes one man to hold another in bondage, any more than the command to honor the king, when that king was Nero, authorized the tyranny of the emperor ; or than the command to turn the other cheek, when one is smitten, justifies the infliction of violence by an injurious man." *

* Wayland's "Elements of Moral Science," pages 225 and 226. The discussion of Slavery, in the chapter from which these extracts are made, is well worthy attention.

How slavery shall be removed, is a question for the slave-holder, and one which he alone can fully answer. He alone has an intimate knowledge of the character and habits of the slaves, to which the means of emancipation should be carefully adapted. General views and principles may and should be suggested at a distance; but the mode of applying them can be understood only by those who dwell on the spot where the evil exists. To the slave-holder belongs the duty of settling and employing the best methods of liberation, and to no other. We have no right of interference, nor do we desire it. We hold that the dangers of emancipation, if such there are, would be indefinitely increased, were the boon to come to the slave from a foreign hand, were he to see it forced on the master by a foreign power. It is of the highest importance that slavery should be succeeded by a friendly relation between master and slave; and to produce this, the latter must see in the former his benefactor and deliverer. His liberty must seem to him an expression of benevolence and regard for his rights. He must put confidence in his superiors, and look to them cheerfully and gratefully for counsel and aid. Let him feel that liberty has been wrung

from an unwilling master, who would willingly replace
the chain, and jealousy, vindictiveness, and hatred would
spring up, to blight the innocence and happiness of his
new freedom, and to make it a peril to himself and all
around him. I believe, indeed, that emancipation, though
so bestowed, would be better than everlasting bondage ;
but the responsibility of so conferring it, is one that none
of us are anxious to assume.

We cannot but fear much from the experiment now
in progress in the West Indies, on account of its being
the work of a foreign hand. The planters, especially of
Jamaica, have opposed the mother-country with a per-
tinaciousness bordering on insánity ; have done much
to exasperate the slaves, whose freedom they could not
prevent ; have done nothing to prepare them for liberty ;
have met them with gloom on their countenances, and
with evil auguries on their lips ; have taught them to
look abroad for relief, and to see in their masters only
obstructions to the amelioration of their lot. It is possible, that, under all these obstacles, emancipation may
succeed. God grant it success ! If it fail, the planter
will have brought the ruin very much on himself. Policy, as well as duty, so plainly taught him to take into
his own hands the work which a superior power had
begun, to spare no effort, no expense, for binding to
him by new ties those who were to throw off their former chains, that we know not how to account for his
conduct, but by supposing that his unhappy position as
a slave-holder had robbed him of his reason, as well as
blunted his moral sense.

In this country no power but that of the Slave-holding
States can remove the evil, and none of us are anxious
to take the office from their hands. They alone can

do it safely. They alone can determine and apply the true and sure means of emancipation. That such means exist I cannot doubt ; for emancipation has already been carried through successfully in other countries ; and even were there no precedent, I should be sure, that, under God's benevolent and righteous government, there could not be a necessity for holding human beings in perpetual bondage. This faith, however, is not universal. Many, when they hear of the evils of slavery, say, " It is bad, but remediless. There are no means of relief." They say, in a despairing tone, " Give us your plan ; " and justify their indifference to emancipation, by what they call its hopelessness. This state of mind has induced me to offer a few remarks on the means of removing slavery ; not that I think of drawing up a plan ; for to this I am necessarily unequal. No individual so distant can do the work, to which the whole intellect and benevolence of the South should be summoned. I wish only to suggest a few principles, which I think would ensure a happy result to the benevolent enterprise, and which may help to remove the incredulity of which I have complained.

What, then, is to be done for the removal of slavery ? In the first place, the great principle, that man cannot rightfully be held as property, should be admitted by the slave-holder. As to any public forms of setting forth this principle, they are of little or no moment, provided it be received into the mind and heart. The slave should be acknowledged as a partaker of a common nature, as having the essential rights of humanity. This great truth lies at the foundation of every wise plan for his relief. The cordial admission of it would give a consciousness of dignity, of grandeur, to efforts for emancipation. There is, indeed, a grandeur in the idea of raising more than two millions of human beings to the enjoyment of human rights, to the blessings of Christian civilization, to the means of indefinite improvement. The Slave-holding States are called to a nobler work of benevolence than is committed to any other communities. They should comprehend its dignity. This they cannot do, till the slave is truly, sincerely, with the mind and heart, recognised as a Man, till he ceases to be regarded as Property.

It may be asked, whether I intend that the slave should be immediately set free from all his present restraints. By no means. Nothing is farther from my thoughts. The slave cannot rightfully, and should not, be owned by the Individual. But, like every other citizen, he is subject to the community, and the community has a right and is bound to continue all such restraints, as its own safety and the well-being of the slave demand. It would be cruelty, not kindness, to the latter to give him a freedom, which he is unprepared to understand or enjoy. It would be cruelty to strike the fetters from a man, whose first steps would infallibly lead him to a precipice. The Slave should not have an owner, but he should have a guardian. He needs authority, to supply the lack of that discretion which he has not yet attained ; but it should be the authority of a friend ; an official authority, conferred by the state, and for which there should be responsibleness to the state ; an authority especially designed to prepare its subjects for personal freedom. The slave should not, in the first instance, be allowed to wander at his will beyond the plantation on which he toils ; and if he cannot be induced to work by rational and natural motives, he should be obliged to labor; on the same principles on which the vagrant in other communities is confined and compelled to earn his bread. The gift of liberty would be a mere name, and worse than nominal, were he to be let loose on society, under circumstances driving him to crimes, for which he would be condemned to severer bondage than he had escaped. Many restraints must be continued; but continued, not because the colored race are property, not because they are bound to live and toil for an owner, but solely and wholly because their own innocence, security, and education, and the public order and peace, require them, during the present incapacity, to be restrained. It should be remembered, that this incapacity is not their fault, but their misfortune; that not they, but the community, are responsible for it; and that the community, without crime, profit by its own wrong. If the government should make any distinction among the citizens, it should be in behalf of the injured. Instead of urging the past existence of slavery, and the incapacity which it has induced, as apologies, or reasons for continuing the yoke, the community should find in these very circumstances new obligations to effort for the wronged.

There is but one weighty argument against immediate emancipation, namely, that the slave would not support himself and his children by honest industry; that, having always worked on compulsion, he will not work without it; that, having always labored from another's will, he will not labor from his own; that there is no spring of exertion in his own mind; that he is unused to forethought, providence, and self-denial, and the responsibilities of domestic life; that freedom would produce idleness; idleness, want; want, crime; and that crime, when it should become the habit of numbers, would bring misery, perhaps ruin, not only on the offenders, but the state. Here lies the strength of the argument for continuing present restraint. Give the slaves disposition and power to support themselves and their families by honest industry, and complete emancipation should not be delayed one hour.

The great step, then, towards the removal of slavery is to prepare the slaves for self-support. And this work seems attended with no peculiar difficulty. The colored man is not a savage, to whom toil is torture, who has centred every idea of happiness and dignity in a wild freedom, who must exchange the boundless forest for a narrow plantation, and bend his proud neck to an unknown yoke. Labor was his first lesson, and he has been repeating it all his life. Can it be a hard task to teach him to labor for himself, to work from impulses in his own breast?

Much may be done at once to throw the slave on himself, to accustom him to work for his own and his family's support, to awaken forethought, and strengthen the habit of providing for the future. On every plantation there are slaves, who would do more for wages than from fear of punishment. There are those, who, if intrusted with a piece of ground, would support themselves and pay a rent in kind. There are those, who, if moderate task-work were given them, would gain their whole subsistence in their own time. Now every such man ought to be committed very much to himself. It is a crime to subject to the whip a man who can be made to toil from rational and honorable motives. This partial introduction of freedom would form a superior class among the slaves, whose example would have

immense moral power on those who needed compulsion.
The industrious and thriving would give an impulse to
the whole race. It is important that the property, thus
earned by the slave, should be made as sacred as that
of any other member of the community, and for this
end he should be enabled to obtain redress of wrongs.
In case of being injured by his master in this or in any
respect, he should either be set free, or, if unprepared
for liberty, should be transferred to another guardian.
This system may seem to many to be attended with insuperable difficulties; but if established and watched
over by a community sincerely desirous of emancipation
(and no other influence can establish it here), it would
find in public sentiment, even more than in law, the
means of execution.

As another means of raising the slave and fitting him
to act from higher motives than compulsion, a system
of bounties and rewards should be introduced. New-
privileges, increased indulgences, honorable distinctions,
expressions of respect, should be awarded to the honest
and industrious. No people are more alive to com-
mendation and honorable distinction than the colored
race. Prizes for good conduct, adapted to their tastes
and character, might in a good degree supersede the
lash. The object is to bring the slave to labor from
other motives than brutal compulsion. Such motives
may easily be found, if the end be conscientiously proposed.

One of the great means of elevating the slave, and
calling forth his energies, is to place his domestic relations on new ground. This is essential. We wish him
to labor for his family. Then he must have a family
to labor for. Then his wife and children must be truly

his own. Then his home must be inviolate. Then the responsibilities of a husband and father must be laid on him. It is agreed that he will be fit for freedom as soon as the support of his family shall become his habit and his happiness; and how can he be brought to this condition, as long as he shall see no sanctity in the marriage bond, as long as he shall see his wife and his children exposed to indignity and to sale, as long as their support shall not be intrusted to his care? No measure for preparing the slave for liberty can be so effectual as the improvement of his domestic lot. The whole power of religion should be employed to impress him with the sacredness and duties of marriage. The chaste and the faithful in this connexion should receive open and strong marks of respect. They should be treated as at the head of their race. The husband and wife, who prove false to each other, and who will not labor for their children, should be visited with the severest rebuke. To create a sense of domestic obligation, to awaken domestic affections, to give the means of domestic happiness, to fix deeply a conviction of the indissolubleness of marriage, and of the solemnity of the parental relation, these are the essential means of raising the slave to a virtuous and happy freedom. All other men labor for their families; and so will the slave, if the sentiments of a man be cherished in his breast. We keep him in bondage, because, if free, he will leave his wife and children to want; and this bondage breaks down all the feelings and habits which would incite him to toil for their support. Not a step will be taken towards the preparation of the slave for voluntary labor, till his domestic rights be respected. The viola-

10 *

tion of these cries to God, more than any other evil of his lot.

To carry this and all other means of improvement into effect, it is essential that the slave should no longer be bought and sold. As long as he is made an article of merchandise, he cannot be fitted for the offices of a man. He will have little motive to accumulate com-forts and ornaments in his hut, if at any moment he may be torn from it. While treated as property, he will have little encouragement to accumulate property, for it cannot be secure. While his wife and children may be exposed at auction, and carried he knows not where, can he be expected to feel and act as a husband and father ? It is time that this Christian and civilized country should no longer be dishonored by one of the worst usages of barbarism. Break up the slave-market, and one of the chief obstructions to emancipation will be removed.

Let me only add, that religious instruction should go hand in hand with all other means for preparing the slave for freedom. The colored race are said to be peculiarly susceptible of the religious sentiment. If this be addressed wisely and powerfully, if the slave be brought to feel his relation and accountableness to God, and to comprehend the spirit of Christianity, he is fit for freedom. To accomplish this work, perhaps preaching should not be the only or chief instrument. Were the colored population to be assembled into Sun-day-schools, and were the whites to become their teach-ers, a new and interesting relation would be formed between the races, and an influence be exerted which would do much to insure safety to the gift of freedom.

In these remarks, I have not intended to say that

emancipation is an easy work, the work of a day, a
good to be accomplished without sacrifices and toil.
The colored man is, indeed, singularly susceptible of
improvement, in consequence of the strength of his
propensities to imitation and sympathy. But all great
changes in society have their difficulties and inconveniences, and demand patient labor. I ask for no precipitate measures, no violent changes. What is needed
is, that the Slave-holding States should resolve conscientiously and in good faith to remove this greatest
of moral evils and wrongs, and should bring immediately to the work their intelligence, virtue, and power.
That its difficulties would yield before such energies,
who can doubt? Our weakness for holy enterprises
lies generally in our own reluctant wills. Breathe into
men a fervent purpose, and you awaken powers before
unknown. How soon would slavery disappear, were
the obligation to remove it thoroughly understood and
deeply felt! We are told that the Slave-holding States
have recently prospered beyond all precedent. This
accession to their wealth should be consecrated to the
work of liberating their fellow-creatures. Not one indulgence should be added to their modes of life, until
the cry of the oppressed has ceased from their fields,
until the rights of every human being are restored.
Government should devote itself to this as its great object. Legislatures should meet to free the slave. The
church should rest not, day or night, till this stain be
wiped away. Let the deliberations of the wise, the
energies of the active, the wealth of the prosperous, the
prayers and toils of the good, have Emancipation for
their great end. Let this be discussed habitually in
the family circle, in the conference of Christians, in

the halls of legislation. Let it mingle with the first thoughts of the slave-holder in the morning and the last at night. Who can doubt that to such a spirit God would reveal the means of wise and powerful action? There is but one obstacle to emancipation, and that is, the want of that spirit in which Christians and freemen should resolve to exterminate slavery.

I have said nothing of colonization among the means of removing slavery, because I believe that to rely on it for this object would be equivalent to a resolution to perpetuate the evil without end. Whatever good it may do abroad, and I trust it will do much, it promises little at home. If the Slave-holding States, however, should engage in colonization, with a firm faith in its practicableness, with an energy proportionate to its greatness, and with a sincere regard to the welfare of the colored race, I am confident it will not fail from want of sympathy and aid on the part of the other States. In truth, these States will not withhold their hearts or hands or wealth from any well-considered plan for the removal of slavery.

I have said nothing of the inconveniences and sufferings, which, it is urged, will follow emancipation, be it ever so safe; for these, if real, weigh nothing against the claims of justice. The most common objection is, that a mixture of the two races will be the result. Can this objection be urged in good faith? Can this mixture go on faster or more criminally than at the present moment? Can the slave-holder use the word " Amalgamation " without a blush? Nothing, nothing, can arrest this evil, but the raising of the colored woman to a new sense of character, to a new self-respect; and this she cannot gain but by being made free. That emancipation will have its evils, we know; for all great changes, however beneficial, in the social condition of a people, must interfere with some interests, must bring loss or hardship to one class or another; but the evils of slavery exceed beyond measure the greatest which can attend its removal. Let the slave-holder desire earnestly, and in the spirit of self-sacrifice, to restore freedom, to secure the rights and the happiness of the slave, and a new light will break upon his path. "Every mountain of difficulty will be brought low, and the rough places be made smooth;" the means of duty will become clear. But without this spirit, no eloquence of man or angel can persuade the slave-holder of the safety of emancipation.

Some readers may perhaps be disappointed, that, in speaking of the means of removing slavery, I have suggested nothing which may be done for the cause by the friends of emancipation in the Free States. On this point my opinions may easily be gathered from what has been already said. Our proper and only means of action is, to spread the truth on the subject of slavery; and let none contemn this means because of its gradual influence. It is not therefore less sure. No state, unless cut off like Paraguay from the communion of nations, can at the present day escape the power of strong, deep, enlightened opinion. Every state, acknowledging Christianity, encouraging education, and holding intercourse with the civilized world, must be pervaded by great and universally acknowledged truths, especially when these, as in the present case, coincide with its prosperity as well as with its honor Let, then, the friends of freedom and humanity be true to their principles, and commend them by wise inculcation to all within their influence. From this work let it be their constant care to exclude the evil passions, which so often bring reproach and failure on a good cause. It is by calm, firm assertion of great principles, and not by personalities and vituperations, that strengh is to be given to the constantly increasing reprobation of slavery through the civilized world.

Objections, however, are made to this mode of acting on slavery. We are told, that, in declaring slavery to be one of the greatest wrongs, we violate the Constitution. What! Can it be that a free constitution, intended to guard all rights, and especially to preserve inviolate the liberty of the press, has in any way foreclosed the discussion of a great moral and religious question? Nothing but express language, too plain to be escaped, can justify us in fastening on this venerable instrument so palpable an inconsistency. But, instead of being embodied in plain words, the doctrine in question is at best a matter of uncertain inference. Admit such licentiousness of construction, and there is no power which may not be grafted on the Constitution; the mercenary and ambitious may warp it into any shape to suit their designs. But on this point no labored reasoning is necessary. It is settled for us by the fathers of our freedom and the framers of our present government. In the period immediately succeeding the adoption of the Constitution, Franklin, the calm and sagacious, and Jay, the inflexibly just, were Presidents of Societies for the Abolition of Slavery Societies of this description were spread over a large part of the country, and were established even in Maryland and Virginia. We have the records of their annual con ventions, and among their delegates we find some of the most honored names in our country. Those of us, whose recollections go back to that period, can bear witness to the freedom with which slavery was then discussed in conversation and by the press. The servile doctrine, which some would now fasten on the Constitution, would have been rejected with indignation by our fathers. That manly generation had not been enervated by long prosperity. The calculations of commerce and the spirit of gain had not then prescribed bounds to speech and the press.

It is further objected to the discussion of slavery, that it will incite the slaves to revolt. This objection is founded on ignorance. A book, addressed to the intelligent of this country and the world, and designed to operate on public opinion, could no more influence the slave, than a speech in an unknown tongue. Unlettered, confined to daily toil, and watched by the overseer, he is in little danger of catching the fever of liberty from discussions intended to act on the minds of the free. — This objection, if fairly carried out, is disproved by its absurdity. The amount of it is, that nothing must be published against slavery. Then the noblest and most popular works of literature must be proscribed. Then the writings of the sainted Cowper must undergo purgation ; for, among the witnesses against slavery, he is perhaps the most awakening. Then the history of the American Revolution must be blotted out. Then the newspapers must beware of speaking of human rights. In truth, our liberty must be kept a secret ; for the great danger of the slave-holder arises from the infusion of liberty into the whole of our social system. A grave book is a dead letter to the slave ; but in our free institutions and manners, there is a living spirit, which he can comprehend and feel. Slavery, under a free government, is a jarring element, a startling contrast; and the most effectual means of preventing disaffection among the enslaved would be, to keep all signs of liberty out of their sight, to cast society in a servile mould, to make it a consistent despotism.

A good book, expounding at once the rights and duties of the slave, if it could be brought down to his comprehension, would rather quiet than disturb him; for it would teach him that submission to wrong is often a duty, and that, in his particular case, revolt would be an infraction of Divine as well as human laws. There are, indeed, some persons among us, so uninstructed in the established principles of moral and political science, as to imagine, that, when a writer pronounces slavery an aggravated wrong, he necessarily and of course summons the slave to insurrection. Such ought to know, what is so generally understood, that insurrection against the civil power is never authorized, but in cases which exclude all other modes of relief, and which give the hope of better institutions. A book, written under the influence to this truth, were it, against all probabilities, to reach the slave, would teach him patience, not exasperation.

It may be added, that, if we must cease to write against slavery, lest we stir up revolt, then we must cease to speak against it, for both must have the same tendency. Speech has wings, as well as the printed word. Sometimes the living voice is more quickening than the press. According to the objection under consideration, we must, then, shut our lips on this great subject. The condemning whisper must not be heard, lest

some rash hearer should echo and spread the fatal truth.
And is it come to this, that freemen must not give
utterance to their deepest moral convictions ? Is slavery
not only to darken the South, but to spread a prison-
gloom over the North ? Are the Free States to renounce one of their dearest rights, because, if they
speak the language of freemen, some dangerous word
may chance to stray beyond their borders, and may
possibly find its way to the hut of the slave ? If so,
all rights must be renounced, as far and as fast as the
fears, passions, and menaces of other parts of the country shall require the surrender.

Undoubtedly, if slavery be discussed, some will write
about it petulantly, passionately, so as to stir up among
the masters much unnecessary irritation. This evil must
be expected and borne, unless we are prepared for a
censorship of the press. There is no subject from
which the rash can be debarred. Even the first principles of morals and religion, on which the order, safety,
and happiness of society mainly rest, are sometimes cov-
ertly, sometimes directly impugned. But must nothing be written on morals and religion, must the wise
and good be put to silence, because, under a system
of freedom, the misguided and depraved will labor to
obscure or subvert the truth ? Would not the whole
activity of life be arrested, if every power, which may
be abused, should be renounced ? Besides, is there
any portion of our country, so wanting in wisdom, self-
respect, and common self-control, as to be driven to
rash and ruinous measures by coarse invectives, which
in a great degree defeat themselves by their very violence ? The declamations of the passionate on the sub-

ject of slavery pass by us at the North as "the idle wind, which we regard not." Liberty naturally runs into these extravagances, and they, who would tame it by laws to such propriety of expression as never to give offence, would leave us only the name of freemen.

CHAPTER VII.

ABOLITIONISM.

The word ABOLITIONIST, in its true meaning, comprehends every man who feels himself bound to exert his influence for removing slavery. It is a name of honorable import, and was worn, not long ago, by such men as Franklin and Jay. Events, however, continually modify terms; and, of late, the word Abolitionist has been narrowed from its original import, and restricted to the members of associations formed among us to promote Immediate Emancipation. It is not without reluctance that I give up to a small body a name which every good man ought to bear. But to make myself intelligible, and to avoid circumlocution, I shall use the word in what is now its common acceptation.

I approach this subject unwillingly, because it will be my duty to censure those, whom at this moment I would on no account hold up to public displeasure. The persecutions, which the Abolitionists have suffered and still suffer, awaken only my grief and indignation, and incline me to defend them to the full extent which truth and justice will admit. To the persecuted of whatever name my sympathies are pledged, and especially to those who are persecuted in a cause substan-

tially good. I would not for worlds utter a word to
justify the violence recently offered to a party, composed very much of men blameless in life, and holding
the doctrine of non-resistance to injuries ; and of women,
exemplary in their various relations, and acting, however mistakenly, from benevolent and pious impulses.

Of the Abolitionists I know very few ; but I am
bound to say of these, that I honor them for their
strength of principle, their sympathy with their fellow-
creatures, and their active goodness. As a party, they
are singularly free from political and religious secta-
rianism, and have been distinguished by the absence of
management, calculation, and wordly wisdom. That
they have ever proposed or desired insurrection or violence among the slaves, there is no reason to believe.
All their principles repel the supposition. It is a remarkable fact, that, though the South and the North
have been leagued to crush them, though they have
been watched by a million of eyes, and though prejudice
has been prepared to detect the slightest sign of corrupt
communication with the slave, yet this crime has not
been fastened on a single member of this body. A few
individuals at the South have, indeed, been tortured
or murdered by enraged multitudes, on the charge of
stirring up revolt ; but their guilt and their connection
with the Abolitionists were not, and, from the peculiar
circumstances of the case, could not be established by
those deliberate and regular modes of investigation,
which are necessary to an impartial judgment. Crimes,
detected and hastily punished by the multitude in a moment of feverish suspicion and wild alarm, are generally creatures of fear and passion. The act, which
caused the present explosion of popular feeling, was

the sending of pamphlets by the Abolitionists into the Slave-holding States. In so doing, they acted with great inconsideration; but they must have been insane, had they intended to stir up a servile war; for the pamphlets were sent, not by stealth, but by the public mail; and not to the slaves, but to the masters; to men in public life, to men of the greatest influence and distinction. Strange incendiaries these! They flourished their firebrands about at noon-day; and, still more, put them into the hands of the very men whom it is said they wished to destroy. They are accused, indeed, of having sent some of the pamphlets to the free colored people, and if so, they acted with great and culpable rashness. But the publicity of the whole transaction absolves them of corrupt design.

The charge of corrupt design, so vehemently brought against the Abolitionists, is groundless. The charge of fanaticism I have no desire to repel. But in the present age it will not do to deal harshly with the characters of fanatics. They form the mass of the people. Religion and Politics, Philanthropy and Temperance, Nullification and Antimasonry, the Levelling Spirit of the working man, and the Spirit of Speculation in the man of business, all run into fanaticism. This is the type of all our epidemics. A sober man who can find? The Abolitionists have but caught the fever of the day. That they should have escaped would have been a moral miracle. — I offer these remarks simply from a sense of justice. Had not a persecution, without parallel in our country, broken forth against this society, I should not have spoken a word in their defence. But whilst I have power, I owe it to the Persecuted. If they have laid themselves open to the laws, let them suffer. For

11 *

all their errors and sins let the tribunal of public opinion inflict the full measure of rebuke which they deserve. I ask no favor for them. But they shall not be stripped of the rights of man, of rights guarantied by the laws and Constitution, without one voice, at least, being raised in their defence.

The Abolitionists have done wrong, I believe; nor is their wrong to be winked at, because done fanatically or with good intention ; for how much mischief may be wrought with good design ! They have fallen into the common error of enthusiasts, that of taking too narrow views, of feeling as if no evil existed but that which they opposed, and as if no guilt could be compared with that of countenancing or upholding it. The tone of their newspapers, as far as I have seen them, has often been fierce, bitter, exasperating. Their imaginations have fed too much on pictures of the cruelty to which the slave is exposed, till not a few have probably conceived of his abode as perpetually resounding with the lash, and ringing with shrieks of agony. I know that many of their publications have been calm, well considered, abounding in strong reasoning, and imbued with an enlightened love of freedom. But some, which have been most widely scattered, and are most adapted to act on the common mind, have had a tone unfriendly both to manners and to the spirit of our religion. I doubt not that the majority of the Abolitionists condemn the coarseness and violence of which I complain. But in this, as in most associations, the many are represented and controlled by the few, and are made to sanction and become responsible for what they disapprove.

One of their errors has been the adoption of "Immediate Emancipation" as their motto. To this they owe not a little of their unpopularity. This phrase has contributed much to spread far and wide the belief, that they wished immediately to free the slave from all his restraints. They made explanations; but thousands heard the motto who never saw the explanation; and it is certainly unwise for a party to choose a watchword, which can be rescued from misapprehension only by labored explication. It may also be doubted, whether they ever removed the objection which their language so universally raised, whether they have not always recommended a precipitate action, inconsistent with the well-being of the slave and the order of the state.

Another objection to their movements is, that they have sought to accomplish their objects by a system of Agitation; that is, by a system of affiliated societies, gathered, and held together, and extended, by passionate eloquence. This, in truth, is the common mode by which all projects are now accomplished. The age of individual action is gone. Truth can hardly be heard unless shouted by a crowd. The weightiest argument for a doctrine is the number which adopts it. Accordingly, to gather and organize multitudes is the first care of him who would remove an abuse or spread a reform. That the expedient is in some cases useful, is not denied. But generally it is a showy, noisy mode of action, appealing to the passions, and driving men into exaggeration; and there are special reasons why such a mode should not be employed in regard to slavery; for slavery is so to be opposed as not to exasperate the slave, or endanger the community in which he lives. The Abolitionists might have formed an association; but it should have been an elective one. Men of strong moral principle, judiciousness, sobriety, should have

been carefully sought as members. Much good might
have been accomplished by the coöperation of such
philanthropists. Instead of this, the Abolitionists sent
forth their orators, some of them transported with fiery
zeal, to sound the alarm against slavery through the
land, to gather together young and old, pupils from
schools, females hardly arrived at years of discretion,
the ignorant, the excitable, the impetuous, and to organize these into associations for the battle against oppression. They preached their doctrine to the colored
people, and collected these into their societies. To
this mixed and excitable multitude, appeals were made
in the piercing tones of passion; and slave-holders were
held up as monsters of cruelty and crime. Now to this
procedure I must object, as unwise, as unfriendly to
the spirit of Christianity, and as increasing, in a degree,
the perils of the Slave-holding States. Among the
unenlightened, whom they so powerfully addressed, was
there no reason to fear that some might feel themselves
called to subvert this system of wrong, by whatever
means? From the free colored people this danger was
particularly to be apprehended. It is easy for us to
place ourselves in their situation. Suppose that millions of white men were enslaved, robbed of all their
rights, in a neighbouring country, and enslaved by a
black race, who had torn their ancestors from the shores
on which our fathers had lived. How deeply should
we feel their wrongs! And would it be wonderful, if,
in a moment of passionate excitement, some enthusiast
should think it his duty to use his communication with
his injured brethren for stirring them up to revolt?

Such is the danger from Abolitionism to the Slave-
holding States. I know no other. It is but justice

to add, that the principle of non-resistance, which the Abolitionists have connected with their passionate appeals, seems to have counteracted the peril. I know not a case in which a member of an anti-slavery society has been proved by legal investigation to have tampered with the slaves ; and, after the strongly pronounced and unanimous opinion of the Free States on the subject, this danger may be considered as having passed away. Still a mode of action requiring these checks is open to strong objections, and ought to be abandoned. Happy will it be, if the disapprobation of friends, as well as of foes, should give to Abolitionsts a caution and moderation, which would secure the acquiescence of the judicious, and the sympathies of the friends of mankind! Let not a good cause find its chief obstruction in its defenders. Let the truth, and the whole truth, be spoken without paltering or fear ; but so spoken as to convince, not inflame, as to give no alarm to the wise, and no needless exasperation to the · selfish and passionate.

I know it is said, that nothing can be done but by excitement and vehemence ; that the zeal which dares every thing is the only power to oppose to long-rooted abuses. But it is not true that God has committed the great work of reforming the world to passion. Love is a minister of good, only when it gives energy to the intellect, and allies itself with wisdom. The Aboli tionists often speak of Luther's vehemence as a model to future reformers. But who, that has read history, does not know, that Luther's reformation was aecompanied by tremendous miseries and crimes, and that its progress was soon arrested ? And is there not reason to fear, that the fierce, bitter, persecuting spirit, which he breathed into the work, not only tarnished its glory, but limited its power? One great principle, which we should lay down as immovably true, is, that, if a good work cannot be carried on by the calm, self-controlled, benevolent spirit of Christianity, then the time for doing it has not come. God asks not the aid of our vices. He can overrule them for good, but they are not the chosen instruments of human happiness.

We, indeed, need zeal, fervent zeal, such as will fear no man's power, and shrink before no man's frown, such as will sacrifice life to truth and freedom. But this energy of will ought to be joined with deliberate wisdom and universal charity. It ought to regard the whole, in its strenuous efforts for a part. Above all, it ought to ask first, not what means are most effectual, but what means are sanctioned by the Moral Law and by Christian Love. We ought to think much more of walking in the right path than of reaching our end. We should desire virtue more than success. If by one wrong deed we could accomplish the liberation of millions, and in no other way, we ought to feel that this good, for which, perhaps, we had prayed with an agony of desire, was denied us by God, was reserved for other times and other hands. The first object of a true zeal is, not that we may prosper, but that we may do right, that we may keep ourselves unspotted from every evil thought, word, and deed. Under the inspiration of such a zeal, we shall not find in the greatness of an enterprise an apology for intrigue or for violence. We shall not need immediate success to spur us to exertion. We shall not distrust God, because he does not yield to the cry of human impatience. We shall not forsake a good work, because it does not advance with a rapid step.

Faith in truth, virtue, and Almighty Goodness, will save us alike from rashness and despair.

In lamenting the adoption by the Abolitionists of the system of agitation or extensive excitement, I do not mean to condemn this mode of action as only evil. There are cases to which it is adapted; and, in general, the impulse which it gives is better than the selfish, sluggish indifference to good objects, into which the multitude so generally fall. But it must not supersede or be compared with Individual action. The enthusiasm of the Individual in a good cause is a mighty power. The forced, artificially excited enthusiasm of a multitude, kept together by an organization which makes them the instruments of a few leading minds, works superficially, and often injuriously. I fear that the native, noble-minded enthusiast often loses that single-heartedness which is his greatest power, when once he strives to avail himself of the machinery of associations. The chief strength of a Reformer lies in speaking truth purely from his own soul, without changing one tone for the purpose of managing or enlarging a party. Truth, to be powerful, must speak in her own words, and in no other's; must come forth, with the authority and spontaneous energy of inspiration, from the depths of the soul. It is the voice of the Individual giving utterance to the irrepressible convictions of his own thoroughly moved spirit, and not the shout of a crowd, which carries truth far into other souls, and insures it a stable empire on earth. For want of this, most which is now done is done superficially. The progress of society depends chiefly on the honest inquiry of the Individual into the particular work ordained him by God, and on his simplicity in following out his convictions. This

moral independence is mightier, as well as holier, than
the practice of getting warm in crowds, and of waiting
for an impulse from multitudes. The moment a man
parts with moral independence ; the moment he judges
of duty, not from the inward voice, but from the interests and will of a party ; the moment he commits himself to a leader or a body, and winks at evil, because
division would hurt the cause; the moment he shakes
off his particular responsibility, because he is but one
of a thousand or million by whom the evil is done ; that
moment he parts with his moral power. He is shorn
of the energy of single-hearted faith in the Right and
the True. He hopes from man's policy what nothing
but loyalty to God can accomplish. He substitutes
coarse weapons forged by man's wisdom for celestial
power.

The adoption of the common system of agitation
by the Abolitionists has not been justified by success.
From the beginning it created alarm in the considerate,
and strengthened the sympathies of the Free States with
the slave-holder. It made converts of a few individuals, but alienated multitudes. Its influence at the South
has been almost wholly evil. It has stirred up bitter
passions and a fierce fanaticism, which have shut every
ear and every heart against its arguments and persuasions.
These effects are more to be deplored, because the
hope of freedom to the slave lies chiefly in the dispositions of his master. The Abolitionist proposed, indeed, to convert the slave-holders ; and for this end he
approached them with vituperation, and exhausted on
them the vocabulary of reproach. And he has reaped
as he sowed. His vehement pleadings for the slaves
have been answered by wilder tones from the slave-

holder; and, what is worse, deliberate defences of slavery have been sent forth, in the spirit of the dark ages, and in defiance of the moral convictions and feelings of the Christian and civilized world. Thus, with good purposes, nothing seems to have been gained. Perhaps (though I am anxious to repel the thought) something has been lost to the cause of freedom and humanity.

I earnestly desire that Abolitionism may lay aside the form of public agitation, and seek its end by wiser and milder means. I desire as earnestly, and more earnestly, that it may not be put down by Lawless Force. There is a worse evil than Abolitionism, and that is the suppression of it by lawless force. No evil greater than this can exist in the state, and this is never heeded. Be it granted, that it is the design, or direct, palpable tendency of Abolitionism to stir up insurrection at the South, and that no existing laws can meet the exigency. It is the solemn duty of the chief magistrate of the state to assemble immediately the legislative bodies; and their duty immediately to apply the remedy of Law. Let every friend of freedom, let every good man lift up his voice against mobs. Through these lies our road to tyranny. It is these which have spread the opinion, so common at the South, that the Free States cannot long sustain republican institutions. No man seems awake to their inconsistency with liberty. Our whole phraseology is in fault. Mobs call themselves, and are called, the People, when in truth they assail immediately the sovereignty of the People, when they involve the guilt of usurpation and rebellion against the People. It is the fundamental principle of our institutions, that the People is Sovereign. But by the People we mean not an individual here and there, not a knot of twenty or a hundred or a thousand individuals in this or that spot, but the community formed into a body politic, and expressing and executing its will through regularly appointed organs. There is but one expression of the will or sovereignty of the People, and that is Law. Law is the voice, the living act, of the people. It has no other. When an individual suspends the operation of Law, resists its established ministers, and forcibly substitutes for it his own will, he is a usurper and rebel. The same guilt attaches to a combination of individuals. These, whether many or few, in forcibly superseding public law and establishing their own, rise up against the People, as truly as a single usurper. The People should assert its insulted majesty, its menaced sovereignty, in one case as decidedly as in the other. The difference between the mob and the individual is, that the usurpation of the latter has a permanence not easily given to the tumultuary movements of the former. The distinction is a weighty one. Little importance is due to sudden bursts of the populace, because they so soon pass away. But when mobs are organized, as in the French Revolution, or when they are deliberately resolved on and systematically resorted to, as the means of putting down an odious party, they lose this apology. A conspiracy exists against the Sovereignty of the People, and ought to be suppressed, as among the chief evils of the state.

In this part of the country our abhorrence of mobs is lessened by the fact, that they were thought to do good service in the beginning of the Revolution. They probably were useful then ; and why ? The work of that day was Revolution. To subvert a government was the fearful task to which our fathers thought themselves summoned. Their duty, they believed, was Insurrection. In such a work mobs had their place. The government of the State was in the hands of its foes. The people could not use the regular organs of administration, for these were held and employed by the power which they wished to crush. Violent, irregular efforts belonged to that day of convulsion. To resist and subvert institutions is the very work of mobs; and when these institutions are popular, when their sole end is to express and execute the will of the people, then mobs are rebellion against the people, and as such should be understood and suppressed. A people is never more insulted than when a mob takes its name. Abolition must not be put down by lawless force. The attempt so to destroy it ought to fail. Such attempts place Abolitionism on a new ground. They make it, not the cause of a few enthusiasts, but the cause of freedom. They identify it with all our rights and popular institutions. If the Constitution and the laws cannot put it down, it must stand; and he who attempts its overthrow by lawless force is a rebel and usurper. The Supremacy of Law and the Sovereignty of the People are one and indivisible. To touch the one is to violate the other. This should be laid down as a first principle, an axiom, a fundamental article of faith which it must be heresy to question. A newspaper, which openly or by innuendoes excites a mob, should be regarded as sounding the tocsin of insurrection. On this subject the public mind slumbers, and needs to be awakened, lest it sleep the sleep of death.

How obvious is it, that pretexts for mobs will never be wanting, if this disorganizing mode of redressing evils be in any case allowed! We all recollect, that, when a recent attempt was made on the life of the

President of the United States, the cry broke forth
from his friends, "that the assassin was instigated by
the continual abuse poured forth on this distinguished
man, and especially by the violent speeches uttered
daily in the Senate of the United States." Suppose,
now, that his adherents, to save the Chief Magistrate
from murder, and to guard his constitutional advisers,
had formed themselves into mobs, to scatter the meetings of his opponents. And suppose that they had resolved to put to silence the legislators, who, it was said,
had abused their freedom of speech to blacken the
character and put in peril the life of the Chief Magistrate. Would they not have had a better pretext than
mobs against abolition? Was not assassination attempted? Had not the President received letters threatening
his life, unless his measures were changed? Can a year
or a month pass, which will not afford equally grave
reasons for insurrections of the populace? A system
of mobs and a free government cannot stand together.
The men who incite the former, and especially those
who organize them, are among the worst enemies of the
state. Of their motives I do not speak. They may
think themselves doing service to their country, for there
is no limit to the delusions of the times. I speak only
of the nature and tendency of their actions. They
should be put down at once by law, and by the moral
sentiment of an insulted people.

In addition to all other reasons, the honor of our nation, and the cause of free institutions, should plead
with us to defend the laws from insult, and social order
from subversion. The moral influence and reputation
of our country are fast declining abroad. A letter, recently received from one of the most distinguished men

of the continent of Europe, expresses the universal feeling on the other side of the ocean. After speaking of the late encroachments on liberty in France, he says, "On your side of the Atlantic, you contribute, also, to put in peril the cause of liberty. We did take pleasure in thinking that there was at least in the New World a country, where liberty was well understood, where all rights were guarantied, where the people was proving itself wise and virtuous. For some time past, the news we receive from America is discouraging. In all your large cities we see mobs after mobs, and all directed to an odious purpose. When we speak of liberty, its enemies reply to us by *pointing to America.*" The persecuted Abolitionists have the sympathies of the civilized world. The country which persecutes them is covering itself with disgrace, and filling the hearts of the friends of freedom with fear and gloom. Already despotism is beginning to rejoice in the fulfilment of its prophecies, in our prostrated laws and dying liberties. Liberty is, indeed, threatened with death in a country, where any class of men are stripped with impunity of their constitutional rights. All rights feel the blow. A community, giving up any of its citizens to oppression and violence, is preparing for itself the same fate. It invites chains for itself, in suffering them to be imposed on any whom it is bound to protect.

12*

CHAPTER VIII.

DUTIES.

A few words remain to be spoken in relation to the duties of the Free States. These need to feel the responsibilities and dangers of their present position. The country is approaching a crisis on the greatest question which can be proposed to it, a question not of profit or loss, of tariffs or banks, or any temporary interests, but a question involving the First Principles of freedom, morals, and religion. Yet who seems to be awake to the solemnity of the present moment? Who seems to be settling for himself the great fundamental truths, by which private efforts and public measures are to be determined

The North has duties to perform towards the South and towards itself. Let it resolve to perform them faithfully, impartially; asking first for the Right, and putting entire confidence in well-doing. The North is bound to frown on all attempts of its citizens, should such be threatened, to excite insurrection at the South, on all attempts to tamper with and to dispose to violence the minds of the slaves. The severest laws, which the Constitutions of the different States admit, may justly be resorted to for this end, and they should be strictly enforced. I believe, indeed, that there is no special need for new legislation on the subject. I believe that there was never a moment, when the Slave-holding States had so little to apprehend from the Free, when the moral feeling of the community in regard to the crime of instigating revolt was so universal, thorough, and inflexible, as at the present moment. Still, if the South needs other demonstrations than it now has of the moral and friendly spirit which in this respect pervades the North, let them be given to the full extent which the spirit and provisions of our respective Constitutions allow. Still more ; it is the duty of the Free States to act by opinion, where they cannot act by law, to discountenance a system of agitation on the subject of slavery, to frown on passionate appeals to the ignorant, and on indiscriminate and inflammatory vituperation of the slave-holder. This obligation, also, has been and will be fulfilled. There was never a stronger feeling of responsibility in this particular than at the present moment.

There are, however, other duties of the Free States, to which they *may* prove false, and which they are too willing to forget. They are bound, not in their public, but individual capacities, to use every virtuous influence for the abolition of slavery. They are bound to encourage that manly, moral, religious discussion of it, through which strength will be given to the continually increasing opinion of the civilized and Christian world in favor of personal freedom. They are bound to seek and hold the truth in regard to human rights, to be faithful to their principles in conversation and conduct, never, never to surrender them to private interest, convenience, flattery, or fear.

The duty of being true to our principles is not easily

to be performed.   At this moment an immense pressure is driving the North from its true ground.   God save it from imbecility, from treachery to freedom and virtue ! I have certainly no feelings but those of good-will towards the South ; but I speak the universal sentiment of this part of the country, when I say, that the tone which the South has often assumed towards the North has been that of a superior, a tone unconsciously borrowed from the habit of command to which it is unhappily accustomed by the form of its society.   I must add, that this high bearing of the South has not always been met by a just consciousness of equality, a just self-respect at the North.   The causes I will not try to explain.   The effect, I fear, is not to be denied.   It is said, that some, who have represented the North in Congress, have not always represented its dignity, its honor ; that they have not always stood erect before the lofty bearing of the South.   Here lies our danger. The North will undoubtedly be just to the South.   It must also be just to itself.   This is not the time for sycophancy, for servility, for compromise of principle, for forgetfulness of our rights.   It is the time to manifest the spirit of Men, a spirit which prizes, more than life, the principles of liberty, of justice, of humanity, of pure morals, of pure religion.

Let it not be thought that I would recommend to the North, what in some parts of our country is called "Chivalry," a spirit of which the duelling pistol is the best emblem, and which settles controversies with blood. A Christian and civilized man cannot but be struck with the approach to barbarism, with the insensibility to true greatness, with the incapacity of comprehending the divine virtues of Jesus Christ, which mark what is called

" chivalry." I ask not the man of the North to borrow it from any part of the country. But I do ask him to stand in the presence of this "chivalry" with the dignity of moral courage and moral independence. Let him, at the same moment, remember the courtesy and deference due to the differing opinions of others, and the sincerity and firmness due to his own. Let him understand the lofty position which he holds on the subject of slavery, and never descend from it for the purpose of soothing prejudice or disarming passion. Let him respect the safety of the South, and still manifest his inflexible adherence to the cause of human rights and personal freedom.

On this point I must insist, because I see the North giving way to the vehemence of the South. In some, perhaps many, of our recent "Resolutions," a spirit has been manifested, at which, if not we, our children will blush. Not long ago there were rumors that some of our citizens wished to suppress by law all discussion, all expression of opinion on slavery, and to send to the South such members of our community as might be claimed as instigators of insurrection. Such encroachments on rights could not, of course, be endured. We are not yet so fallen. Some generous inspirations, some echoes of the old eloquence of liberty, still come down to us from our fathers. Could such encroachments be borne, would not the soil of New England, so long trodden by freemen, quake under the steps of her degenerate sons? We are not prepared for these. But a weak, yielding tone, for which we seem to be prepared, may be the beginning of concessions which we shall one day bitterly rue.

The means used at the South to bring the North

to compliance, seem to demand particular attention. I will not record the contemptuous language which has been thrown on the money-getting habits of New England, or the menaces which have been addressed to our cupidity, for the purpose of putting us to silence on the subject of slavery. Such language does in no degree move me. I only ask that we may give no ground for its application. We can easily bear it, if we do not deserve it. Our mother-country has been called a nation of shopkeepers, and New England ought not to be provoked by the name. Only let us give no sanction to the opinion that our spirit is narrowed to our shops; that we place the art of bargaining above all arts, all sciences, accomplishments, and virtues; that, rather than lose the fruits of the slave's labor, we would rivet his chains; that, sooner than lose a market, we would make shipwreck of honor; that, sooner than sacrifice present gain, we would break our faith to our fathers and our children, to our principles and our God. To resent or retaliate reproaches would be unwise and unchristian. The only revenge worthy of a good man is, to turn reproaches into admonitions against baseness, into incitements to a more generous virtue. New England has long suffered the imputation of a sordid, calculating spirit, of supreme devotion to gain. Let us show that we have principles, compared with which the wealth of the world is light as air. It is a common remark here, that there is not a community under heaven, through which there is so general a diffusion of intelligence and healthful moral sentiment as in New England. Let not the just influence of such a society be impaired by any act, which would give to prejudice the aspect of truth.

The Free States, it is to be feared, must pass through

a struggle. May they sustain it as becomes their freedom ! The present excitement at the South can hardly be expected to pass away, without attempts to wrest from them unworthy concessions. The tone in regard to slavery in that part of our country is changed. It is not only more vehement, but more false than formerly. Once slavery was acknowledged as an evil. Now it is proclaimed to be a good. We have even been told, not by a handful of enthusiasts in private life, but by men in the highest station and of widest influence at the South, that slavery is the soil into which political freedom strikes its deepest roots, and that republican institutions are never so secure as when the laboring class is reduced to servitude. Certainly, no assertion of the wildest Abolitionist could give such a shock to the slave-holder, as this new doctrine is fitted to give to the people of the North. Liberty, with a slave for her pedestal and a chain in her hand, is an image, from which our understandings and hearts alike recoil. A doctrine, more wounding or insulting to the mechanics, farmers, laborers of the North than this strange heresy, cannot well be conceived. A doctrine more irreverent, more fatal to republican institutions, was never fabricated in the councils of despotism. It does not, however, provoke us. I recall it only to show the spirit in which slavery is upheld, and to remind the Free States of the calm energy which they will need, to keep themselves true to their own principles of liberty.

There is a great dread in this part of the country, that the union of the States may be dissolved by the conflict about slavery. To avert this evil, every sacrifice should be made but that of honor, freedom, and principle. No one prizes the Union more than myself.

Perhaps I may be allowed to say, that I am attached to it by no common love. Most men value the Union as a Means; to me it is an End. Most would preserve it for the prosperity of which it is the instrument; I love and would preserve it for its own sake. Some value it as favoring public improvements, facilities of commercial exchange, &c.; I value these improvements and exchanges chiefly as favoring union. I ask of the General Government to unite us, to hold us together as brethren in peace; and I care little whether it does any thing else. So dear to me is union. Next to liberty, it is our highest national interest. All the pecuniary sacrifices which it can possibly demand should be made for it. The politicians in some parts of our country, who are calculating its value, and are willing to surrender it because they may grow richer by separation, seem to me bereft of reason. Still, if the Union can be preserved only by the imposition of chains on speech and the press, by prohibition of discussion on a subject involving the most sacred rights and dearest interests of humanity, then union would be bought at too dear a rate; then it would be changed from a virtuous bond into a league of crime and shame. Language cannot easily do justice to our attachment to the Union. We will yield every thing to it but Truth, Honor, and Liberty. These we can never yield.

Let the Free States be firm, but also patient, forbearing, and calm. From the slave-holder they cannot look for perfect self-control. From his position he would be more than man, were he to observe the bounds of moderation. The consciousness which tranquillizes the mind can hardly be his. On this subject he has always been sensitive to excess. Much exasperation is to be expected. Much should be borne. Every thing may be surrendered but our principles and our rights.

· The work, which I proposed to myself, is now completed. I ask and hope for it the Divine blessing, as far as it expresses Truth, and breathes the spirit of Justice and Humanity. If I have written any thing under the influence of prejudice, passion, or unkindness to any human being, I ask forgiveness of God and man. I have spoken strongly, not to offend or give pain, but to produce in others deep convictions corresponding to my own. Nothing could have induced me to fix my thoughts on this painful subject, but a conviction, which pressed on me with increasing weight, that the times demanded a plain and free exposition of the truth. The few last months have increased my solicitude for the country. Public sentiment has seemed to me to be losing its healthfulness and vigor. I have seen symptoms of the decline of the old spirit of liberty. Servile opinions have seemed to gain ground among us. The faith of our fathers in free institutions has waxed faint, and is giving place to despair of human improvement. I have perceived a disposition to deride abstract rights, to speak of freedom as a dream, and of republican governments as built on sand. I have perceived a faintheartedness in the cause of human rights. The condemnation, which has been passed on Abolitionists, has seemed to be settling into acquiescence in slavery. The sympathies of the community have been turned from the slave to the master. The impious doctrine, that human laws can repeal the Divine, can convert unjust and oppressive power into a moral right, has more and more tinctured the style of conversation and the press. With these sad and solemn views of society, I could not be silent; and I thank God, amidst the consciousness of great weakness and imperfection, that I have been able to offer this humble tribute, this sincere though feeble testimony, this expression of heart-felt allegiance, to the cause of Freedom, Justice, and Humanity.

Having stated the circumstances which have moved me to write, I ought to say, that they do not discourage me. Were darker omens to gather round us, I should not despair. With a faith like his, who came to prepare the way for the Great Deliverer, I feel and can say, " The Kingdom of Heaven," the Reign of Justice and Disinterested Love, " is at hand, and All Flesh shall see the salvation of God." I know, and rejoice to know, that a power, mightier than the prejudices and oppression of ages, is working on earth for the world's redemption, the power of Christian Truth and Goodness. It descended from Heaven in the person of Christ. It was manifest in his life and death. From his cross it went forth conquering and to conquer. Its mission is, " to preach deliverance to the captive, and to set at liberty them that are bound." It has opened many a prison-door. It is ordained to break every chain. I have faith in its triumphs. I do not, cannot despair.

NOTE.

I<small>T</small> was my purpose to address a chapter to the South, but I have thought fit to omit it. I beg, however, to say, that nothing which I have written can have proceeded from unkind feeling towards the South ; for in no other part of the country have my writings found a more gratifying reception ; from no other part have I received stronger expressions of sympathy. To these I am certainly not insensible. My own feelings, had I consulted them, would have led me to stifle every expression, which could give pain to those from whom I have received nothing but good-will.

I wished to suggest to the slave-holders that the excitement now prevalent among themselves is incomparably more perilous, more fitted to stir up insurrection, than all the 'efforts of Abolitionists, allowing these to be ever so corrupt. I also wished to remind the men of principle and influence in that part of the country, of the necessity of laying a check on lawless procedures, in regard to the citizens of the North. We have heard of large subscriptions at the South for the apprehension of some of the Abolitionists in the Free States, and for the transportation of them to parts of the country where they would meet the fate, which, it is said, they deserve. Undoubtedly, the respectable portion of the slave-holding communities are not answerable for these measures. But does not policy, as well as principle, require such men steadily to discountenance them ? At present, the Free States have stronger sympathies with the South than ever before. But can it be supposed that they will suffer their citizens to be stolen, exposed to violence, and murdered by other States ? Would not such an outrage rouse them to feel and act as one man ? Would it not identify the Abolitionists with our most sacred rights ? One kidnapped, murdered Abolitionist would do more for the violent destruction of slavery than a thousand societies. His name would be sainted. The day of his death would be set apart for solemn, heart-stirring commemoration. His blood would cry through the land with a thrilling voice, would pierce every dwelling, and find a response in every heart. Do men, under the light of the present day, need to be told, that enthusiasm is not a flame to be quenched with blood ? On this point, good and wise men, and the friends of the country at the North and South, can hold but one opinion ; and if the press, which, I grieve to say, has kept an ominous silence amidst the violations of law and rights, would but speak plainly and strongly, the danger would be past.

The views and principles, supported in this short work, will, of course, provoke much opposition, and, what I greatly lament, they will excite the displeasure not only of the selfish and violent, but of good and honorable men, whose unfavorable position hardly admits an impartial judgment of slavery, and renders them excessively sensitive to every exposition of it. I shall not, however, be anxious to defend what I have written. The principles, here laid down, if true, will stand. I should anticipate little good from engaging in controversies with individuals. The selfish passions, awakened by such collisions, too often prevail over the love of truth ; and without this, the truth cannot be worthily maintained. In regard to slavery, it is peculiarly important, that discussion should be calm, general, unmixed with personalities. In this way, I trust that the subject will be better understood by all parties. I should rejoice to be convinced, that slavery is a less debasing influence than I have affirmed. How welcome would be brighter views of life and of mankind! Still, we must see things as they are, and not turn away from the most painful truth.

I have only to add, that I alone am responsible for what I have now written. I represent no society, no body of men, no part of the country. I have written by no one's instigation, and with no one's encouragement, but solely from my own convictions. If cause of offence is given, the blame ought to fall on me alone.

NOTE FOR THE FOURTH EDITION.

In commencing the chapter on Abolitionism, I have expressed my respect for the few Abolitionists whom I have known. I am bound to say, that, in consequence of hearing and seeing more of this body, I have an increasing persuasion of the purity of purpose, and the moral worth of its members generally. I have spoken freely of their errors ; but these ought not to blind us to their virtues and sacrifices, and especially ought not to prejudice us against the truths which they contend for. We must not abandon great principles, because asserted unwisely. We must not grow cold to a good cause, because reproach is brought on it by defenders who have more zeal than discretion. Its dangers should attach us to it more closely, and we should do what we can to lead its friends to the use of means corresponding to its dignity, and fitted to insure its success.

In the chapter on the Means of removing Slavery, I have expressed my fears as to the result of the experi-

13*

ment now going on in the English West Indies. I rejoice to say, that recent accounts from those islands have
diminished my apprehensions. It is stated, that in some of
the islands real estate has risen in value since the emancipation, and that imports are considerably increased.
I have just heard, that a West Indian planter residing in
this country, who was strenuously opposed to the Act of
Emancipation, speaks now of his estate as more productive than formerly. That no disturbance of the peace
has followed this great change, is well understood, and
this is the essential point. Undoubtedly the experiment
is not yet decided, and reports are to be received with
caution ; but the success of the measure has as yet sur-
passed the expectations of all except the Abolitionists.
As yet they have proved the truest prophets. May events
set the seal of truth on all their predictions ! This country is interested in nothing more than in the success of
emancipation in the West Indies. With this example
before us, the destruction of slavery would be as speedy
as it is sure.

No part of my book on Slavery seems to have given
so much offence as that in which I have spoken of conjugal infidelity on the part of the master as increased by
slavery. Of the abuse heaped on me for this opinion I
shall, of course, say nothing. Had I received nothing
but abuse, the remarks now to be made would not be
offered to the public ; but a gentleman of high character,
Mr. Leigh of Virginia, has solemnly protested against
my statement in the senate of the United States, and I
should do him great wrong were I to confound him with
the vulgar politicians, too common in Congress as well
as out of it, who are ready to say any thing and every
thing which may serve their cause. Mr. Leigh expresses
his deliberate conviction, that conjugal fidelity is not more

respected in any part of the country than in the Slave-holding States. It will be observed, in recurring to my book, that I said nothing of the Slave-holding States, but of slave countries generally, and that I argued not from reports or documents, but from the principles of human nature and from the very nature of slavery. I feel as if such reasoning could not deceive me ; but I will now say, what I forbore to say in the first instance, that I should not have brought this charge against slavery, had not the general argument, drawn from human nature, been corroborated by all the evidence which the case will well admit. In that part of my work, I expressed not my own opinion alone, but the common, and perhaps I should say the universal opinion of the North, and, still more, the public opinion of the civilized world. During my whole life, I have not met an individual, who has questioned, whether slavery exerts a disastrous influence on the domestic relations. I do not believe, that, among the well-informed at the North, an individual is to be found, who supposes that the obligations of marriage are as much respected in the Slave-holding States as in the Free. On reading Mr. Leigh's speech, I determined to make inquiries, with the purpose of retracting my error in the face of the world, if I should find reason to charge myself with rashness. I have obtained the opinions of those whose authority in such a case seems to me most worthy of confidence, and in every instance I have been assured that I have uttered only the truth. I know not how many have spoken to me on this point in the most undoubting tone. In my book, I have only given expression to the public sentiment of the North, and I as little expected to hear my correctness questioned, as to hear the existence of slavery denied. I do not, of course, intend to impute the least unfairness to Mr. Leigh, who is known among us only as a virtuous man, who does honor to his country

I presume, that, in the comparison which he made between the Slave-holding States and other parts of the
country, he spoke without a sufficient knowledge of the
latter. I cannot, therefore, I dare not, expunge from my
book the offensive passage, though in the revised edition
I have somewhat changed its form. If I know my own
heart, I should rejoice to be able to expunge it.

I have regretted, that a passage, which I prepared for
this work at the time of its composition, was not inserted.
In the chapter of Explanations, after speaking of the examples of moral and religious excellence to be found in
the Slave-holding States, I expressed, in a few sentences,
my deep sense of the virtues, as well as the accomplishments of the women of the South. I wrote this passage
with a fervent heart, because it was dictated, in a measure, by the grateful recollection of unwearied kindnesses
received from woman during a residence in that part of the
country in my youth. I should be glad to publish it now,
had it not been destroyed with the manuscript of which it
formed a part, for it expressed feelings which time has
only strengthened. After much deliberation I omitted it
in the first edition, and did so from considerations which
I cannot now approve. I feared that what I had written
would be set down by strangers as a common-place of
flattery. I feared that I might seem desirous to expiate
by this praise the censures contained in other parts of the
book, desirous to shield myself from the obloquy to which
I was exposing myself in publishing unpopular truth. I
did on this occasion what I have too often done. In
shrinking from the appearance of vices which I abhor, I
was unjust to my convictions and affections. The reader
will excuse this reference to myself, when he learns that I
have been shamelessly accused of casting reproach on
the purity of the women at the South. I should not, however, have noticed this calumny, had not the preceding

part of this note almost compelled me to refer to it. I feel too much about the great subject on which I have written, to be very solicitous about what is said of myself. I feel that I am nothing, that my reputation is nothing, in comparison with the fearful wrong and evil, which I have labored to expose ; and I should count myself unworthy the name of a man or a Christian, if the calumnies of the bad, or even the disapprobation of the good, could fasten my thoughts on myself and turn me aside from a cause, which, as I believe, truth, humanity, and God call me to maintain.

THE ABOLITIONISTS

LETTER TO JAMES G. BIRNEY

THE following letter was prepared for "The Philanthropist," an anti-slavery paper, published at Cincinnati, and edited by James G. Birney, — a gentleman, highly respected for his intellectual and moral endowments. It was occasioned by the attempt made in that city to suppress the anti-slavery party by force. Mr. Birney was driven from Cincinnati, and the press, at which "The Philanthropist" was printed, was broken up. A particular account of this disgraceful affair may be found in the "Narrative of the late riotous proceedings against the liberty of the press at Cincinnati," prepared by Mr. Birney and his associates. The following letter, besides appearing in "The Philanthropist," has been published as a pamphlet for distribution at the West, and the author now submits it to the community here in the same form, with a few slight changes, and with some new matter in a note.

BOSTON, *December* 20, 1836.

THE ABOLITIONISTS.

BOSTON, *Nov.* 1, 1836.

MY DEAR SIR,

I have not the pleasure of knowing you personally ; but your history and writings have given me an interest in you, which induces and encourages me to address you with something of the freedom of acquaintance. I feel myself attracted to the friends of humanity and freedom, however distant ; and when such are exposed by their principles to peril and loss, and stand firm in the evil day, I take pleasure in expressing to them my sympathy and admiration. The first accounts which reached me of the violence which drove you from Cincinnati, inclined me to write to you ; but your " Narrative of those riotous proceedings," which I have lately received and read, does not permit me to remain longer silent. The subject weighs much on my mind. I feel that I have a duty to perform in relation to it, and I cannot rest till I yield to this conviction, till I obey what seems to me the voice of God. I think it best, however, not to confine myself to the outrage at Cincinnati, but to extend my remarks to the spirit of violence and persecution, which has broken out against the Abolitionists through the whole country. This, I know, will be more acceptable to you, than any expression of sympathy with you as an individual. You look beyond yourself to the cause which you have adopted, and to the much injured body of men, with whom you are associated.

It is not my purpose to speak of the Abolitionists as Abolitionists. They now stand before the world in another character, and to this I shall give my present attention. Of their merits and demerits as Abolitionists, I have formerly spoken. In my short work on Slavery, I have expressed my fervent attachment to the great end to which they are pledged, and at the same time my disapprobation, to a certain extent, of their spirit and measures. I have no disposition to travel over this ground again. Had the Abolitionists been left to pursue their object with the freedom which is guarantied to them by our civil institutions; had they been resisted only by those weapons of reason, rebuke, reprobation, which the laws allow, I should have no inducement to speak of them again either in praise or censure. But the violence of their adversaries has driven them to a new position. Abolitionism forms an era in our history, if we consider the means by which it has been opposed. Deliberate, systematic efforts have been made, not here or there, but far and wide, to wrest from its adherents that liberty of speech and the press, which our fathers asserted unto blood, and which our national and state governments are pledged to protect as our most sacred right. Its most conspicuous advocates have been hunted and stoned, its meetings scattered, its presses broken up, and nothing but the patience,

constancy, and intrepidity of its members, has saved it
from extinction. The Abolitionists then not only appear in the character of champious of the colored race.
In their persons the most sacred rights of the white
man and the free man have been assailed. They are
sufferers for the liberty of thought, speech, and the
press ; and, in maintaining this liberty amidst insult and
violence, they deserve a place among its most honored defenders. In this character I shall now speak of
them.

In regard to the methods adopted by the Abolitionists of promoting emancipation, I might find much to
censure ; but when I regard their firm, fearless assertion of the rights of free discussion, of speech and the
press, I look on them with unmixed respect. I see
nothing to blame, and much to admire. To them has
been committed the most important bulwark of liberty,
and they have acquitted themselves of the trust like
men and Christians. No violence has driven them from
their post. Whilst, in obedience to conscience, they
have refrained from opposing force to force, they have
still persevered amidst menace and insult, in bearing
their testimony against wrong, in giving utterance to
their deep convictions. Of such men, I do not hesitate
to say, that they have rendered to freedom a more essential service, than any body of men among us. The
defenders of freedom are not those, who claim and exercise rights which no one assails, or who win shouts
of applause by well turned compliments to liberty in the
days of her triumph. They are those, who stand up for
rights which mobs, conspiracies, or single tyrants put
in jeopardy ; who contend for liberty in that particular
form, which is threatened at the moment by the many

or the few. To the Abolitionists this honor belongs.
The first systematic effort to strip the citizen of freedom of speech they have met with invincible resolution.
From my heart I thank them. I am myself their debt-
or. I am not sure, that I should this moment write in
safety, had they shrunk from the conflict, had they shut
their lips, imposed silence on their presses, and hid
themselves before their ferocious assailants. I know not
where these outrages would have stopped, had they not
met resistance from their first destined victims. The
newspaper press, with a few exceptions, uttered no genuine indignant rebuke of the wrong-doers, but rather
countenanced, by its gentle censures, the reign of Force.
The mass of the people looked supinely on this new
tyranny, under which a portion of their fellow-citizens
seemed to be sinking. A tone of denunciation was beginning to proscribe *all* discussion of slavery; and had
the spirit of violence, which selected associations as its
first objects, succeeded in this preparatory enterprise,
it might have been easily turned against any and every
individual, who might presume to agitate the unwelcome
subject. It is hard to say, to what outrage the fettered
press of the country might not have been reconciled.
I thank the Abolitionists, that in this evil day, they
were true to the rights which the multitude were ready
to betray. Their purpose to suffer, to die, rather than
surrender their dearest liberties, taught the lawless, that
they had a foe to contend with, whom it was not safe
to press, whilst, like all manly appeals, it called forth
reflection and sympathy in the better portion of the
community. In the name of freedom and humanity,
I thank them. Through their courage, the violence,
which might have furnished a precedent fatal to free-

dom, is to become, I trust, a warning to the lawless, of the folly as well as crime of attempting to crush opinion by Force.

Of all powers, the last to be intrusted to the multitude of men, is that of determining what questions shall be discussed. The greatest truths are often the most unpopular and exasperating ; and were they to be denied discussion, till the many should be ready to accept them, they would never establish themselves in the general mind. The progress of society depends on nothing more, than on the exposure of time-sanctioned abuses, which cannot be touched without offending multitudes, than on the promulgation of principles, which are in advance of public sentiment and practice, and which are consequently at war with the habits, prejudices, and immediate interests of large classes of the community. Of consequence, the multitude, if once allowed to dictate or proscribe subjects of discussion, would strike society with spiritual blindness, and death. The world is to be carried forward by truth, which at first offends, which wins its way by degrees, which the many hate and would rejoice to crush. The right of free discussion is therefore to be guarded by the friends of mankind, with peculiar jealousy. It is at once the most sacred, and most endangered of all our rights. He who would rob his neighbour of it, should have a mark set on him as the worst enemy of freedom.

I do not know that our history contains a page, more disgraceful to us as freemen, than that which records the violences against the Abolitionists. As a people, we are chargeable with other and worse misdeeds, but none so flagrantly opposed to the spirit of liberty, the very spirit of our institutions, and of which we make

14 *

our chief boast. Who, let me ask, are the men, whose offences are so aggravated, that they must be denied the protection of the laws, and be given up to the worst passions of the multitude? Are they profligate in principle and life, teachers of impious or servile doctrines, the enemies of God and their race? I speak not from vague rumor, but from better means of knowledge, when I say, that a body of men and women, more blameless than the Abolitionists in their various relations, or more disposed to adopt a rigid construction of the Christian precepts, cannot be found among us. Of their judiciousness and wisdom, I do not speak; but I believe they yield to no party in moral worth. Their great crime, and one, which in this land of liberty is to be punished above all crimes, is this, that they carry the doctrine of human equality to its full extent, that they plead vehemently for the oppressed, that they assail wrong-doing however sanctioned by opinion or intrenched behind wealth and power, that their zeal for human rights is without measure, that they associate themselves fervently with the Christians and philanthropists of other countries against the worst relic of barbarous times. Such is the offence, against which mobs are arrayed, and which is counted so flagrant, that a summary justice, too indignant to wait for the tardy progress of tribunals, must take the punishment into its own hands.

How strange in a free country, that the men, from whom the liberty of speech is to be torn, are those who use it in pleading for freedom, who devote themselves to the vindication of human rights! What a spectacle is presented to the world by a republic, in which sentence of proscription is passed on citizens, who labor, by addressing men's consciences, to enforce the truth, that slavery is the greatest of wrongs ! Through the civilized world, the best and greatest men are bearing joint witness against slavery. Christians of all denominations and conditions, rich and poor, learned and ignorant, are bound in a holy league against this most degrading form of oppression. But in free America, the language which despots tolerate, must not be heard. One would think, that freemen might be pardoned, if the view of fellow-creatures stripped of all human rights should move them to vehemence of speech. But, whilst, on all other subjects, the deeply stirred feelings may overflow in earnest remonstrance, on slavery the freemen must speak in whispers, or pay the penalty of persecution for the natural utterance of strong emotion.

I am aware, that the outrages on the Abolitionists are justified or palliated by various considerations; nor is this surprising; for when did violence ever want excuse ? It is said, that Abolitionism tends to stir up insurrection at the South, and to dissolve the Union. Of all pretences for resorting to lawless force, the most dangerous is the *tendency* of measures or opinions. Almost all men see ruinous tendencies in whatever opposes their particular interests or views. All the political parties, which have convulsed our country, have seen tendencies to national destruction in the principles of their opponents. So infinite are the connexions and consequences of human affairs, that nothing can be done in which some dangerous tendency may not be detected. There is a tendency in arguments against any old establishment to unsettle all institutions, because all hang together. There is a tendency in the laying bare of deep-rooted abuses to throw a community into a storm. Liberty tends to licentiousness, government

to despotism.   Exclude all enterprises which *may* have
evil results, and human life will stagnate.   Wise men
are not easily deterred by difficulties and perils from a
course of action, which promises great good.   Especially when justice and humanity cry aloud for the removal of an enormous social evil, it is unworthy of men
and Christians to let the imagination run riot among possible dangers, instead of rousing every energy of mind
to study how the evil may be taken away, and the
perils, which accompany beneficial changes, may he
escaped.

As to the charge brought against the Abolitionists,
of stirring up insurrection at the South, I have never
met the shadow of a proof that this nefarious project
was meditated by a single member of their body.   The
accusation is repelled by their characters and principles
as well as by facts; nor can I easily conceive of a sane
man giving it belief.   As to the "tendency" of their
measures to this result, it is such only as we have seen
to belong to all human affairs, and such as may easily
be guarded against.   The truth is, that any exposition
of Slavery, no matter from whom it may come, may
chance to favor revolt.   It may chance to fall into the
hands of a fanatic, who may think himself summoned
by Heaven to remove violently this great wrong; or it
may happen to reach the hut of some intelligent daring
slave, who may think himself called to be the avenger
of his race.   All things are possible.   A casual, innocent remark in conversation, may put wild projects into
the unbalanced or disordered mind of some hearer.
Must we then live in perpetual silence?   Do such
chances make it our duty to shut our lips on the subject
of an enormous wrong, and never to send from the

press a reprobation of the evil ? .The truth is, that the great. danger to the slave-holder comes from slavery itself, from the silent innovations of time, from political conflicts and convulsions, and not from the writings of strangers. I readily grant that the Abolitionists, in consequence of their number and their systematic and public efforts, are more likely to be heard of by the slave, than a solitary individual who espouses his cause. But when I consider, how steadily they have condemned the resort to force on the part of the oppressed; when I consider what power the master possesses of excluding incendiary influences, if such are threatened from abroad ; when I remember, that, during the late unparalleled excitement at the South, not a symptom of revolt appeared ; and when to all this, I add the strongly manifested purpose of the Free States to put forth their power, if required, for the suppression of insurrection, it seems to me that none but the most delicate nerves can be disturbed by the movements of the Abolitionists. Can any man, who has a sense of character, affect to believe, that the tendency of Abolitionism to stir up a servile war, is so palpable and resistless as to require the immediate application of Force for its suppression, as to demand the substitution of mobs for the action of. law, as to justify the violation of the most sacred right of the citizen ?

As to the other charge, that the measures of the Abolitionists endanger our National Union, and must therefore be put down by any and every means, it is weaker than the former. Against whom has not this charge been hurled ? What party among us has not been loaded with this reproach ? Do not we at the North almost unanimously believe, that the spirit and measures of Nullification have a direct and immediate tendency to dissolve the Union? But are we therefore authorized to silence the nullifier by violence? Should a leader of that party travel among us, is he to be mobbed? Let me farther ask, how is it, that the Abolitionists endanger the Union? The only reply, which I have heard, is, that they exasperate the South. And is it a crime to exasperate men? Who then so criminal as the Founder and primitive teachers of our faith? Have we yet to learn, that, in cases of exasperation, the blame is as apt to lie with those who take, as with those who occasion, offence? How strange the doctrine, that men are to be proscribed for uttering language which gives offence, are to be outlawed for putting their neighbours into a passion! Let it also be considered, that the Abolitionists are not the only people who exasperate the South. Can the calmest book be written on Slavery, without producing the same effect? Can the Chief Justice of Massachusetts expound the constitution and laws of that commonwealth according to their free spirit, and of course in opposition to Slavery, without awakeuing indignation? Is not the doctrine, that Congress has the right of putting an end to Slavery in the District of Columbia, denounced as fiercely as the writings and harangues of Abolitionists? Where then shall mobs stop, if the crime of exasperating the South is so heinous as to deserve their vengeance? If the philanthropist and Christian must be silenced on the subject of Slavery, lest they wound the sensitive ears of the South, ought the judge and legislator to be spared? Who does not see, that these apologies for lawless force, if they have any validity, will bring every good man under its iron sway?

In these remarks you learn my abhorrence of the violence offered to the Abolitionists, and my admiration of the spirit they haye opposed to it. May they vindicate to the end the rights which in their persons have been outraged. Allow me now to express my earnest desire and hope, that the Abolitionists will maintain the liberty of speech and the press, not only by asserting it firmly, but by using it wisely, deliberately, generously, and under the control of the severest moral principle. It is my earnest desire, that they will exercise it in the spirit of Christians and philanthropists, with a supreme love of truth, without passion or bitterness, and without that fanaticism which cannot discern the true proportions of things, which exaggerates or distorts whatever favors or conflicts with its end, which sees no goodness except in its own ranks, which shuts itself up in one object and is blind to all besides. Liberty suffers from nothing more, than from licentiousness, and I fear that Abolitionists are not to be absolved from this abuse of it. It seems to me that they are particularly open to one reproach. Their writings have been blemished by a spirit of intolerance, sweeping censure, and rash, injurious judgment. I do not mean to bring this charge against all their publications. Yours, as far as I have seen them, are an honorable exception; and others, I know, deserve the same praise. But Abolitionism, in the main, has spoken in an intolerant tone, and in this way has repelled many good minds, given great advantage to its opponents, and diminished the energy and effect of its appeals. I should rejoice to see it purified from this stain.

Abolitionism seems to me to have been intolerant towards the slave-holders, and towards those in the Free

States who oppose them, or who refuse to take part in their measures. I say, first, towards the slave-holder. The Abolitionist has not spoken, and cannot speak, against slavery too strongly. No language can exceed the enormity of the wrong. But the whole class of slave-holders often meets a treatment in anti-slavery publications which is felt to be unjust, and is certainly unwise. We always injure ourselves, in placing our adversary on the footing of an injured man. One groundless charge helps him to repel many which are true. There is indeed a portion of slave-holders who deserve the severest reprobation. In every such community, there are many who hold their fellow-creatures in bondage for gain, for mere gain. They perpetuate this odious system not reluctantly, but from choice ; not because the public safety compels them, as they think, to act the part of despots, but because they love despotism, and count money their supreme good. Provided they can be supported in ease and indulgence, can be pampered and enriched, they care not for the means. They care not what wrongs or stripes are inflicted, what sweat is extorted, what powers of the immortal soul are crushed. For such men no rebuke can be too severe. If any vehemence of language can pierce their consciences, let it be used. The man who holds slaves for gain is, in effect, though unconsciously, the worst of robbers ; for he selfishly robs his fellow-creatures not only of their property, but of themselves. He is the worst of tyrants, for, whilst absolute governments spoil men of civil, he strips them of personal rights. But I do not, cannot believe, that the majority of slave-holders are of the character now described. I believe that the majority, could they be persuaded of the consistency of emancipation with the well-being of the colored race and with social order, would relinquish their hold on the slave, and sacrifice their imagined property in him to the claims of justice and humanity. They shrink from emancipation, because it seems to them a precipice. Having seen the colored man continually dependent on foreign guidance and control, they think him incapable of providing for himself. Having seen the laboring class kept down by force, they feel as if the removal of. this restraint would be a signal to universal lawlessness and crime. That such opinions absolve from all blame those who perpetuate slavery, I do not say. That they are often strengthened by the self-interest of the master, I cannot doubt ; for we see men everywhere grasping and defending doctrines which confirm their property and power. I acknowledge, too, that the ready, unhesitating acquiescence of the slave-holder in such loose notions, especially at the present moment, .is a . bad symptom. In the present age, when a flood of light has been thrown on the evils of slavery, and when the whole civilized world cries out against it as the greatest of wrongs ; and in this country, where the doctrine of human rights has been expounded by the profoundest minds, and sealed with the best blood, a fearful, responsibility is assumed by masters, who, pronouncing emancipation hopeless, make no serious, anxious inquiry after the means of accomplishing it, and no serious effort to remove the supposed unfitness of the slave for freedom. Still, while there is much to be condemned in the prevalent opinions and feelings at the South, we have no warrant for denying to all slave-holders moral and religious excellence. The whole history of the world shows us, that a culpable blindness in regard to one class of obligations may consist with a sincere reverence for religious and moral principles, as far as they are understood. In estimating men's characters, we must never forget the disadvantages under which they labor. Slavery, upheld, as it is at the South, by the deepest prejudices of education, by the sanction of laws, by the prescription of ages, and by real difficulties attending emancipation, cannot easily be viewed in that region as it appears to more distant and impartial observers. The hatefulness of the system ought to be strongly exposed, and it cannot be exposed too strongly; but this hatefulness must not be attached to all who sustain slavery. There are pure and generous spirits at the South, and they are to be honored the more for the sore trials amidst which their virtues have gained strength. The Abolitionists, in their zeal, seem to have overlooked these truths in a great degree, and by their intolerance towards the slave-holder, have awakened towards him sympathy rather than indignation, and weakened the effect of their just invectives against the system which he upholds.

I think, too, that they are chargeable with a like intolerance towards those in the Free States, who oppose them, or who refuse to participate in their operations. They have been apt to set down opposition to themselves as equivalent to attachment to slavery. Regarding their own dogmas as the only true faith, and making their own zeal the standard of a true interest in the oppressed, they have been apt to cast scornful looks and reproaches on those who have spoken in doubt or displeasure of their movements. This has made them

-many foes. They have been too belligerent to make friends. I do not mean in these remarks, that the Abolitionists have had nothing to blame in their opponents. Among these, are not a few deserving severe reprehension, and I have no desire to shield them from it. But the great mass, who have refused to take part in the anti-slavery movement, have been governed by pure motives. If they have erred, they have not erred willingly, or from the influence of low and servile passions. They have consequently been wronged by the treatment they have received at the hands of the Abolitionists, and men are not brought over by wrongs 'to a good cause.

I have said that I have no desire to shield the unworthy among ourselves. We have those, whose opposition to Abolitionism has been wicked, and merits reprobation. Such are to be found in all classes, forming indeed a minority in each, yet numerous enough to deserve attention and to do much harm. Such are to be found in what is called the highest class of society, that is, among the rich and fashionable ; and the cause is obvious. The rich and fashionable belong to the same caste with the slave-holder ; and men are apt to sympathize with their own caste more readily than with those beneath them. The slave is too low, too vulgar, to awaken interest in those, who abhor vulgarity more than oppression and crime, and who found all their self-admiration on the rank they occupy in the social scale. Far be it from me to charge on the rich or fashionable, as a class, this moral degradation ; but among them are the worshippers of high degree, who would think their dignity soiled, by touching the cause of a menial, degraded race, and who load its advocates with ridicule and scorn.

Then, in the commercial class, there are unworthy opposers of Abolitionism. There are those, whose interests rouse them to withstand every movement, which may offend the South. They have profitable connexions with the slave-holder, which must not be endangered by expressions of sympathy with the slave. Gain is their god, and they sacrifice on this altar without compunction the rights and happiness of their fellow-creatures. To such, the philanthropy, which would break every chain, is fanaticism, or a pretence. Nothing in their own souls helps them to comprehend the fervor of men, who feel for the wronged, and who hazard property and life in exposing the wrong. Your "Narrative of the Riotous Proceedings at Cincinnati," shows to what a fearful extent the spirit of humanity, justice, and freedom may be supplanted by the accursed lust of gain. This, however, cannot surprise us. Our present civilization is characterized and tainted by a devouring greediness of wealth; and a cause, which asserts right against wealth, must stir up bitter opposition, especially in cities where this divinity is most adored. Every large city will furnish those, who would sooner rivet the chain on the slave than lose a commission, or retrench an expenditure. I would on no account intimate, that such men constitute the majority of the commercial class. I rejoice to know that a more honorable spirit prevails in the community which falls more immediately under my notice. Still, the passion for gain is everywhere sapping pure and generous feeling, and everywhere raises up bitter foes against any reform which may threaten to turn aside a stream of wealth. I sometimes feel as if a great social revolution were necessary to break up our present mercenary civilization, in order that Christianity, now repelled by the almost universal worldliness, may come into new contact with the soul, and may reconstruct society after its own pure and disinterested principles.

In another class, which contains many excellent people, may also be found unworthy opposers of all anti-slavery movements. I refer to the Conservative class, to those who are tremblingly alive to the spirit of innovation now abroad in the world, who have little or no faith in human progress, who are anxious to secure what is now gained rather than to gain more, to whom that watchword of the times, Reform, sounds like a knell. Among these are to be found individuals, who, from no benevolent interest in society, but simply because they have drawn high prizes in the lottery of life, are unwilling that the most enormous abuses should be touched, lest the established order of things, so propitious to themselves, should be disturbed. A palsying, petrifying order, keeping things as they are, seems to them the Ideal of a perfect community, and they have no patience with the rude cry of reformers for the restoration of human beings to their long-lost rights.

I will only add the politicians, as another class, which has furnished selfish assailants of Abolitionism. Among our politicians are men, who regard public life as a charmed circle into which moral principle must not enter, who know no law but expediency, who are prepared to kiss the feet of the South for southern votes, and who stand ready to echo all the vituperations of the slave-

15 *

holder against the active enemies of slavery in the Free
States.

For these various descriptions of selfish opponents of
Abolitionism, I make no apology.   Let them be visited
with just rebuke.   But they, after all, form but a small
part of that great body in the Free States, who look on
the present anti-slavery movement with distrust and disapprobation.   The vast majority in the Free States,
who refuse communion with you, are not actuated by
base considerations.   The fear of a servile war, the
fear of political convulsions, a perception of the difficulties of great social changes, self-distrust, a dread of
rashness, these, and the like motives, have great influence in deterring multitudes from giving their countenance to what seem to them violent movements for the
abolition of slavery.   That a culpable insensibility to the
evils and wrongs of this nefarious institution is too common in the class of which I now speak, I do not mean
to deny.   Still, how vast a proportion of the intelligence, virtue, and piety of the country is to be found in
their ranks !   To speak of them slightly, contemptu-
ously, bitterly, is to do great wrong, and such speaking,
I fear, has brought much reproach on Abolitionism.

The motives which have induced me to make this
long communication to you will not, I trust, be misun-
derstood.   I earnestly desire, my dear Sir, that you
and your associates will hold fast the right of free discussion by speech and the press, and, at the same time,
that you will exercise it as Christians, and as friends of
your race.   That you, Sir, will not fail in these duties, I rejoice to believe.   Accept my humble tribute
of respect and admiration for your disinterestedness, for

your faithfulness to your convictions, under the peculiar sacrifices to which you have been called. It is my prayer, that, by calm, fearless perseverance in well-doing, you may guide and incite many to a like virtue.

It may be said, that it is easy for one, living, as I do, at a distance from danger, living in prosperity and ease, to preach exposure and suffering to you and your friends. I can only say in reply, that I lay down no rule for others, which I do not feel to be binding on myself. What I should do in the hour of peril may be uncertain ; but what I ought to do is plain. What I desire to do, is known to the Searcher of all hearts. It is my earnest desire, that prosperity may not unnerve me, that no suffering may shake my constancy in a cause which my heart approves. I sometimes indeed fear for myself, when I think of untried persecutions. I know not what weaknesses the presence of great danger may call forth. But in my most deliberate moments, I see nothing worth living for, but the divine virtue which endures and surrenders all things for truth, duty, and mankind. I look on reproach, poverty, persecution, and death, as light evils compared with unfaithfulness to pure and generous principles, to the spirit of Christ, and to the will of God. With these impressions, I ought not to be deterred by self-distrust, or by my distance from danger, from summoning and cheering others to conflict with evil. Christianity, as I regard it, is designed throughout to fortify us for this warfare. Its great lesson is self-sacrifice. Its distinguishing spirit is Divine Philanthropy suffering on the cross. The Cross, the Cross, this is the badge and standard of our religion. I honor all who bear it. I look with scorn on the self ish greatness of this world, and with pity on the most gifted and prosperous in the struggle for office and power; but I look with reverence on the obscurest man, who suffers for the right, who is true to a good but persecuted cause.

With these sentiments, I subscribe myself your sincere friend,

WILLIAM E. CHANNING.

NOTE.

As the preceding letter was prepared for a newspaper, I was obliged, by the narrowness of my limits, to pass over some topics, on which I should have been glad to offer a few remarks. — In expressing my conviction of the moral worth of the Abolitionists, I wished to say, that they are in danger, as a body, of forfeiting this praise. Let them gather numbers and strength, and they may be expected to degenerate. The danger is greater, now that they have begun to add the ballot-box, or political action, to their other modes of operation. It is one of the evils attending associations and an argument against them, that, by growing popular, they attract to themselves unworthy members, lose their original simplicity of purpose, become aspiring, and fall more and more under the control of popular leaders. Intriguers will never be wanting to press them, if possible, into the service of one or another of the great parties which divide the country, and by becoming political machines, they only increase the confusion of public affairs.

I have spoken in the letter, of "the fettered press" of the country, a subject of much moral interest. The newspaper press is fettered among us by its dependence on subscribers, among whom there are not a few intolerant enough to withdraw their patronage, if an editor give publicity to articles which contradict their cherished opinions, or shock their party prejudices, or seem to clash with their interests. In such a state of things, few newspapers can be expected to afford to an unpopular in-

dividual or party, however philanthropic or irreproach-
able, an opportunity of being heard by the public. Edi-
tors engage in their vocation like other men, for a support;
and communications, which will thin their subscription-
lists, will of course find little favor at their hands. Much
reproach is sometimes thrown on them for their want of
moral independence ; but the root of the evil lies in the
intolerance of the community. One result of this state
of things is, that the newspaper press fails of one of its
chief duties, which is to stem corrupt opinion, to stay the
excesses of popular passions. It generally swells, seldom
arrests, the violence of the multitude. The very subjects,
on which the public mind may most need to be reformed,
are most likely to be excluded from its columns. Another
evil result is, the increase of the number and violence of
parties. Conscientious men, who cannot obtain a hearing
through the common newspapers, are compelled to league
for the support of papers of their own, and, in speaking
through these organs, they are tempted to an extravagance and bitterness which they would have shunned, had
they used other vehicles. It may be doubted, whether
Abolitionism would have taken the form of organized and
affiliated societies, if the subject of slavery could have
been discussed in the common papers with the same freedom as other topics. That Abolitionism has owed not a
little of its asperity to its having been proscribed from
the beginning, and to its having been denied the common
modes of addressing the public mind, I cannot doubt.
Toleration seems to be the last virtue which individuals
or communities learn. One would think, that experience
had sufficiently taught men, that persecution is not the
way to put down opinions. The selfish may indeed be
disheartened by opposition ; but conscientious men are
strengthened by it in their convictions. Persecution
drives and knits them together ; and when formed into a

party by this bond, their zeal becomes more intense, their prejudices more inveterate, their opinions more extravagant, their means more violent, than if they had continued to be scattered through the community. If Abolitionism should convulse the country, as some seem to fear, a large share of the blame will belong to that intolerance, which has heaped on the most respectable men every epithet of scorn and vituperation, and has driven them to assume a separate and belligerent attitude in the community.

I cannot easily conceive of a greater good to a city, than the establishment of a newspaper by men of superior ability and moral independence, who should judge all parties and public measures by the standard of the Christian law, who should uncompromisingly speak the truth and adhere to the Right, who should make it their steady aim to form a just and lofty public sentiment, and who should at the same time give to upright and honorable men an opportunity of making known their opinions on matters of general interest, however opposed to the opinions and passions of the day. In the present stage of society, when newspapers form the reading of all classes, and the chief reading of multitudes, the importance of the daily press cannot be overrated. It is one of the mightiest instruments at work among us. It may and should take rank among the most effectual means of social order and improvement. It is a power, which should be wielded by the best minds in the community. The office of editor is one of solemn responsibility, and the community should encourage the most gifted and virtuous men to assume it, by liberally recompensing their labor, and by according to them that freedom of thought and speech, without which no mind puts forth all its vigor, and which the highest minds rank among their dearest rights and blessings.

In speaking of the unworthy opponents of Abolitionism in the preceding letter, I proposed to say something of those unhappy men, who, in one part of our country, have proclaimed Slavery to be a good, a domestic blessing, and an essential support or condition of free institutions. But I felt that I could not easily speak on this point in measured terms; and in such cases I prefer silence, unless a clear conviction of duty forbids it. Happily this detestable doctrine needs no effort to expose it; for it carries its refutation in its own absurdity, and in its repugnance to all moral and religious feeling. The Southern States would be grievously wronged by being made responsible for this insane estimate of Slavery. It is confined, I trust, to a small number, who have been hardy enough to set at defiance the judgment of the Christian and civilized world, and whom nothing but oblivion can screen from that condemning sentence, which future times will pass more and more sternly on the advocates of oppression, on the foes of freedom and human rights.

A

LETTER TO THE HON. HENRY CLAY,

ON

THE ANNEXATION OF TEXAS

TO

THE UNITED STATES.

THE ANNEXATION OF TEXAS

TO THE UNITED STATES.

———

My Dear Sir,

I trust that you will excuse the liberty which I take in thus publicly addressing you. If you could look into my heart, I am sure you would not condemn me. You would discover the motives of this act, in my respect for your eminent powers, and in my confidence that you are disposed to use them for the honor and happiness of your country. Were you less distinguished, or less worthy of distinction, I should not trouble you with this letter. I write you, because I am persuaded, that your great influence, if exerted in promoting just views on the subject of this communication, would accomplish a good, to which, perhaps, no other man in the country is equal. I am bound, in frankness, to add another reason for addressing you. I hope that your name, prefixed to this letter, may secure to it an access to some, perhaps to many, who would turn away, were its thoughts presented in a more general form. Perhaps by this aid it may scale the barrier, which now excludes

from the South a certain class of the writings of the
North. I am sure your hospitality would welcome me
to Kentucky ; and your well-known generosity, I believe, will consent that I should use your name, to gain
a hearing in that and the neighbouring States.

It is with great reluctance that I enter on the topic of
this letter. My tastes and habits incline me to very
different objects of thought and exertion. I had hoped,
that I should never again feel myself called to take part
in the agitations and exciting discussions of the day,
especially in those of a political character. I desire
nothing so much as to devote what remains of life to the
study and exposition of great principles and universal
truths. But the subject of Texas weighs heavily on
my mind, and I cannot shake it off. To me, it is more
than a political question. It belongs eminently to morals
and religion. I have hoped, that the attention of the
public would be called to it by some more powerful
voice. I have postponed writing, until the national
legislature is about to commence the important session,
in which, it is thought, this subject may be decided.
But no one speaks, and therefore I cannot be silent.
Should Texas be annexed to our country, I feel that I
could not forgive myself, if, with my deep, solemn impressions, I should do nothing to avert the evil. I cannot easily believe, that this disastrous measure is to be
adopted, especially at the present moment. The annexation of Texas, under existing circumstances, would
be more than rashness ; it would be madness. That
opposition to it must exist at the South, as well as at
the North, I cannot doubt. Still, there is a general impression, that great efforts will be made to accomplish
this object at the approaching session of Congress, and

that nothing but strenuous resistance can prevent their success. I must write, therefore, as if the danger were real and imminent ; and if any should think that I am betrayed into undue earnestness by a false alarm, they will remember that there are circumstances, in which excess of vigilance is a virtue.

In the course of this discussion, I shall be forced to speak on one topic, which can hardly be treated so as to give no offence. I am satisfied that in this, as in all cases, it is best, safest, as well as most right and honorable, to speak freely and plainly. Nothing is to be gained by caution, circumlocution, plausible softenings of language, and other arts, which, in destroying confidence, defeat their own end. In discussions of an irritating nature, the true way of doing good is, to purify ourselves from all unworthy motives, to cherish disinterested sentiments and unaffected good-will towards those from whom we differ, and then to leave the mind to utter itself naturally and spontaneously. How far I have prepared myself for my work, by this self-purification, it becomes not me to say ; but this I may say, that I am not conscious of the slightest asperity of feeling towards any party or any individual. I have no private interests to serve, no private passions to gratify. The strength of my conviction may be expressed in strong, perhaps unguarded language ; but this want of caution is the result of the consciousness, that I have no purpose or feeling which I need conceal.

I shall, in one respect, depart from the freedom of a letter. I shall arrange my thoughts under distinct heads ; and I shall do this, because I wish to put my reader in full possession of my views. I wish to use no vague declamation, to spread no vague alarm, but to bring out

16 *

as clearly as possible the precise points of objection to the measure I oppose.*

I. We have a strong argument against annexing Texas to the United States, in the Criminality of the revolt which threatens to sever that country from Mexico. On this point our citizens need light. The Texan insurrection is seriously regarded by many among us as a struggle of the oppressed for freedom. The Texan revolution is thought to resemble our own. Our own is contaminated by being brought into such relationship, and we owe to our fathers and ourselves a disclaimer of affinity with this new republic. The Texan revolt, if regarded in its causes and its means of success, is

---

* It may be well to state the principal authorities on which I rely for the statements in this letter. I am most indebted, perhaps, to an article on Mexico and Texas, in the July number of the North American Review for the year 1836. This article, as I understood at the time, was written by an enlightened and respected citizen of the South. The quotations in the first head of this letter, without a marginal reference, are taken from this tract, with a few unimportant exceptions. I have also made use of a pamphlet, bearing the title of the "War in Texas," written by Mr. Benjamin Lundy, a man of unimpeachable character, and who professes to have given particular attention to the subject. With his reasonings and opinions, I have nothing to do ; but his statement of facts has been represented to me as worthy of full credit. I have also consulted a "History of Texas, by David B. Edwards." I know not that this has furnished me any thing of importance. But, by its undesigned coincidence, it corroborates the preceding articles. My chief reliance, however, is not on books, but on the notoriety of the facts here given, which may be considered as a testimony borne to them by the whole people. This is a singularly unexceptionable testimony in the present case ; because it is well known, that the advocates of the Texan revolt have had possession, to a great degree, of the press of the country, and unfavorable accounts could not have obtained general currency, without a foundation in truth. Let me add, that by "the North," I understand in this letter all the Free States, and by "the South," all the Slave-holding States except where the terms are plainly restricted by the connexion.

criminal ; and we ought in no way to become partakers in its guilt. You, I doubt not, are familiar with its history ; but for the benefit of some, into whose hands this letter may fall, I will give the leading facts.

The first grant of land in Texas to our citizens was made under the Royal Government ; and, in accepting it, the obligation was expressly incurred, of submission to the civil and religious despotism which then crushed the country. It was understood, that the settlers were to adopt the Catholic faith, and to conform in all other respects to the institutions of Mexico. Under the revolutionary governments, which succeeded the fall of the Spanish power, the original grant was confirmed, and new ones made, on condition of subjection to the laws of the land. The terms were very liberal, except that adherence to the Catholic religion was required as the condition of settlement. These facts will help us to understand the reasonableness of some of the complaints, under which the colonists seek to shelter their revolt.

Mexico, on declaring her independence on the mother country, established a republican government, and was unfortunately betrayed by her admiration of this country into the adoption of a Federal system, for which no foundation had been laid in her previous history. From this cause, added to her inexperience in self-government, and to the want of intelligence among the mass of her population, her institutions have yielded very imperfectly the fruits of freedom. The country has been rent by factions, the capital convulsed by revolutions, and the chief office of the state been secured by the military to popular chieftains. The emigrants from this country to Texas went with open eyes, with full knowledge of the unsettled state of affairs, into this region of misrule and agitation.   Happily their distance from the seat of government prevented their being drawn into the whirlpool of civil contests, which threatened at times the destruction of the metropolis.   Whilst the city of Mexico was pillaged or laid under martial law, Texas found security in her remoteness ; and, had her colonists proved loyal citizens, this security might have been undisturbed.

Complaints of one another soon sprung up between the General Government and Texas.   Mexico complained of the gross infraction of her laws, and Texas of the violence of the means by which it was attempted to enforce them.   That both parties had ground of reproach, we cannot doubt ; nor is it easy to strike the balance between them, or to say where the chief blame lies.   The presumption is strong, that the fault began with the colonists.   We of this country, receiving our accounts of the controversy from Texans, are in danger of being warped in our judgments.   But we have for our guidance our knowledge of human nature, which helps us to construe the testimony of interested witnesses, and which, in the present case, cannot easily deceive us.   If we consider the distance of Texas from the seat of government, her scattered population, her vicinity to a slave country, the general character of the first settlers in a wilderness, and the difficulty of subjecting them to regular tribunals ; can we doubt, for a moment, that Mexico had cause for the complaints, which she urged, of the gross infractions and evasions of her laws in Texas, especially of the laws relating to revenue, and to the exclusion of slaves ?   On the other hand, if we consider the circumstances of Mexico, can we doubt, that the military force sent by her to Texas, and needed there to enforce the laws, abused its power more or less ?, That lawless men should be put down by lawless means, especially in a country swept by the spirit of revolution, is an effect too common and natural to excite wonder. The wonder is, that Texas escaped with so little injury. Whether she would have suffered at all, had she submitted in good faith to the laws which she had pledged herself to obey, may be fairly questioned. I ask you, Sir, whether it is not your deliberate conviction, that Mexico, from the beginning of her connexion with the colonists, has been more sinned against than sinning. But allowing that the violent means, used by Mexico, for enforcing her authority, were less provoked than we believe them to have been ; did not the Texans enter, the country with a full knowledge of its condition ? Did they not become citizens of a state, just escaped from a grinding despotism, just entered into the school of freedom, which had been inured for ages to abuses of - military power, and whose short republican history had been made up of civil agitation ? In swearing allegiance to such a state, did they not consent to take their chance of the evils, through which it must have been expected to pass in its way to firm and free institutions ? Was there, or could there be in so unsettled a society, that deliberate, settled, inflexible purpose of spoiling the colonists of their rights, which alone absolves a violation of allegiance from the guilt of treason ?

Some of the grounds, on which the Texans justify their conflict for independence, are so glaringly deficient in truth and reason, that it is hard to avoid suspicion of every defence set up for their revolt. They complain of being denied the right of worshipping God according to the dictates of their consciences ; and this they do, though they entered the country and swore allegiance to its government, with full knowledge that the Catholic religion was the religion of the state and alone tolerated by the constitution. What increases the hollowness and criminality of the pretence is, that notwithstanding the provision of the constitution, Protestant sects had held their meetings undisturbed in Texas, and no persecution had ever taken place on account of difference of creed.

Another grievance by which they justify their revolt is, that the trial by jury had been withheld; and this complaint they have the courage to make, although they were fully aware, before becoming the adopted citizens of the country, that this mode of trial was utterly unknown to its jurisprudence, and though, in the constitution of the State of Coahuila and Texas, the following article had been introduced: "One of the principal subjects for the attention of Congress [State Legislature] shall be to establish in criminal cases the trial by jury, extending it gradually, and even adopting it in civil cases, in proportion as the advantages of this precious institution may be practically developed."

One of the greatest grievances in the eyes of Texas, was the change of the Mexican government from a Federal to a Central or Consolidated form. But this change, however violently brought about, was ratified by the national Congress according to the rules prescribed by the constitution, and was sanctioned by the Mexican people. The decree of Congress, introducing this " reform " of the national institutions, declares the system of government " republican, popular, and representative," and provides all the organs by which such a government is characterized. What also deserves our consideration,

in estimating this measure, is, that the whole history of
Mexico has proved the necessity of substituting a Central for a Federal government.   Liberty and order can
be reconciled and preserved to that country by no process but by the introduction of more simple and efficient
institutions.   And yet the Texans, a handful of strangers, raised the standard of revolt, because the government was changed by a nation of nine millions without
their consent.

I have spoken of the Texans as a handful of people.
At the breaking out of the insurrection they were about
twenty thousand, including women and children.   They
were, of course, wholly unable to achieve or maintain
national independence ; so that one condition which is
required to authorize revolution, namely, the ability to
sustain a government, to perform the duties of sovereignty, they could not pretend to fulfil.   Twenty thousand men, women, and children, raising the standard of
war, and proposing to dismember a mighty empire !   It
is very possible that there are suburbs of London con-
taining an equal number of discontented people, who
suffer under and have reason to complain of municipal
or national injustice.   And may these fly to arms, set
up for a nation, and strive to break the unity of the
British dominions ?   It should also be remembered,
that the Texans were not only a drop of the bucket
compared with the Mexican population, but that they
were a decided minority in the particular State to which
they belonged ; so that their revolt may be compared
to the rising of a county in Massachusetts or Virginia
for the purpose of establishing a separate sovereignty,
on the ground of some real or imagined violation of
right on the part of the Federal or the State govern-

ment.   Still more, this little knot of Texans were far
from being unanimous as to the revolt.   The older and
wealthier inhabitants favored peace.   " There were great
differences of opinion among the colonists, and even
violent party dissensions.   Many, who were in the
quiet enjoyment of their property, were opposed to all
these hostile movements.   The first public declaration
of independence was adopted, not by persons assuming
to act in a representative capacity, but by about *nine-
ty individuals,* all, except two, Americans, if we may
judge by their names, acting for themselves, and recommending a similar course to their fellow-citizens.   That
declaration furnishes proofs of the dissensions and jealousies of which we have spoken. — It proves another
fact, that the ancient population of the province was
favorable to the new views of the government of Mexico."   In some letters written by Colonel S. T. Austin,
the founder of the colony, in the year 1834, whilst
imprisoned in Mexico on the charge of encouraging
revolutionary movements in Texas, we have some remarkable passages, showing the aversion of the sounder
part of the population to violent measures.   " I wish
my friends and all Texas to adopt and firmly adhere to
the motto and rule I have stated in this letter.   The
rule is, to discountenance, in the most unequivocal and
efficient manner, all persons who are in the habit of
speaking or writing in violent or disrespectful terms of
the Mexican people or authorities. — I have been led
into so much difficulty, and Texas has been so much
jeopardized in its true and permanent interests, by
inflammatory men, political fanatics, political adventurers, would-be-great men, vain talkers, and visionary
fools, that I begin to lose all confidence except for

those who seek their living between the plough-handles ; and, alas for them ! they are too often sacrificed before they know it.—Tolerate no more violent measures, and you will prosper, and obtain from the government all that reasonable men ought to ask for." * It is very plain, that, of this diminutive colony, the more reasonable men, had they not been overborne by the more violent, would have averted the civil war. Such was the number which set up for a nation !

I have no disposition to deny that Texas had grievances to justify complaint. In proof of this I need no documents. That she was not always wisely governed, that her rights were not always respected, who can doubt? What else could be expected? Mexico is not wise. Mexico is not skilled in the science of human rights. Her civilization is very imperfect, as we and the Texans have always known ; and a good government is one of the slowest fruits of civilization. In truth a good government exists nowhere. The errors and vices of rulers entail evils on every state. Especially in an extensive community, some districts will always suffer from unwise, partial, unjust legislation. If every town or county may start up into a sovereign state, whenever it is wronged, society will be given up to perpetual convulsion, and history be one bloody record of revolt. The right of insurrection is to be exercised most rarely, fearfully, reluctantly, and only in cases of fixed, pronounced, persevering oppression, from which no relief can be found but in force. Nothing is easier than for any and every people to draw up a list of wrongs ; nothing more ruinous than to rebel because

---

* History of Texas, p. 210, Austin's Correspondence.

every claim is not treated with respect. The United States did not throw off the British yoke, because every human right, which could be demonstrated by moral science, was not granted them ; but because they were denied the rights which their fathers had enjoyed, and which had been secured to the rest of the empire. They began with pleading precedent. They took their first stand on the British constitution. They claimed the rights of Englishmen. They set up the case of peculiar oppression ; and did not appeal to arms, until they had sought redress, for years, by patient and respectful remonstrance ; until they had exhausted every means of conciliation which wisdom could devise or a just self-respect would allow. Such was the code of national morality to which our fathers bowed ; and in so doing they acknowledged the sacredness of allegiance, and manifested their deep conviction of the fearful responsibility of subverting a government and of rupturing national ties. A province, in estimating its grievances, should have respect to the general condition of the country to which it belongs. A colony, emigrating from a highly civilized country, has no right to expect in a less favored state the privileges it has left behind. The Texans must have been insane, if, on entering Mexico, they looked for an administration as faultless as that under which they had lived. They might with equal reason have planted themselves in Russia, and then have unfurled the banner of independence near the throne of the Czar, because denied the immunities of their native land.

Having thus considered the grievances of the Texans, I now proceed to consider the real and great causes of the revolt. These are matters of notoriety, so as to need no minute exposition. The first great cause was the unbounded, unprincipled spirit of land speculation, which so tempting a prize as Texas easily kindled in multitudes in the United States, where this mode of gambling is too common a vice. Large grants of land in Texas were originally made to individuals, chiefly citizens of our country, who, in many cases, transferred their claims to joint-stock companies in some of our cities. A quotation will illustrate the nature of these grants and the frauds and speculations to which they gave birth. " The nominal grantee is called the *empresario*. He is considered, by the terms of the contract, merely as a trustee of the government, having no title himself to the land within the limits of his future colony, except upon condition of settling a number of families [within a given time]. The settlers themselves receive a title for each family for a league square, upon the express condition of settlement and cultivation, and the payment of certain very moderate charges within a limited period. It is believed, that these conditions were by the colonization laws of Mexico the basis of all the land-titles in Texas, together with the further condition, that all right and title should be forfeited, if the grantee [or new settler] should abandon the country, or sell his land before having cultivated it. An inspection of the various maps of Texas will show how numerous have been these privileges conceded to various *empresarios*. The face of the province, from Nueces to Red River, and from the Gulf to the mountains, is nearly covered by them. It became at last a matter of greedy speculation ; and it is a notorious fact, that many of the *empresarios*, forgetting the contingent character of their own rights to the soil, and the conditions upon which their future colonists were to receive allotments of land, proceeded at once to make out scrip, which has been sold in the United States to an incalculable amount. In addition to this, we are informed on the best authority, that the manufacture of land-titles, having no foundation whatever, has been carried on as a regular business. That frauds of these different kinds have been practised on the cupidity and credulity of the people of the United States, is beyond doubt. Had the close of the present campaign been what its opening seemed to portend, and the colonies been broken up, it would be impossible to calculate the losses which would be sustained by those who have never seen the land which they have bought. It is not hazarding too much to say, that millions have been expended in the Southern and Southwestern States."

Texas, indeed, has been regarded as a prey for land speculators within its own borders and in the United States. To show the scale on which this kind of plunder has been carried on, it may be stated, that the legislature of Coahuila and Texas, in open violation of the laws of Mexico, were induced " by a company of land speculators, never distinctly known, to grant them, in consideration of twenty thousand dollars, the extent of four hundred square leagues of the public land.* This transaction was disavowed, and the grant annulled, by the Mexican government, and led to the dispersion of. the legislature, and the imprisonment of the governor, Viesca. And yet this unauthorized, and, perhaps, corrupt, grant of public lands formed the basis of new speculation and frauds. A new scrip was formed ; and, according to the best information we have been able to

* Another account says, 411 leagues for 30,000 dollars.

obtain, four hundred leagues became, in the hands of speculators, as many thousands. The extent of these frauds is yet to be ascertained ; for such is the blindness of cupidity, that any thing which looks fair on paper passes without scrutiny for a land-title in Texas." The indignation excited in the Mexican government by this enormous grant, and the attempt to seize the legislators who perpetrated it, were among the immediate excitements to the revolt. In consequence of these lawless proceedings, great numbers in this country and Texas have nominal titles to land, which can only be substantiated by setting aside the authority of the General Congress of Mexico, and are, of consequence, directly and strongly interested in severing this province from the Mexican confederacy. Texan independence can alone legalize the mighty frauds of the land speculator. Texas must be wrested from the country to which she owes allegiance, that her soil may pass into the hands of cheating and cheated foreigners. We have here one explanation of the zeal, with which the Texan cause was embraced in the United States. From this country the great impulse has been given to the Texan revolution ; and a principal motive has been, the unappeasable hunger for Texan land. An interest in that soil, whether real or fictitious, has been spread over our country. Thus "the generous zeal for freedom," which has stirred and armed so many of our citizens to fight for Texas, turns out- to be a passion for unrighteous spoil.

I proceed to another cause of the revolt ; and this was, the resolution to throw Texas open to slave-holders and slaves. Mexico, at the moment of throwing off the Spanish yoke, gave a noble testimony of her loyalty to

17 *

free principles, by decreeing, " that no person there-
after should be born a slave or introduced as such into
the Mexican States; that all slaves then held should
receive stipulated wages, and be subject to no punishment but on trial and judgment by the magistrate." The
subsequent acts of the government carried out fully these
constitutional provisions.   It is matter of deep grief
and humiliation, that the emigrants from this country,
whilst boasting of superior civilization, refused to second this honorable policy, intended to set limits to one
of the greatest social evils.   Slaves were brought into
Texas with their masters from the neighbouring States
of this country.   One mode of evading the laws was,
to introduce slaves under formal indentures for long periods, in some cases it is said for ninety-nine years.   By
a decree of the State Legislature of Coahuila and Texas, all indentures for a longer period than ten years were
annulled, and provision was made for the freedom of
children born during this apprenticeship.   This settled,
invincible purpose of Mexico to exclude slavery from
her limits, created as strong a purpose to annihilate her
authority in Texas.   By this prohibition, Texas was
virtually shut against emigration from the Southern and
Western portions of this country; and it is well known
that the eyes of the South and West had for some time
been turned to this province, as a new market for slaves,
as a new field for slave labor, and as a vast accession
of political power to the Slave-holding States.   That
such views were prevalent, we know; for, nefarious as
they are, they found their way into the public prints.
The project of dismembering a neighbouring republic,
that slave-holders and slaves might overspread a region
which had been consecrated to a free population, was

discussed in newspapers as coolly as if it were a matter of obvious right and unquestionable humanity. A powerful interest was thus created for severing from Mexico her distant province. We have here a powerful incitement to the Texan revolt, and another explanation of the eagerness, with which men and money were thrown from the United States into that region to carry on the war of revolution.

I proceed to another circumstance, which helped to determine or at least to hasten the insurrection ; and that was, the disappointment of the Texans in their efforts to obtain for themselves an organization as a separate State. Texas and Coahuila had hitherto formed a single State. But the colonists, being a minority in the joint legislature, found themselves thwarted in their plans. Impatient of this restraint, and probably suffering at times from a union which gave the superiority to others, they prepared for themselves a constitution, by which they were to be erected into a separate State, neglecting in their haste the forms prescribed by the Mexican law. This instrument they forwarded to the capital for the sanction of the General Congress, by whom it was immediately rejected. Its informality was a sufficient reason for its finding no better reception ; but the omission of all provision to secure the country against slavery, was a more serious obstacle to its ratification. The irritation of the Texans was great. Once invested with the powers of a State, they would not have found it difficult, in their remoteness from the capital and in the unsettled state of the nation, to manage their affairs in their own way. A virtual independence might have been secured, and the laws of Mexico evaded with impunity. Their exasperation was increased by the imprisonment of the agent who had carried the instrument to Mexico, and who had advised them, in an intercepted letter, to take matters into their own hands, or to organize a State Government without authority from the National Congress.   Thus denied the privilege of a separate State, and threatened with new attempts on the part of the General Government to enforce the laws, they felt that the critical moment had arrived; and, looking abroad for help, resolved to take the chances of a conflict with the crippled power of Mexico.

Such were the chief excitements to the revolt.   Undoubtedly, the Texans were instigated by the idea of wrongs, as well as by mercenary hopes.   But had they yielded true obedience to the country of which they had, with their own free will, become a part; had they submitted to the laws relating to the revenue, to the sale of lands, and to slavery ; the wrongs of which they complained might never have been experienced, or might never have been construed into a plea for insurrection. The great motives to revolt on which I have insisted are so notorious, that it is wonderful that any among us could be cheated into sympathy with the Texan cause, as the cause of freedom.   Slavery and fraud lay at its very foundation.   It is notorious, that land speculators, slave-holders, and selfish adventurers were among the foremost to proclaim and engage in the crusade for " Texan liberties."   From the hands of these we are invited to receive a province, torn from a country to which we have given pledges of amity and peace. — In these remarks, I do not, of course, intend to say that every invader of Texas was carried thither by selfish motives.   Some, I doubt not, were impelled by a generous interest in what bore the name of liberty ; and more by that natural sympathy which incites a man to take part with his countrymen against a stranger, without stopping to ask whether they are right or wrong. But the motives, which rallied the great efficient majority round the standard of Texas, were such as have been exposed, and should awaken any sentiment but respect.

Having considered the motives of the revolution, I proceed to inquire, How was it accomplished? The answer to this question will show more fully the criminality of the enterprise. The Texans, we have seen, were a few thousands, as unfit for sovereignty as one of our towns; and, if left to themselves, must have utterly despaired of achieving independence. They looked abroad; and to whom did they look? To any foreign state? To the government under which they had formerly lived? No; their whole reliance was placed on selfish individuals in a neighbouring republic at peace with Mexico. They looked wholly to private individuals, to citizens of this country, to such among us, as, defying the laws of the land, and hungry for sudden gain, should be lured by the scent of this mighty prey, and should be ready to stain their hands with blood for spoil. They held out a country as a prize to the reckless, lawless, daring, avaricious, and trusted to the excitements of intoxicated imagination and insatiable cupidity, to supply them with partners in their scheme of violence.

By whom has Texas been conquered? By the colonists? By the hands which raised the standard of revolt? By foreign governments espousing their cause? No; it has been conquered by your and my countrymen, by citizens of the United States, in violation of our laws and of the laws of nations. We, we have filled the ranks which have wrested Texas from Mexico. In the army of eight hundred men who won the victory which scattered the Mexican force, and made its chief a prisoner, "not more than fifty were citizens of Texas having grievances of their own to seek relief from on that field." The Texans in this warfare are little more than a name, a cover, under which selfish adventurers from another country have prosecuted their work of plunder.

Some crimes, by their magnitude, have a touch of the sublime; and to this dignity the seizure of Texas by our citizens is entitled. Modern times furnish no example of individual rapine on so grand a scale. It is nothing less than the robbery of a realm. The pirate seizes a ship. The colonists and their coadjutors can satisfy themselves with nothing short of an empire. They have left their Anglo-Saxon ancestors behind them. Those barbarians conformed to the maxims of their age, to the rude code of nations in time of thickest heathen darkness. They invaded England under their sovereigns, and with the sanction of the gloomy religion, of the North. But it is in a civilized age, and amidst refinements of manners; it is amidst the lights of science and the teachings of Christianity, amidst expositions of the law of nations and enforcements of the law of universal love, amidst institutions of religion, learning, and humanity, that the robbery of Texas has found its instruments. It is from a free, well-ordered, enlightened Christian country, that hordes have gone forth, in open day, to perpetrate this mighty wrong.

Let me now ask, are the United States prepared to receive from these hands the gift of Texas? In annexing it to this country, shall we not appropriate to ourselves the fruits of a rapine which we ought to have suppressed ? We certainly should shrink from a propositiou to receive a piratical state into our confederacy. And of whom does Texas consist ? Very much of our own citizens, who have won a country by waging war against a foreign nation, to which we owed protection against such assaults. Does it consist with national honor, with national virtue, to receive to our embrace men who have prospered by crimes which we were bound to reprobate and repress ?

Had this country resisted with its whole power the lawlessness of its citizens; had these, notwithstanding such opposition, succeeded in extorting from Mexico a recognition of independence; and were their sovereignty acknowledged by other nations; we should stand acquitted, in the sight of the civilized world, of participating in their crime, were considerations of policy to determine us to admit them into our Union. Unhappily, the United States have not discharged the obligations of a neutral state. They have suffered, by a culpable negligence, the violation of the Mexican territory by their citizens; and if now, in the midst of the conflict, whilst Mexico yet threatens to enforce her claims, they should proceed to incorporate Texas with themselves, they would involve themselves, before all nations, in the whole infamy of the revolt. The United States have not been just to Mexico. Our citizens did not steal singly, silently, in disguise, into that land. Their purpose of dismembering Mexico, and attaching her distant province to this country, was not wrapped in mystery. It was proclaimed in our public prints. Expeditions were openly fitted out within our borders for the Texan

war. Troops were organized, equipped, and marched
for the scene of action. Advertisements for volunteers,
to be enrolled and conducted to Texas at the expense
of that territory, were inserted in our newspapers. The
government, indeed, issued its proclamation, forbidding
these hostile preparations; but this was a dead letter.
Military companies, with officers and standards, in defiance of proclamations, and in the face of day, directed
their steps to the revolted province. We had, indeed,
an army near the frontiers of Mexico. Did it turn
back these invaders of a land with which we were at
peace? On the contrary, did not its presence give
confidence to the revolters? After this, what construction of our conduct shall we force on the world, if we
proceed, especially at this moment, to receive into our
Union the territory, which, through our neglect, has
fallen a prey to lawless invasion? Are we willing to
take our place among robber-states? As a people,
have we no self-respect? Have we no reverence for
national morality? Have we no feeling of responsibility to other nations, and to Him by whom the fates
of nations are disposed?

II. Having unfolded the argument against the annexation of Texas from the criminality of the revolt, I
proceed to a second very solemn consideration, namely,
that by this act our country will enter on a career of
encroachment, war, and crime, and will merit and incur
the punishment and woe of aggravated wrong-doing.
The seizure of Texas will not stand alone. It will
darken our future history. It will be linked by an iron
necessity to long-continued deeds of rapine and blood.
Ages may not see the catastrophe of the tragedy, the

first scene of which we are so ready to enact. It is strange that nations should be so much more rash than individuals ; and this, in the face of experience, which has been teaching, from the beginning of society, that, of all precipitate and criminal deeds, those perpetrated by nations are the most fruitful of misery.

Did this country know itself, or were it disposed to profit by self-knowledge, it would feel the necessity of laying an immediate curb on its passion for extended territory. It would not trust itself to new acquisitions. It would shrink from the temptation to conquest. We are a restless people, prone to encroachment, impatient of the ordinary laws of progress, less anxious to consolidate and perfect than to extend our institutions, more ambitious of spreading ourselves over a wide space than of diffusing beauty and fruitfulness over a narrower field. We boast of our rapid growth, forgetting that, throughout nature, noble growths are slow. Our people throw themselves beyond the bounds of civilization, and expose themselves to relapses into a semi-barbarous state, under the impulse of wild imagination, and for the name of great possessions. Perhaps there is no people on earth, on whom the ties of local attachment sit so loosely. Even the wandering tribes of Scythia are bound to one spot, the graves of their fathers ; but the homes and graves of our fathers detain us feebly. The known and familiar is often abandoned for the distant and untrodden ; and sometimes the untrodden is not the less eagerly desired because belonging to others. We owe this spirit, in a measure, to our descent from men who left the old world for the new, the seats of ancient cultivation for a wilderness, and who advanced by driving before them the old occupants of the soil. To this spirit we have sacrificed justice and humanity ; and, through its ascendency, the records of this young nation are stained with atrocities, at which communities grown gray in corruption might blush.

It is full time, that we should lay on ourselves serious, resolute restraint. Possessed of a domain, vast enough for the growth of ages, it is time for us to stop in the career of acquisition and conquest. Already endangered by our greatness, we cannot advance without imminent peril to our institutions, union, prosperity, virtue, and peace. Our former additions of territory have been justified by the necessity of obtaining outlets for the population of the South and the West. No such pretext exists for the occupation of Texas. We cannot seize upon or join to ourselves that territory, without manifesting and strengthening the purpose of setting no limits to our empire. We give ourselves an impulse, which will and must precipitate us into new invasions of our neighbours' soil. Is it by pressing forward in this course that we are to learn self-restraint ? Is cupidity to be appeased by gratification ? Is it by unrighteous grasping, that an impatient people will be instructed how to hem themselves within the rigid bounds of justice ?

Texas is a country conquered by our citizens ; and the annexation of it to our Union will be the beginning of conquests, which, unless arrested and beaten back by a just and kind Providence, will stop only at the Isthmus of Darien. Henceforth, we must cease to cry, Peace, peace. Our Eagle will whet, not gorge its appetite on its first victim ; and will snuff a more tempting quarry, more alluring blood, in every new region which opens southward. To annex Texas is to declare perpetual war with Mexico. That word, *Mexico*, associated in men's minds with boundless wealth, has already awakened rapacity. Already it has been proclaimed, that the Anglo-Saxon race is destined to the sway of this magnificent realm, that the rude form of society, which Spain established there, is to yield and vanish before a higher civilization. Without this exposure of plans of rapine and subjugation, the result, as far as our will can determine it, is plain. Texas is the first step to Mexico. The moment we plant our authority on Texas, the boundaries of those two countries will become nominal, will be little more than lines on the sand of the sea-shore. In the fact, that portions of the Southern and Western States are already threatened with devastation, through the impatience of multitudes to precipitate themselves into the Texan land of promise, we have a pledge and earnest of the flood which will pour itself still farther south, when Texas shall be but partially overrun.

Can Mexico look without alarm on the approaches of this ever-growing tide? Is she prepared to be a passive prey? to shrink and surrender without a struggle? Is she not strong in her hatred, if not in her fortresses or skill? Strong enough to make war a dear and bloody game? Can she not bring to bear on us a force, more formidable than fleets, the force of priva teers, that is, of legalized pirates, which, issuing from her ports, will scour the seas, prey on our commerce, and add to spoliation, cruelty and murder?

Even were the dispositions of our government most pacific and opposed to encroachment, the annexation of Texas would almost certainly embroil us with Mexico. This territory would be overrun by adventurers; and the most unprincipled of these, the proscribed, the disgraced, the outcasts of society, would, of course, keep always in advance of the better population. These would represent our republic on the borders of the Mexican States. The history of the connexion of such men with the Indians, forewarns us of the outrages which would attend their contact with the border inhabitants of our southern neighbour. Texas, from its remoteness from the seat of government, would be feebly restrained by the authorities of the nation to which it would belong. Its whole early history would be a lesson of scorn for Mexico, an education for invasion of her soil. Its legislature would find in its position some color for stretching to the utmost the doctrine of state-sovereignty. It would not hear unmoved the cries for protection and vengeance, which would break from the frontier, from the very men whose lawlessness would provoke the cruelties so indignantly denounced; nor would it sift very anxiously the question, on which side the wrong began. To the wisdom, moderation, and tender mercies of the back-settlers and law-givers of Texas, the peace of this country would be committed.

Have we counted the cost of establishing and making perpetual these hostile relations with Mexico? Will wars, begun in rapacity, carried on so far from the centre of the confederation, and, of consequence, little checked or controlled by Congress, add strength to our institutions, or cement our union, or exert a healthy moral influence on rulers or people? What limits can be set to the atrocities of such conflicts? What limits to the treasures, which must be lavished on such distant borders? What limits to the patronage and power, which such distant expeditions must accumulate in the hands of the Executive? Are the blood and hard-earned wealth of the older States to be poured out like water, to protect and revenge a new people, whose character and condition will plunge them into perpetual wrongs?

Is the time never to come, when the neighbourhood of a more powerful and civilized people will prove a blessing, instead of a curse, to an inferior community? It was my hope, when the Spanish colonies of this continent separated themselves from the mother country, and, in admiration of the United States, adopted republican institutions, that they were to find in us friends to their freedom, helpers to their civilization. If ever a people were placed by Providence in a condition to do good to a neighbouring state, we of this country sustained such a relation to Mexico. That nation, inferior in science, arts, agriculture, and legislation, looked to us with a generous trust. She opened her ports and territories to our farmers, mechanics, and merchants. We might have conquered her by the only honorable arms, by the force of superior intelligence, industry, and morality. We might silently have poured in upon her our improvements; and by the infusion of our population have assimilated her to ourselves. Justice, good-will, and profitable intercourse, might have cemented a lasting friendship. And what is now the case? A deadly hatred burns in Mexico towards this country. No stronger national sentiment now binds her scattered provinces together than dread and detestation of Republican America. She is ready to attach herself to Europe for defence from the United States. All the moral power, which we might have gained over Mexico,

18 *

we have thrown away ; and suspicion, dread, and abhorrence, have supplanted respect and trust.

I am aware that these remarks are met by a vicious reasoning, which discredits a people among whom it finds favor. It is sometimes said, that nations are swayed by laws, as unfailing as those which govern matter ; that they have their destinies ; that their character and position carry them forward irresistibly to their goal ; that the stationary Turk must sink under the progressive civilization of Russia, as inevitably as the crumbling edifice falls to the earth ; that, by a like necessity, the Indians have melted before the white man, and the mixed, degraded race of Mexico must melt before the Anglo-Saxon. Away with this vile sophistry ! There is no necessity for crime. There is no Fate to justify rapacious nations, any more than to justify gamblers and robbers, in plunder. We boast of the progress of society, and this progress consists in the substitution of reason and moral principle for the sway of brute force. It is true, that more civilized must always exert a great power over less civilized communities in their neighbourhood. But it may and should be a power to enlighten and improve, not to crush and destroy. We talk of accomplishing our destiny. So did the late conqueror of Europe ; and destiny consigned him to a lonely rock in the ocean, the prey of an ambition which destroyed no peace but his own.

Hitherto I have spoken of the annexation of Texas as embroiling us with Mexico ; but it will not stop here. It will bring us into collision with other states. It will, almost of necessity, involve us in hostility with European powers. Such are now the connexions of nations, that Europe must look with jealousy on a country, whose ambition, seconded by vast resources, will seem to place within her grasp the empire of the new world. And not only general considerations of this nature, but the particular relation of certain foreign states to this continent, must tend to destroy the peace now happily subsisting between us and the kingdoms of Europe. England, in particular, must watch us with suspicion, and cannot but resist our appropriation of Texas to ourselves. She has at once a moral and political interest in this question, which demands and will justify interference.

First, England has a moral interest in this question. The annexation of Texas is sought by us for the very porpose of extending slavery, and thus will necessarily give new life and extension to the slave-trade. A new and vast market for slaves cannot, of course, be opened, without inviting and obtaining a supply from abroad, as well as from this country. The most solemn treaties, and ships of war lining the African coast, do not and cannot suppress this infernal traffic, as long as the slaver, freighted with stolen, chained, and wretched captives, can obtain a price proportioned to the peril of the undertaking. Now, England has long made it a part of her foreign policy to suppress the slave-trade; and, of late, a strong public feeling impels the government to resist, as far as may be, the extension of slavery. Can we expect her to be a passive spectator of a measure, by which her struggles for years in the cause of humanity, and some of her strongest national feelings, are to be withstood?

England is a privileged nation. On one part of her history she can look with unmixed self-respect. With the exception of the promulgation of Christianity, I know not a moral effort so glorious, as the long, painful, victorious struggle of her philanthropists against that concentration of all horrors, cruelties and crimes, the slave-trade. Next to this, her recent Emancipation Act is the most signal expression, afforded by our times, of the progress of civilization and a purer Christianity. Other nations have won imperishable honors by heroic struggles for their own rights. But there was wanting the example of a nation espousing, with disinterestedness, and amidst great obstacles, the rights of others, the rights of those who had no claim but that of a common humanity, the rights of the most fallen of the race. Great Britain, loaded with an unprecedented debt and with a grinding taxation, contracted a new debt of a hundred million dollars, to give freedom, not to Englishmen, but to the degraded African. This was not an act of policy, not a work of statesmen. Parliament but registered the edict of the people. The English nation, with one heart and one voice, under a strong Christian impulse, and without distinction of rank, sex, party or religious names, decreed freedom to the slave. I know not that history records a national act so disinterested, so sublime. In the progress of ages, England's naval triumphs will shrink into a more and more narrow space in the records of our race. This moral triumph will fill a broader, brighter page. Is not England, representing, as she does in this case, the civilized world, authorized, and even bound, to remonstrate, in the name of humanity and religion, against a measure, by which the great work, for which she has so long toiled, is to be indefinitely postponed ?

But England has a political as well as a moral interest in this question. By the annexation of Texas we shall approach her liberated colonies; we shall build up a power in her neighbourhood, to which no limits can be prescribed. By adding Texas to our acquisition of Florida, we shall do much toward girdling the Gulf of Mexico; and I doubt not, that some of our politicians will feel, as if our mastery in that sea were sure. The West Indian Archipelago, in which the European is regarded as an intruder, will, of course, be embraced in our ever-growing scheme of empire. In truth, collision with the West Indies will be the most certain effect of the extension of our power in that quarter. The example, which they exhibit, of African freedom, of the elevation of the colored race to the rights of men, is, of all influences, most menacing to slavery at the South. It must grow continually more perilous. These islands, unless interfered with from abroad, seem destined to be nurseries of civilization and freedom to the African race. The white race must melt more and more before the colored, if both are left to free competition. The Europeans, unnerved by the climate, and forming but a handful of the population, cannot stand before the African, who revels in the heat of the tropics, and is to develope under it all his energies. Will a slave-holding people, spreading along the shores of the Mexican Gulf, cultivate friendly sentiments towards communities, whose whole history will be a bitter reproach to their institutions, a witness against their wrongs, and whose ardent sympathies will be enlisted in the cause of the slave? Cruel, ferocious conflicts must grow from this neighbourhood of hostile principles, of communities regarding one another with unextinguishable hatred. All the islands of the Archipelago will have cause to dread our power, but none so much as the emancipated. Is it not more than possible, that wars, having for an object the subjugation of the colored race, the destruction of this tempting example of freedom, should spring from the proposed extension of our dominion along the Mexican Gulf? Can England view our encroachments without alarm? I know it is thought, that, staggering, as she does, under her enormous debt, she will be slow to engage in war. But other nations of Europe have islands in the same neighbourhood, to induce them to make common cause with her.   Other nations look with jealousy on our peculiar institutions and our growing maritime power. Other nations are unwilling that we should engross or control the whole commerce of the Mexican Gulf.   We ought to remember, that this jealousy is sanctioned by our example.   It is understood, that, at one period of the internal disorders of Spain, which rendered all her foreign possessions insecure, we sought from France and Great Britain assurances that they would not possess themselves of Cuba.   Still more, after the revolt of her colonies from Spain, and after our recognition of their independence, it was announced to the nations of Europe, in the message of the President, that we should regard as hostile, any interference, on their part, with these new-governments, " for the purpose of oppressing them, or controlling their destiny in any other way." I, of course, have no communication with foreign cabinets ; but I cannot doubt that Great Britain has remonstrated against the annexation of Texas to this country. An English minister would be unworthy of his office, who should see another state greedily swallowing up territories in the neighbourhood of British colonies, and not strive, by all just means, to avert the danger.   I have just referred to the warning given by us to the powers of Europe, to abstain from appropriating to themselves the colonies torn from Spain. How will Europe interpret our act, if we now seize Texas, and take this stride towards Mexico ? Will she not suspect, that we purposed to drive away the older vultures, in order to keep the victim to ourselves ; that, conscious of growing power, we foresaw, in the exclusion of foreign states, the sure extension of our own dominion over the new world ? Can we expect those powers, with such an example before them, to heed our warning ? Will they look patiently on, and see the young vulture feasting on the nearest prey, and fleshing itself for the spoils which their own possessions will next present ? Will it be strange, if hunger for a share of the plunder, as well as the principle of self-defence, should make this continent the object of their policy to an extent we have never dreamed ?

It is of great and manifest importance, that we should use every just means to separate this continent from the politics of Europe, that we should prevent, as far as possible, all connexion, except commercial, between the old and the new world, that we should give to foreign states no occasion or pretext for insinuating themselves into our affairs. For this end, we should maintain towards our sister republics a more liberal policy than was ever adopted by nation towards nation. We should strive to appease their internal divisions, and to reconcile them to each other. We should even make sacrifices to build up their strength. Weak and divided, they cannot but lean upon foreign support. No pains should be spared to prevent or allay the jealousies, which the great superiority of this country is suited to awaken. By an opposite policy we shall favor foreign interference. By encroaching on Mexico, we shall throw her into the arms of European states, shall compel her to seek defence in transatlantic alliance. How plain is it, that alliance with Mexico will be hostility to the United States, that her defenders will repay themselves by making her subservient to their views, that they will thus strike root in her soil, monopolize her trade, and control her resources. And with what face can we resist the aggressions of others on our neighbour, if we give an example of aggression? Still more, if by our advances we put the colonies of England in new peril, with what face can we oppose her occupation of Cuba? Suppose her, with that magnificent island in her hands, to command the Mexican Gulf and the mouths of the Mississippi; will the Western States find compensation for this formidable neighbourhood, in the privilege of flooding Texas with slaves?

Thus, wars with Europe and Mexico are to be entailed on us by the annexation of Texas. And is war the policy by which this country is to flourish? Was it for interminable conflicts that we formed our Union? Is it blood, shed for plunder, which is to consolidate our institutions? Is it by collision with the greatest maritime power, that our commerce is to gain strength? Is it by arming against ourselves the moral sentiments of the world, that we are to build up national honor? Must we of the North buckle on our armour, to fight the battles of slavery; to fight for a possession, which our moral principles and just jealousy forbid us to incorporate with our confederacy? In attaching Texas to ourselves, we provoke hostilities, and at the same time expose new points of attack to our foes. Vulnerable at so many points, we shall need a vast military force

Great armies will require great revenues, and raise up great chieftains. Are we tired of freedom, that we are prepared to place it under such guardians ? Is the republic bent on dying by its own hands ? Does not every man feel, that, with war for our habit, our institutions cannot be preserved? If ever a country were bound to peace, it is this. Peace is our great interest. In peace our resources are to be developed, the true interpretation of the constitution to be established, and the interfering claims of liberty and order to be adjusted. In peace we are to discharge our great debt to the human race, and to diffuse freedom by manifesting its fruits. A country has no right to adopt a policy, however gainful, which, as it may foresee, will determine it to a career of war. A nation, like an individual, is bound to seek, even by sacrifices, a position, which will favor peace, justice, and the exercise of a beneficent influence on the world. A nation, provoking war by cupidity, by encroachment, and, above all, by efforts to propagate the curse of slavery, is alike false to itself, to God, and to the human race.

III. I proceed now to a consideration of what is to me the strongest argument against annexing Texas to the United States. This measure will extend and perpetuate slavery. I have necessarily glanced at this topic in the preceding pages ; but it deserves to be brought out distinctly. I shall speak calmly, but I must speak earnestly ; and I feel, and rejoice to feel, that, however you may differ from some of my views, yet we do not differ as to the great principle on which all my remarks and remonstrances are founded. Slavery seems to you, as to me, an evil and a wrong. Your language on this subject has given me a satisfaction, for which I owe you thanks ; and if, in what I am now to say, I may use expressions which you may think too strong, I am sure your candor will recognise in them the signs of deep conviction, and will acquit me of all desire to irritate or give pain.

The annexation of Texas, I have said, will extend and perpetuate slavery. It is fitted, and, still more, intended to do so. On this point there can be no doubt. As far back as the year 1829, the annexation of Texas was agitated in the Southern and Western States ; and it was urged on the ground of the strength and extension it would give the slave-holding interest. In a series of essays, ascribed to a gentleman now a senator in Congress, it was maintained, that five or six slave-holding States would by this measure be added to the Union ; and he even intimated that as many as nine States as large as Kentucky might be formed within the limits of Texas. In Virginia, about the same time, calculations were made as to the increased value which would thus be given to slaves, and it was even said, that this acquisition would raise the price fifty per cent. Of late the language on this subject is most explicit. The great argument for annexing Texas is, that it will strengthen "the pecular institutions" of the South, and open a new and vast field for slavery.

By this act, slavery will be spread over regions to which it is now impossible to set limits. Texas, I repeat it, is but the first step of aggressions. I trust, indeed, that Providence will beat back and humble our cupidity and ambition. But one guilty success is often suffered to be crowned, as men call it, with greater ; in order that a more awful retribution may at length

vindicate the justice of God, and the rights of the oppressed. Texas, smitten with slavery, will spread the
infection beyond herself. We know that the tropical
regions have been found most propitious to this pestilence ; nor can we promise ourselves, that its expulsion
from them for a season forbids its return. By annexing Texas, we may send this scourge to a distance,
which, if now revealed, would appall us, and through
these vast regions every cry of the injured will invoke
wrath on our heads.

By this act, slavery will be perpetuated in the old
States, as well as spread over new. It is well known,
that the soil of some of the old States has become exhausted by slave cultivation. Their neighbourhood to
communities, which are flourishing under free labor,
forces on them perpetual arguments for adopting this
better system. They now adhere to slavery, not on
account of the wealth which it extracts from the soil,
but because it furnishes men and women to be sold in
newly settled and more southern districts. It is by
slave-breeding and slave-selling that these States subsist.
Take away from them a foreign market, and slavery
would die. Of consequence, by opening a new market,
it is prolonged and invigorated. By annexing Texas,
we shall not only create it where it does not exist, but
breathe new life into it, where its end seemed to be
near. States, which might and ought to throw it off,
will make the multiplication of slaves their great aim and
chief resource.

Nor is the worst told. As I have before intimated,
and it cannot be too often repeated, we shall not only
quicken the domestic slave-trade ; we shall give a new
impulse to the foreign. This, indeed, we have pro-

nounced in our laws to be felony ; but we make our laws cobwebs, when we offer to rapacious men strong motives for their violation.   Open a market for slaves in an unsettled country, with a sweep of sea-coast, and at such a distance from the seat of government that laws may be evaded with impunity, and how can you exclude slaves from Africa ?   It is well known that cargoes have been landed in Louisiana.   What is to drive them from Texas ?   In incorporating this region with the Union to make it a slave-country, we send the kidnapper to prowl through the jungles, and to dart, like a beast of prey, on the defenceless villages of Africa ; we chain the helpless, despairing victims ; crowd them into the fetid, pestilential slave-ship ; expose them to the unutterable cruelties of the middle passage, and, if they survive it, crush them with perpetual bondage.

I now ask, whether, as a people, we are prepared to seize on a neighbouring territory for the end of extending slavery ?   I ask, whether, as a people, we can stand forth in the sight of God, in the sight of the nations, and adopt this atrocious policy ?   Sooner perish ! Sooner be our name blotted out from the record of nations !

This is no place for entering into the argument against slavery.   I have elsewhere given my views of it.   In truth, no argument is needed.   The evil of slavery speaks for itself.   It is one of those primary, intuitive truths, which need only a fair exhibition to be immediately received.   To state is to condemn this institution. The choice which every freeman makes of death for his child and for every thing he loves, in preference to slavery, shows what it is.   The single consideration, that, by slavery, one human being is placed powerless and defenceless in the hands of another, to be driven to whatever labor that other may impose, to suffer whatever punishment he may inflict, to live as his tool, the instrument of his pleasure, this is all that is needed, to satisfy such as know the human heart and its unfitness for irresponsible power, that, of all conditions, slavery is the most hostile to the dignity, self-respect, improvement, rights, and happiness of human beings. Is it within the bounds of credibility, that a people, boasting of freedom, of civilization, of Christianity, should systematically strive to spread this calamity over the earth?

To perpetuate and extend slavery is not now, in a moral point of view, what it once was. We cannot shelter ourselves under the errors and usages of our times. We do not belong to the dark ages, or to heathenism. We have not grown up under the prejudices of a blinding, crushing tyranny. We live under free institutions and under the broad light of Christianity. Every principle of our government and religion condemns slavery. The spirit of our age condemns it. The decree of the civilized world has gone out against it. England has abolished it. France and Denmark meditate its abolition. The chain is falling from the serf in Russia. In the whole circuit of civilized nations, with the single exception of the United States, not a voice is lifted up in defence of slavery. All the great names in legislation and religion are against it. The most enduring reputations of our times have been won by resisting it. Recall the great men of this and the last generation, and, be they philosophers, philanthropists, poets, economists, statesmen, jurists, all swell the reprobation of slavery. The leaders of opposing religious sects, Wesley, the patriarch of Methodism,

19*

Edwards and Hopkins, pillars of Calvinism, join as brothers in one solemn testimony against slavery. And is this an age in which a free and Christian people shall deliberately resolve to extend and perpetuate the evil? In so doing, we cut ourselves off from the communion of the nations; we sink below the civilization of our age; we invite the scorn, indignation, and abhorrence of the world.

Let it not be said, that this opposition of our times to slavery is an accident, a temporary gust of opinion, an eddy in the current of human thought, a fashion to pass away with the present actors on the stage. He who so says must have read history with a superficial eye, and is strangely blind to the deepest and most powerful influences which are moulding society. Christianity has done more than all things to determine the character and direction of our present civilization; and who can question or overlook the tendency and design of this religion? Christianity has no plainer purpose than to unite all men as brethren, to make man unutterably dear to man, to pour contempt on outward distinctions, to raise the fallen, to league all in efforts for the elevation of all. Under its influence, the differences of nations and rank are softening. To the establishment of a fraternal relation among men, the science, literature, commerce, education of the Christian world are tending. Who cannot see this mighty movement of Providence? Who is so blind as to call it a temporary impulse? Who so daring, so impious, as to strive to arrest it?

What is the tendency of all governments in the Christian world? To secure more and more to every man his rights, be his condition what it may. Even in despotisms, where political rights are denied, private rights are held more and more sacred. The absolute monarch is more and more anxious to improve the laws of the state, and to extend their protection and restraints over all classes and individuals without distinction. Equality before the law is the maxim of the civilized world. To place the rights of a large part of the community beyond the protection of law, to place half a people under private, irresponsible power, is to oppose one of the most characteristic and glorious tendencies of modern times. Who has the courage to set down this reverence for private rights among the fashions and caprices of the day? Is it not founded in everlasting truth? And dare we, in the face of it, extend and perpetuate an institution, the grand feature of which is, that it tramples private rights in the dust?

Whoever studies modern history with any care must discern in it a steady, growing movement towards one most interesting result, — I mean, towards the elevation of the laboring class of society. This is not a recent, accidental turn of human affairs. We can trace its beginning in the feudal times, and its slow advances in subsequent periods, until it has become the master movement of our age. Is it not plain, that those who toil with their hands, and whose productive industry is the spring of all wealth, are rising from the condition of beasts of burden, to which they were once reduced, to the consciousness, intelligence, self-respect, and proper happiness of men? Is it not the strong tendency of our times to diffuse among the many the improvements once confined to the few? He who overlooks this has no comprehension of the great work of Providence, or of the most signal feature of his times ; and is this an age for efforts to extend and perpetuate an institution, the very object of which is to keep down the laborer, and to make him a machine for another's gratification ?

I know it has been said, in reply to such views, that, do what we will with the laborer, call him what we will, he is and must be in reality a slave. The doctrine has been published at the South, that nature has made two · classes, the rich and the poor, the employer and the employed, the capitalist and the operative, and that the class who work are, to all intents, slaves to those in whose service they are engaged. In a report on the mail, recently offered to the Senate of the United States, an effort was made to establish resemblances between slavery and the condition of free laborers, for the obvious purpose of showing, that the shades of difference between them are not very strong. Is it possible that such reasonings escaped from a man who has trod the soil of New England, and was educated at one of her colleges ? Whom did he meet at that college ? The sons of her laborers, young men whose hands had been hardened at the plough. Does he not know, that the families of laborers have furnished every department in life among us with illustrious men, have furnished our heroes in war, our statesmen in council, our orators in the pulpit and at the bar, our merchants whose enterprises embrace the whole earth ? What ! the laborer of the Free State a slave, and to be ranked with the despised negro, whom the lash drives to toil, and whose dearest rights are at the mercy of irresponsible power ? If there be a firm, independent spirit on earth, it is to be found in the man, who ·tills the fields ˙of the Free ·States, and moistens them with the sweat of his brow. I recently heard of a visiter from the South compassionating the operatives of our manufactories, as in a worse condition than the slave. What carries the young woman to the manufactory ? Not, generally, the want of a comfortable home ; but sometimes the desire of supplying herself with a wardrobe which ought to satisfy the affluent, and oftener the desire of furnishing in more than decent style the home, where she is to sustain the nearest relations, and perform the most sacred duties of life. Generally speaking, each of these young women has her plan of life, her hopes, her bright dreams, her spring of action in her own free will, and amidst toil she contrives to find seasons for intellectual and religious culture. It is common in New England for the sons of farmers to repair to the large towns, and there to establish themselves as domestics in families, a condition which the South will be peculiarly disposed to identify with slavery. But what brings these young men to the city ? The hope of earning in a shorter time a sum, with which to purchase a farm at home or in the West, perhaps to become traders ; and in these vocations they not unfrequently rise to consideration, and to what, in their places of residence, is called wealth. I have in my thoughts an individual distinguished alike by vigor and elevation of mind, who began life by hiring himself as a laborer to a farmer, and then entered a family as a domestic ; and now he is the honored associate of the most enlightened men, and devotes himself to the highest subjects of human thought. It is true, that much remains to be done for the laboring class in the most favored regions ; but the intelligence already spread through this class is an earnest of a brighter day, of the most glorious revolution in history, of the elevation of the mass of men to the dignity of human beings.

It is the great mission of this country to forward this
revolution, and never was a sublimer work committed
to a nation.   Our mission is, to elevate society through
all its conditions, to secure to every human being the
means of progress, to substitute the government of equal
laws for that of irresponsible individuals, to prove that,
under popular institutions, the people may be carried
forward, that the multitude who toil are capable of en-
joying the noblest blessings of the social state.   The
prejudice, that labor is a degradation, one of the worst
prejudices handed down from barbarous ages, is to receive here a practical refutation.   The power of liberty
to raise up the whole people, this is the great Idea, on
which our institutions rest, and which is to be wrought
out in our history.   Shall a nation having such a mission
abjure it, and even fight against the progress which it is
specially called to promote ?

The annexation of Texas, if it should be aecom-
plished, would do much to determine the future history
and character of this country.   It is one of those measures, which call a nation to pause, reflect, look forward,
because their force is not soon exhausted.   Many acts
of government, intensely exciting at the moment, are
yet of little importance, because their influence is too
transient to leave a trace on history.   A bad administration may impoverish a people at home, or cripple its
energies abroad, for a year or more.   But such wounds
heal soon.   A young people soon recruits its powers,
and starts forward with increased impulse, after the momentary suspension of its activity.   The chief interest
of a people lies in measures, which, making, perhaps,
little noise, go far to fix its character, to determine its
policy and fate for ages, to decide its rank among na-

tions. A fearful responsibility rests on those who originate or control these pregnant acts. The destiny of millions is in their hands. The execration of millions may fall on their heads. Long after present excitements shall have passed away, long after they and their generation shall have vanished from the earth, the fruits of their agency will be reaped. Such a measure is that of which I now write. It will commit us to a degrading policy, the issues of which lie beyond human foresight. In opening to ourselves vast regions, through which we may spread slavery, and in spreading it for this, among other ends, that the Slave-holding States may bear rule in the national councils, we make slavery the predominant interest of the state. We make it the basis of power, the spring or guide of public measures, the object for which the revenues, strength, and wealth of the country are to be exhausted. Slavery will be branded on our front, as the great Idea, the prominent feature of the country. We shall renounce our high calling as a people, and accomplish the lowest destiny to which a nation can be bound.

And are we prepared for this degradation ? Are we prepared to couple with the name of our country the infamy of deliberately spreading slavery ? and especially, of spreading it through regions from which the wise and humane legislation of a neighbouring republic had excluded it ? We call Mexico a semi-barbarous people ; and yet we talk of planting slavery where Mexico would not suffer it to live. What American will not blush to lift his head in Europe, if this disgrace shall be fastened on his country ? Let other calamities, if God so will, come on us. Let us be steeped in poverty. Let pestilence stalk through our land. Let famine thin our population.   Let the world join hands against our free institutions, and deluge our shores with blood.   All this can be endured.   A few years of industry and peace will recruit our wasted numbers, and spread fruitfulness over our desolated fields.   But a nation, devoting itself to the work of spreading and perpetuating slavery, stamps itself with a guilt and shame, which generations may not be able to efface.   The plea on which we have rested, that slavery was not our choice, but a sad necessity bequeathed us by our fathers, will avail us no longer.   The whole guilt will be assumed by ourselves.

It is very lamentable, that, among the distinguished men of the South, any should be found so wanting to their own fame, as to become advocates of slavery. That vulgar politicians, who look only at the interests of the day and the chances of the next election, should swell the madness of the passions, by which they hope to rise, is a thing of course.   But that men, who might leave honorable and enduring record of themselves in their country's history, who might associate their names with their country's progress, and who are solemnly bound by their high gifts to direct and purify public sentiment, that such men should lend their great powers to the extension of slavery, is among the dark symptoms of the times.   Can such men be satisfied with the sympathies and shouts of the little circle around them, and of the passing moment ?   Have they nothing of that prophetic instinct, by which truly great men read the future ?   Can they learn nothing from the sentence now passed on men, who, fifty years ago, defended the slave-trade ?   We have to rejoice, Sir, that you, amidst the excitements of the time, have always given your testimony against slavery.   You have adhered to the doctrine, which the great men of the South of the last generation asserted, that it is a great evil. We shall not forget this among the good services, which you have rendered to your country.

I have expressed my fears, that by the annexation of Texas, slavery is to be continued and extended. But I wish not to be understood, as having the slightest doubt as to the approaching fall of the institution. It may be prolonged, to our reproach and greater ultimate suffering. But fall it will and must. This, Sir, you know, and I doubt not, rejoice to know. The advocates of slavery must not imagine, that to carry a vote is to sustain their cause. With all their power, they cannot withstand the providence of God, the principles of human nature, the destinies of the race. To succeed, they must roll back time to the dark ages, must send back Luther to the cell of his monastery, must extinguish the growing light of Christianity and moral science, must blot out the declaration of American Independence. The fall of slavery is as sure as the descent of your own Ohio. Moral laws are as irresistible as physical. In the most enlightened countries of Europe, a man would forfeit his place in society, by vindicating slavery. The slave-holder must not imagine, that he has nothing to do but fight with a few societies. These, of themselves, are nothing. He should not waste on them one fear. They are strong, only as representing the spirit of the Christian and civilized world. His battle is with the laws of human nature and the irresistible tendencies of human affairs. These are not to be withstood by artful strokes of policy, or by daring crimes. The world is against him, and the world's Maker. Every day the sympathies of the world are forsaking him. Can' he hope to sustain slavery against the moral feeling, the solemn sentence of the human race ?

The South, cut off by its " peculiar institutions " from close connexion with other communities, comprehends little the progress of the civilized world. The spirit, which is spreading through other communities, finds no organ within its borders, and the strength of this is therefore little understood. Hence, it looks on anti-slavery movements in any part of the country, as an accident, which a little force can put down. It might as well think of imprisoning the winds. The South is ignorant of what it most needs to know. A very intelligent gentleman from that quarter told me, not long ago, that he could not learn at home the working of Emancipation in the West Indies ; so that an experiment of infinite interest to the slave-holder is going on at his door, and he knows little more of it than if it were occurring in another planet. Of course, there are exceptions. There are at the South philosophical observers of the progress of human affairs. But in such a state of society, it is hard to realize the truth on this subject. Were it known, the project of building a power on the diffusion of slavery would seem to be an act of madness, as truly as of crime.

I suppose that I shall be charged with unfriendly feelings towards the South. All such I disclaim. Strange as it may seem, if I have partialities, they are rather for the South. I spent a part of my early life in that region, when manners probably retained more of their primitive character than they now do ; and to a young man, unaccustomed to life and its perils, there was something singularly captivating in the unbounded hospitality, the impulsive generosity, the carelessness of the future, the frank, open manners, the buoyant spirit and courage, which marked the people ; and though I have since learned to interpret more wisely what I then, saw, still the impressions which I then received, and the friendships .formed at a yet earlier age with the youth of the South, have always given me a leaning towards that part of the country. I am unconscious of local prejudices. My interest in the South strengthens my desire to avert the annexation of Texas to the Union. That act, I feel, will fix an indelible stain on the South. It will conflict with the generous elements of character, which I take pleasure in recollecting there. The South will cease to be what it was. In the period to which I have referred, slavery was acknowledged there to be a great evil. I heard it spoken of freely with abhorrence. The moral sentiment of the community on this point was not corrupt. The principles of Mr. Jefferson in relation to it found a wide response. The doctrine, that slavery is a good, if spread by the seizure of Texas, will work a moral revolution, the most disastrous which can befall the South. It will paralyze every effort for escape from this enormous evil. A deadly sophistry will weigh on men's consciences and hearts, until terrible convulsions, — God's just judgments, — will hasten the deliverance which human justice and benevolence were bound to accomplish.

IV. I now proceed to another important argument against the annexation of Texas to our country, the argument drawn from the bearings of the measure on our National Union. Next to liberty, union is our great political interest, and this cannot but be loosened, it may be dissolved, by the proposed extension of our territory. I will not say that every extension must be pernicious, that our government cannot hold together even our present confederacy, that the central heart cannot send its influences to the remote States which are to spring up within our present borders. Old theories must be cautiously applied to the institutions of this country. If the Federal government will abstain from minute legislation, and rigidly confine itself within constitutional bounds, it may be a bond of union to more extensive communities than were ever comprehended under one sway. Undoubtedly, there is peril in extending ourselves, and yet the chief benefit of the Union, which is the preservation of peaceful relations among neighbouring States, is so vast, that some risk should be taken to secure it in the greatest possible degree. The objection to the annexation of Texas, drawn from the unwieldiness it would give to the country, though very serious, is not decisive. A far more serious objection is, that it is to be annexed to us for the avowed purpose of multiplying slave-holding States, and thus giving political power. This cannot, ought not to be borne. It will justify, it will at length demand, the separation of the States.

We maintain that this policy is altogether without reason on the part of the South. The South has exerted, and cannot help exerting, a disproportionate share of influence on the confederacy. The Slave-holding States have already advantages for coöperation, and for swaying the country, which the others do not possess. The Free States have no great common interest, like slavery, to hold them together. They differ in character, feelings, and pursuits. They agree but on one

point, and that a negative one, the absence of slavery;
and this distinction, as is well-known, makes no lively
impression on the consciousness, and in no degree coun-
teracts the influences which divide them from one another. To this may be added the well-known fact, that
in the Free States, the subject of politics is of secondary importance, whilst at the South it is paramount.
At the North every man must toil for subsistence, and,
amidst the feverish competitions and anxieties of the
eager and universal pursuit of gain, political power is
sought with little comparative avidity. In some districts
it is hard to find fit representatives for Congress, so
backward are superior men to forego the emoluments of
their vocation, the prospects of independence, for the
uncertainties of public life. At the North, too, a vast
amount of energy is absorbed in associations of a religious, philanthropic, literary character. The apathy of
the Free States in regard to Texas, an apathy from
which they are just beginning to be roused, is a striking
proof of their almost incredible' indifference to political
power. Perhaps no parallel to it can be found in the
history of confederations. What a contrast does the
South form with the divided and slumbering North!
There, one strong, broad distinction exists, of which all
the members of the community have a perpetual consciousness; there, a peculiar element is found, which
spreads its influence through the mass, and impresses
itself on the whole constitution of society. Slavery is
not a superficial distinction. Nothing decides the character of a people more than the form and determination
of labor. Hence we find a unity at the South unknown
at the North. At the South, too, the proprietors, released from the necessity of labor, and having little of

20 *

the machinery of associations to engage their attention, devote themselves to politics with a concentration of zeal, which a Northern man can only comprehend by residing on the spot. Hence the South has professional politicians, a character hardly known in the Free States. The result is plain. The South has generally ruled the country. It must always have an undue power. United, as the North cannot be, it can always link with itself some discontented portion at the North, which it can liberally reward by the patronage which the possession of the government confers. That the constitutional rights of the South should be prejudiced by the North is one of those moral impossibilities, against which it is folly to ask security.

We cannot consent, that the South should extend its already disproportionate power by an indefinite extension of territory, because we maintain, that its dispositions towards us gives us no pledge, that its power will be well used. It is unhappily too well known, that it wants friendly feelings towards the North. Divided from us by an institution, which gives it a peculiar character, which lays it open to reproach, and which will never suffer it to rival our prosperity, it cannot look on us with favor. It magnifies our faults. It is blind to our virtues. At the North, no unfriendly disposition prevails towards the South. We are too busy and too prosperous for hatred. We complain, that our good-will is not reciprocated. We complain, that our commerce and manufactures have sometimes found little mercy at the hands of the South. Still more, we feel, though we are slow to complain of it, that in Congress, the common ground of the confederacy, we have had to encounter a tone and bearing, which it has required the colder temperament

of the North to endure. We cannot consent to take a
lower place than we now hold. We cannot consent,
that our confederacy should spread over the wilds of
Mexico, to give us more powerful masters. The old
balance of the country is unfavorable enough. We
cannot consent, that a new weight should be thrown in,
which may fix the political inferiority of ourselves and
our posterity. I give you, Sir, the feelings of the
North. In part they may be prejudices. Jealousies,
often groundless, are the necessary fruits of confederations. On that account, measures must not be adopted,
disturbing violently, unnaturally, unexpectedly, the old
distributions of power, and directly aimed at that result.

In other ways the annexation of Texas is to endanger
the Union. It will give new violence and passion to the
agitation of the question of slavery. It is well known,
that a majority at the North have discouraged the discussion of this topic, on the ground, that slavery was imposed on the South by necessity, that its continuance
was not of choice, and that the States in which it subsists, if left to themselves, would find a remedy in their
own way. Let slavery be systematically proposed as
the policy of these States, let it bind them together in
efforts to establish political power, and a new feeling
will burst forth through the whole North. It will be a
concentration of moral, religious, political, and patriotic
feelings. The fire, now smothered, will blaze out, and,
of consequence, new jealousies and exasperations will
be kindled at the South. Strange, that the South
should think of securing its " peculiar institutions " by
violent means. Its violence necessarily increases the
evils it would suppress. For example, by denying the
right of petition to those who sought the abolition of

slavery within the immediate jurisdiction of the United States, it has awakened a spirit, which will overwhelm Congress with petitions till this right be restored. The annexation of Texas would be a measure of the same injurious character, and would stir up an open, uncompromising hostility to slavery, of which we have seen no example, and which would produce a reaction very dangerous to union.

The annexation of Texas will give rise to constitutional questions and conflicts, which cannot be adjusted. It is well known, that the additions to our territory of Louisiana and Florida were acceded to by the North, though very reluctantly, on account of their obvious utility. But it has been seriously doubted, whether the powers given by the Constitution were not in both cases transcended. "At the time Louisiana was acquired, Mr. Jefferson himself was deliberately of opinion, that the treaty-making authority, under the Constitution of the United States, was incompetent to make such an acquisition from a foreign power, and annex it to the Union, and that an amendment of the Constitution would be necessary to sanction it. In a letter to Governor Lincoln he even furnishes the formula of a proposed amendment, for the purpose of admitting Louisiana into the Union ; but adds, that the less that is said about the constitutional difficulty the better. Very little *was* said about it, and there was a general and tacit acquiescence, in consequence of the great and incalculable advantages expected from the acquisition in a national point of view. The purchase of Texas, under existing circumstances, might present a very different question." *

* North American Review, July, 1836.

It is true, that, as a general rule, the right to purchase territory is incident to sovereignty. But the sovereignty of our national government is a limited one. The Constitution was a compromise among independent States, and it is well known that geographical relations and local interests were among the essential conditions on which the compromise was made. We are willing, for the sake of universally acknowledged public interests, that additions of territory should be made to our country. But can it be admitted, that the Constitution gives power to the President and Senate to add a vast realm to the United States, for the very purpose of disturbing the balance between different sections, or of securing ascendency to certain parts of the confederacy? Was not the Constitution founded on conditions or considerations, which are even more authoritative than its particular provisions, and the violation of which must be death to our Union? Besides, a new question is to be opened by the admission of Texas. We shall not purchase a territory, as in the case of Louisiana, but shall admit an independent community, invested with sovereignty, into the confederation; and can the treaty-making power do this? Can it receive foreign nations, however vast, to the Union? Does not the question carry its own answer? By the assumption of such a right, would not the old compact be at once considered as dissolved?

To me it seems not only the right, but the duty of the Free States, in case of the annexation of Texas, to say to the Slave-holding States, "We regard this act as the dissolution of the Union. The essential conditions of the national compact are violated. To you we will faithfully adhere, but will not join ourselves to this new

and iniquitous acquisition. We will not become partners in your wars with Mexico and Europe, in your
schemes of spreading and perpetuating slavery, in your
hopes of conquest, in your unrighteous spoils." No
one prizes the Union more than myself, as the means of
peace. But, with Texas, we shall have no peace.
Texas, brought into the confederacy, will bring with it
domestic and foreign strife. It will change our relations
to other countries, and to one another. A pacific division in the first instance seems to me to threaten less
contention than a lingering, feverish dissolution of the
Union, such as must be expected under this fatal innovation.

I am but one of a nation of fifteen millions, and, as
such, may seem too insignificant to protest against a
public measure. But in this country every man, even
the obscurest, participates in the sovereignty, and is responsible for public acts, unless by some mode of oppo-
sitiou, proportioned to his sense of the evil, he absolves
himself from the guilt. For one then, I say, that, earnestly as I deprecate the separation of these States, and
though this event would disappoint most cherished hopes
for my country, still I can submit to it more readily than
to the reception of Texas into the confederacy. I
shrink from that contamination. I shrink from an act,
which is to pledge us as a people to robbery and war,
to the work of upholding and extending slavery without
limitation or end. I do not desire to share the responsibility, or to live under the laws of a government,
adopting such a policy, and swayed by such a spirit, as
would be expressed by the incorporation of Texas with
our country.

In truth, if the South is bent on incorporating Texas with itself, as a new prop to slavery, it would do well to insist on the division of the States. It would, in so doing, consult best its own safety. It should studiously keep itself from communion with the free part of the country. It should suffer no railroad from that section to cross its borders. It should block up intercourse with us by sea and land. Still more, it should abjure connexion with the whole civilized world; for, from every country it would be invaded by an influence hostile to slavery. It should borrow the code of the Dictator of Paraguay, and seal itself hermetically against the infectious books, opinions, and visits of foreigners. Its pride, as well as safety, should teach it this insulation; for, having once taken the ground, that slavery is a good, to be spread and made perpetual, it does by that act forfeit the rank which it covets among civilized and improving communities. It cannot be recognised as an equal by other states. On this point the decree of the world has gone forth, and no protests or clamors can drown the deep, solemn voice of humanity, gathering strength with every new generation. A community, acknowledging the evils of slavery, and continuing it only because the first law of nature, self-preservation, seems to require gradual processes of change, may retain the respect of those who deem their fears unfounded. But a community, wedding itself to slavery inseparably, with choice and affection, and with the purpose of spreading the plague far and wide, must become a by-word among the nations; and the friend of humanity will shake off the dust of his feet against it, in testimony of his reprobation.

V. I proceed now to the last head of this communication. I observe, that the cause of Liberty, of free institutions, a cause more sacred than union, forbids the annexation of Texas. It is plain from the whole preceding discussion, that this measure will exert a disastrous influence on the moral sentiments and principles of this country, by sanctioning plunder, by inflaming cupidity, by encouraging lawless speculation, by bringing into the confederacy a community whose whole history and circumstances are adverse to moral order and wholesome restraint, by violating national faith, by proposing immoral and inhuman ends, by placing us as a people in opposition to the efforts of philanthropy, and the advancing movements of the civilized world. It will spread a moral corruption, already too rife among us, and, in so doing, it will shake the foundations of freedom at home, and bring reproach on it abroad. It will be treachery to the great cause which has been confided to this above all nations.

The dependence of freedom on morals is an old subject, and I have no thought of enlarging on the general truth. I wish only to say, that it is one which needs to be brought home to us at the present moment, and that it cannot be trifled with but to our great peril. There are symptoms of corruption amongst us, which show us that we cannot enter on a new career of crime without peculiar hazard. I cannot do justice to this topic without speaking freely of our country, as freely as I should of any other; and unhappily we are so accustomed, as a people, to receive incense, to be soothed by flattery, and to account reputation as a more important interest than morality, that my freedom may be construed into a kind of disloyalty. But it would be wrong to make concessions to this dangerous weakness. I believe that morality is the first interest of a people, and that this requires self-knowledge in nations, as truly as in individuals. He who helps a community to comprehend itself, and to apply to itself a higher rule of action, is the truest patriot, and contributes most to its enduring fame.

I have said, that we shall expose our freedom to great peril by entering on a new career of crime. We are corrupt enough already. In one respect, our institutions have disappointed us all. They have not wrought out for us that elevation of character, which is the most precious, and, in truth, the only substantial blessing of liberty. Our progress in prosperity has indeed been the wonder of the world; but this prosperity has done much to counteract the ennobling influence of free institutions. The peculiar circumstances of the country and of our times have poured in upon us a torrent of wealth; and human nature has not been strong enough for the assault of such severe temptation. Prosperity has become dearer than freedom. Government is regarded more as a means of enriching the country, than of securing private rights. We have become wedded to gain, as our chief good. That, under the predominance of this degrading passion, the higher virtues, the moral independence, the simplicity of manners, the stern uprightness, the self-reverence, the respect for man as man, which are the ornaments and safeguards of a republic, should wither, and give place to selfish calculation and indulgence, to show and extravagance, to anxious, envious, discontented strivings, to wild adventure,

and to the gambling spirit of speculation, will surprise
no one who has studied human nature. The invasion
of Texas by our citizens is a mournful comment on our
national morality. Whether without some fiery trial,
some signal prostration of our prosperity, we can rise
to the force and self-denial of freemen, is a question not
easily solved.

There are other alarming views. A spirit of lawlessness pervades the community, which, if not repress-
ed, threatens the dissolution of our present forms of
society. Even in the old States, mobs are taking the
government into their hands, and a profligate newspaper
finds little difficulty in stirring up multitudes to violence.
When we look at the parts of the country nearest Texas, we see the arm of the law paralyzed by the passions
of the individual. Men take under their own protection the rights which it is the very office of government
to secure. The citizen, wearing arms as means of defence, carries with him perpetual proofs of the weakness of the authorities under which he lives. The
substitution of self-constituted tribunals for the regular
course of justice, and the infliction of immediate punishment in the moment of popular frenzy, are symptoms
of a people half reclaimed from barbarism. I know
not, that any civilized country on earth has exhibited,
during the last year, a spectacle so atrocious, as the
burning of a colored man by a slow fire, in the neighbourhood of St. Louis; and this infernal sacrifice was
offered not by a few fiends selected from the whole
country, but by a crowd gathered from a single spot.
Add to all this, the invasions of the rights of speech
and of the press by lawless force, the extent and tol-

eration of which oblige us to believe, that a considerable portion of our citizens have no comprehension of the first principles of liberty.

It is an undeniable fact, that, in consequence of these and other symptoms, the confidence of many reflecting men in our free institutions is very much impaired. Some despair. That main pillar of public liberty, mutual trust among citizens, is shaken. That we must seek security for property and life in a stronger government is a spreading conviction. Men, who in public talk of the stability of our institutions, whisper their doubts (perhaps their scorn) in private. So common are these apprehensions, that the knowledge of them has reached Europe. Not long ago, I received a letter from an enlightened and fervent friend of liberty, in Great Britain, beseeching me to inform him, how far he was to rely on the representations of one of his countrymen just returned from the United States, who had reported to him, that, in the most respectable society, he had again and again been told, that the experiment of freedom here was a failure, and that faith in our institutions was gone. That the traveller misinterpreted in a measure what he heard, we shall all acknowledge. But is the old enthusiasm of liberty unchilled among us? Is the old jealousy of power as keen and uncompromising? Do not parties more unscrupulously encroach on the constitution and on the rights of minorities? In one respect we must all admit a change. When you and I grew up, what a deep interest pervaded this country in the success of free institutions abroad! With what throbbing hearts did we follow the struggles of the oppressed! How many among

us were ready to lay down their lives for the cause oi
liberty on the earth!` And now who cares for free in-
stitutions abroad ?   How seldom does the topic pass
men's lips !   Multitudes, discouraged by the licentiousness at home, doubt the value of popular institutions,
especially in less enlightened countries ; whilst greater
numbers, locked up in gain, can spare no thought on
the struggles of liberty, and, provided they can drive a
prosperous trade with foreign nations, care little whether they are bond or free.

I may be thought inclined to draw a dark picture of
our moral condition.   But at home I am set down
among those who hope against hope ; and I have never
ceased to condemn as' a crime the despondence of those,
who, lamenting the corruptions of the times, do not lift
a finger to withstand it.   I am far, very far from despair.   I have no fears but such as belong to a friend
of freedom.   Among dark omens, I see favorable influences, remedial processes, counteracting agencies.   I
well know, that the vicious part of our system makes
more noise and show than the sound.   I know, that the
prophets of ruin to our institutions are to be found most
frequently in the party out of power, and that many
dark auguries must be set down to the account of disappointment and irritation.   I am sure, too, that imminent peril would wake up the spirit of our fathers in
many who slumber in these days of ease and security.
It is also true, that, with all our defects, there is a wider
diffusion of intelligence, moral restraint, and self-respect
among us, than through any other community.   Still, I
am compelled to acknowledge an extent of corruption
among us, which menaces freedom and our dearest in-

terests ; and a policy, which will give new and enduring impulse to corruption, which will multiply indefinitely public and private crime, ought to be reprobated as the sorest calamity we can incur. Freedom is fighting her battles in the world with sufficient odds against her. Let us not give new chances to her foes.

That the cause of republicanism is suffering abroad, through the defects and crimes of our countrymen, is as true, as that it is regarded with increased skepticism among ourselves. Abroad, republicanism is identified with the United States, and it is certain that the American name has not risen of late in the world. It so happens, that, whilst writing, I have received a newspaper from England, in which Lynch law is as familiarly associated with our country, as if it were one of our establishments. We are quoted as monuments of the degrading tendencies of popular institutions. When I visited England fifteen years ago, republican sentiments were freely expressed to me. I should probably hear none now. Men's minds seem to be returning to severer principles of government ; and this country is responsible for a part of this change. It is believed abroad, that property is less secure among us, order less stable, law less revered, social ties more easily broken, religion less enforced, life held less sacred, than in other countries. Undoubtedly, the prejudices of foreign nations, the interests of foreign governments, have led to gross exaggeration of evils here. The least civilized parts of the country are made to represent the whole, and occasional atrocities are construed into habits. But who does not feel, that we have given cause of reproach ? and shall we fix this reproach, and exasperate it into indignation and hatred, by adopting a policy against which the moral sentiments of the Christian world revolt? Shall we make the name of republic "a stench in the nostrils" of all nations, by employing our power to build up and spread slavery, by resisting the efforts of other countries for its abolition, by falling behind monarchies in reverence for the rights of men?

When we look forward to the probable growth of this country; when we think of the millions of human beings who are to spread over our present territory; of the career of improvement and glory opened to this new people; of the impulse which free institutions, if prosperous, may be expected to give to philosophy, religion, science, literature, and arts; of the vast field in which the experiment is to be made, of what the unfettered powers of man may achieve; of the bright page of history which our fathers have filled, and of the advantages under which their toils and virtues have placed us for carrying on their work; when we think of all this, can we help, for a moment, surrendering ourselves to bright visions of our country's glory, before which all the glories of the past are to fade away? Is it presumption to say, that, if just to ourselves and all nations, we shall be felt through this whole continent, that we shall spread our language, institutions, and civilization through a wider space than any nation has yet filled with a like beneficent influence? And are we prepared to barter these hopes, this sublime moral empire, for conquests by force? Are we prepared to sink to the level of unprincipled nations, to content ourselves with a vulgar, guilty greatness, to adopt in our youth maxims and ends which must brand our future with sordidness, oppression, and shame? This country cannot without peculiar infamy run the common race of national rapacity. Our origin, institutions, and position are peculiar, and all favor an upright, honorable course. We have not the apologies of nations hemmed in by narrow bounds, or threatened by the overshadowing power of ambitious neighbours. If we surrender ourselves to a selfish policy, we shall sin almost without temptation, and forfeit opportunities of greatness vouchsafed to no other people, for a prize below contempt.

I have alluded to the want of wisdom with which we are accustomed to speak of our destiny as a people. We are *destined* (that is the word) to overspread North America; and, intoxicated with the idea, it matters little to us how we accomplish our fate. To spread, to supplant others, to cover a boundless space, this seems our ambition, no matter what influence we spread with us. Why cannot we rise to noble conceptions of our destiny? Why do we not feel, that our work as a nation is, to carry freedom, religion, science, and a nobler form of human nature over this continent? and why do we not remember, that to diffuse these blessings we must first cherish them in our own borders; and that whatever deeply and permanently corrupts us will make our spreading influence a curse, not a blessing, to this new world? It is a common idea in Europe, that we are destined to spread an inferior civilization over North America; that our slavery and our absorption in gain and outward interests mark us out, as fated to fall behind the old world in the higher im-

provements of human nature, in the philosophy, the
refinements, the enthusiasm of literature and the arts,
which throw a lustre round other countries. I am not
prophet enough to read our fate. I believe, indeed,
that we are to make our futurity for ourselves. I believe, that a nation's destiny lies in its character, in the
principles which govern its policy and bear rule in the
hearts of its citizens. I take my stand on God's moral
and eternal law. A nation, renouncing and defying
this, cannot be free, cannot be great.

Religious men in this community, and they are many,
are peculiarly bound to read the future history of their
country, not in the flattering promises of politicians,
but in the warnings of conscience, and in the declaration of God's word. They know, and should make it
known, that nations cannot consolidate free institutions
and secure a lasting prosperity by crime. They know,
that, retribution awaits communities as well as individuals ; and they should tremble amidst their hopes, when,
with this solemn truth on their minds, they look round
on their country. Let them consider the clearness
with which God's will is now made known, and the
signal blessings of his Providence poured out on this
people, with a profusion accorded to no other under
heaven ; and then let them consider our ingratitude for
his boundless gifts, our abuse of his beneficence to sensual and selfish gratification, our unmeasured, unrighteous love of gain, our unprincipled party-spirit, and
our faithless and cruel wrongs toward the Indian race ;
and can they help fearing, that the cup of wrath is filling for this people ? Men, buried in themselves and in
outward interests, atheists in heart and life, may scoff

at the doctrine of national retribution, because they do not see God's hand stretched out to destroy guilty communities. But does not all history teach, that the unlicensed passions of a guilty people are more terrible ministers of punishment than miraculous inflictions? To chastise and destroy, God needs not interfere by supernatural judgments. In every community, there are elements of discord, revolution, and ruin, pent up in the human soul, which need only to be quickened and set free by a new order of events, to shake and convulse the whole social fabric. Never were the causes of disastrous change in human affairs more active than at the present moment. Society heaves and trembles, from the struggle of opposing principles, as the earth quakes through the force of central fires. This is not the time for presumption, for defying Heaven by new crimes, for giving a new range to cupidity and ambition. Men who fear God must fear for their country, in this " day of provocation," and they will be false to their country, if they look on passively, and see without remonstrance the consummation of a great national crime, which cannot fail to bring down awful retribution.

I am aware, that there are those, who, on reading these pages, will smile at my simplicity in urging moral and religious motives, disinterested considerations, lofty aims, on a politician. The common notion is, that the course of a man embarked in public life will be shaped by the bearing of passing events on his immediate popularity ; that virtue and freedom, however they may round his periods in the senate, have little influence on his vote. But I do not believe, that public life is necessarily degrading, or that a statesman is incapable of looking above himself. Public life appeals to the noblest, as well as basest principles of human nature. It holds up for pursuit enduring fame, as well as the notoriety of the passing hour. By giving opportunities of acting on the vast and permanent interests of a nation, it often creates a deep sense of responsibility, and a generous self-oblivion. I have too much faith in human nature to distrust the influence of great truths and high motives on any class of men, especially on men of commanding intelligence. There is a congeniality between vast powers of thought and dignity of purpose. None are so capable of sacrificing themselves, as those who have most to sacrifice, who, in offering themselves, make the greatest offerings to humanity. With this conviction, I am not discouraged by the anticipated smiles and scoffs of those, who will think, that, in insisting on national purity as the essential condition of freedom and greatness, I have " preached " to the winds. To you, Sir, rectitude is not an empty name, nor will a measure, fraught with lasting corruption and shame to your country, seem to you any thing but a fearful calamity.

I have now finished the task which I have felt myself bound to undertake. That I have escaped all error, I cannot hope. That I may have fallen into occasional exaggeration, I ought perhaps to fear, from the earnestness with which I have written. But of the essential truth of the views here communicated, I cannot doubt. It is exceedingly to be regretted, that the subject of this letter has as yet drawn little attention at the North. The unprecedented pecuniary difficulties, pressing now on the country, have absorbed the public mind. And yet these difficulties, should they be aggravated and continued far beyond what is most dreaded, would be a light national evil, compared with the annexation of Texas to the Union. I trust the people will not slumber on the edge of this precipice, till it shall be too late to reflect and provide for safety. Too much time has been given for the ripening of this unrighteous project. I doubt not, as I have said, that opposition exists to it in the Slave-holding States. This, if manifested in any strength, would immediately defeat it. The other States should raise a voice against it, like the voice of many waters. Party dissensions should be swallowed up in this vast common interest. The will of the people, too strong and fixed to be resisted, should be expressed to Congress, in remonstrances from towns, cities, counties, and legislatures. Let no man, who feels the greatness of the evil which threatens us, satisfy himself with unprofitable regrets ; but let each embody his opposition in a form which will give incitement to his neighbours, and act on men in power.

I take it for granted, that those who differ from me will ascribe what I have written to unworthy motives. This is the common mode of parrying unwelcome truths ; and it is not without influence, where the author is unknown. May I then be allowed to say, that I have strong reasons for believing, that, among the many defects of this letter, those of unworthy intention are not to be numbered. The reluctance, with which I have written, satisfies me, that I have not been impelled by any headlong passion. Nor can I have been impelled by party-spirit. I am pledged to no party. In truth, I do not feel myself able to form a decisive opinion on the subjects, which now inflame and divide the country, and which can be very little understood except by men who have made a study of commerce and finance. As to having written from that most common motive, the desire of distinction, I may be permitted to say, that, to win the public ear, I need not engage in a controversy which will expose me to unmeasured reproach. May I add, that I have lived long enough to learn the worth of applause. Could I, indeed, admit the slightest hope of securing to myself that enduring fame, which future ages award to the lights and benefactors of their race, I could not but be stirred by the prospect. But notoriety among contemporaries, obtained by taking part in the irritating discussions of the day, I would no stretch out a hand to secure.

I cannot but fear, that the earnestness with which I have written may seem to indicate an undue excitement of mind. But I have all along felt distinctly the importance of calmness, and have seemed to myself to maintain it. I have prepared this letter, not amidst the goadings, irritations, and feverish tumults of a crowded city, but in the stillness of retirement, amid scenes of peace and beauty. Hardly an hour has passed, in which I have not sought relief from the exhaustion of writing, by walking abroad amidst God's works, which seldom fail to breathe tranquillity, and which, by their harmony and beneficence, continually cheer me, as emblems and prophecies of a more harmonious and blessed state of human affairs than has yet been known. Perhaps some will object it to me, that a man, living in such retirement, unfits himself to judge of passing events, that he is prone to substitute his visions for realities, and to legislate for a world which does not exist. I acknowledge the danger of such a position. On the other hand, it is equally true, that the man, who lives in a crowd and receives perpetual impulse from its prejudices and passions, who connects himself with a party and looks to it for reward, cannot easily keep his mind open to truth, or sacrifice the interests of the moment to everlasting principles and the enduring welfare of his country. Everywhere our frail nature is severely tried. All circumstances have their perils. In every condition, there are biases to wrong judgment and incitements to wrong action. Through such discipline, we are to make our way to truth and perfection. The dread of these dangers must not keep us inactive. Having sought to understand the difficulties in our respective paths, and having done what we can to learn the truth, we must commit ourselves to our convictions without fear, expressing them in word and action, and leaving results to Him, who will accept our pure purpose, and whose providence is the pledge of the ultimate triumphs of humanity and uprightness.

You and I, my dear Sir, are approaching that period of life, when the passions lose much of their force, when disappointment, bereavement, the fall of our contemporaries on the right hand and the left, and long experience of the emptiness of human favor and of the instability of all earthly goods, are teaching us the lofty lessons of superiority to the fleeting opinion of our day, of reliance on the everlasting law of Right, of reference to a Higher Judge than man, of solemn anticipation of our final account. Permit me to close this letter, with desiring for you in your commanding station, what I ask for myself in private life, that we may be faithful to ourselves, to our country, to mankind, to the benevolent principles of the Christian faith, and to the common Father of the whole human race.

 Very respectfully,
  Your friend and servant,
   William E. Channing.
Newport, R. I., *August* 1, 1837.

NOTE.

A few remarks, which have been suggested since the completion of the preceding letter, I shall throw into a note.

The recognition of the independence of Texas by our government is to be lamented, as unbecomingly hasty, and as a violation of the principle adopted by Mr. Monroe, in regard to the Spanish colonies. "These new states," he says, " had completely established their independence, before we acknowledged them." We have recognised Texas as a nation, having all the attributes of sovereignty, and competent to the discharge of all the obligations of an independent state. And what is Texas ? A collection of a few settlements, which would vanish at once, were a Mexican army of any force to enter the country. One decisive victory would scatter all Texas like a horde of Tartars, and not a trace of its institutions and population would remain. We have been accustomed to think of a nation as something permanent, as having some fixtures, some lasting bond of union. There would be nothing to hold Texas together, were her single, small army to be routed in one battle. To send a minister plenipotentiary to such a handful of people, made up chiefly of our own citizens, is to degrade the forms of national intercourse. This new republic, with its president and diplomatic corps, has been called a Farce. But the tragic element prevails so much over the farcical in this whole business, that we cannot laugh at it. The movements of our government in regard to Texas are chiefly interesting, as they are thought to indicate a disposition favorable to its annexation to our country. But we will not believe, that the government is resolved on this great wrong, unless we are compelled so to do. We hope, that the present administration will secure the confidence of good men by well-considered and upright measures, looking beyond momentary interests, to the lasting peace, order, and strength of the country.

There is another objection to the annexation of Texas, which, after our late experience, is entitled to attention. This possession will involve us in new Indian wars. Texas, besides being open to the irruption of the tribes within our territories, has a tribe of its own, the Camanches, which is described as more formidable than any in North America. Such foes are not to be coveted. The Indians! that ominous word, which ought to pierce the conscience of this nation, more than the savage war-cry pierces the ear. The Indians! Have we not inflicted and endured evil enough in our intercourse with this wretched people, to abstain from new wars with them? Is the tragedy of Florida to be acted again and again in our own day, and in our children's?

In addition to what I have said of the constitutional objections to the annexation of Texas to our country, I would observe, that we may infer, from the history and language of the Constitution, that our national Union was so far from being intended to spread slavery over new countries, that, had the possibility of such a result been anticipated, decided provisions would have been introduced for its prevention. It is worthy of remark, how anxious the framers of that instrument were to exclude from it the word Slavery. They were not willing, that this feature of our social system should be betrayed in the construction of our free government. A stranger might read it, without suspecting the existence of this institution among us. Were slavery to be wholly abolished here, no change would be needed in the Constitution, nor would any part become obsolete, except an obscure clause, which, in apportioning the representatives, provides that there shall be added to the whole number of free persons " three fifths of other persons." Slavery is studiously thrown into the back-ground. How little did our forefathers suppose, that it was to become a leading interest of the government, to which our peace at home and abroad was to be made a sacrifice !

I have said, that I desire no political union with communities bent on spreading and perpetuating slavery. It is hardly necessary to observe, that this was not intended to express a desire to decline friendly intercourse with the members of those communities. Individuals, who have received from their ancestors some pernicious prejudice or institution, may still, in their general spirit, be disinterested and just. Our testimony against the wrong which such men practise, is not to be stifled or impaired by the feelings of interest or attachment which they inspire ; nor, on the other hand, must this wrong be spread by our imaginations over their whole characters, so as to seem their sole attribute, and so as to hide all their claims to regard. In an age of reform, one of the hardest duties is, to be inflexibly hostile to the long-rooted corruptions of society, and at the same time to be candid and just to those who uphold them. It is true, that, with the most friendly feelings, we shall probably give offence to those, who are interested in abuses which we condemn. But we are not on this account absolved from the duty of cultivating and expressing kindness and justice, of laying strong restraint on our passions, and of avoiding all needless provocation.

The speech of Mr. Adams on the subject of the preceding letter, delivered in Congress, in December, 1835,

22 *

should be republished and circulated. It deserves to be read as a specimen of parliamentary eloquence ; and its moral and political views are worthy of its eminent author.

There seems to be an apprehension at the South, that the Free States, should they obtain the ascendency, might be disposed to use the powers of the government for the abolition of slavery. On this point, there is but one feeling at the North. The Free States feel, that they have no more right to abolish slavery in the Slave-holding States than in a foreign country. They regard the matter as wholly out of their reach. They, indeed, claim the right of setting forth the evils of slavery, as of any other pernicious and morally wrong institution. But the thought of touching the laws which established it in any State, they reject without a discordant voice. In regard to the District of Columbia, many of us feel, that slavery continues there by the action of *all* the States, that the Free States, therefore, are responsible for it ; and we maintain that it is most unreasonable, that an institution should be sustained by those who hold it to be immoral and pernicious. But we feel no such responsibility for slavery in the Slave-holding States. These States must determine for themselves how long it shall continue, and by what means it shall be abolished. We solemnly urge them to use their power for its removal ; but nothing would tempt us to wrest the power from them, if we could. The South has fears, that the Free States may be hurried away by " enthusiasm " into usurpation of unconstitutional powers on the subject. One is tempted to smile at the want of acquaintance with the North, which such an apprehension betrays. This enthusiasm, to endanger the South, must spread through all the Free States ; for, as the slave-holders are unanimous, nothing but a like unanimity in their opponents can expose them to harm. And is it possible, that a large number of communities, spread over a vast surface, having a diversity of interests, and all absorbed in the pursuit of gain, to a degree, perhaps, without a parallel, should be driven by a moral, philanthropic enthusiasm, into violations of a national compact, by which their peace and prosperity would be put in peril, and into combined and lawless efforts against other communities, with whom they sustain exceedingly profitable connexions, and from whom they could not be sundered without serious loss ? Whoever is acquainted with the Free States knows, that the excesses, to which they are exposed, are not so much those of enthusiasm, as of caution and worldly prudence. The patience, with which they have endured recent violent measures directed against their citizens, shows little propensity to rashness. The danger is, not so much that they will invade the rights of other members of the confederacy, as that they will be indifferent to their own.

I have spoken in this letter of the estimation in which this country is held abroad. I hope I shall not be numbered among those, too common here, who are irritably alive to the opinions of other nations, to the censures and misrepresentations of travellers. To a great and growing people, how insignificant is the praise or blame of a traveller or a nation! " None of these things move me." But one thing does move me. It is a sore evil, that freedom should be blasphemed, that republican institutions should forfeit the confidence of mankind, through the unfaithfulness of this people to their trust.

In reviewing this letter, I perceive that I have used the strong language, in which the apprehension of great evils naturally expresses itself. I hope this will not be construed as betokening any anxieties or misgivings in regard to the issues of passing events. I place a cheerful trust in Providence. The triumphs in evil, which men call great, are but clouds passing over the serene and everlasting heavens. Public men may, in craft or passion, decree violence and oppression. But silently, irresistibly, they and their works are swept away. A voice of encouragement comes to us from the ruins of the past, from the humiliations of the proud, from the prostrate thrones of conquerors, from the baffled schemes of statesmen, from the reprobation with which the present age looks back on the unrighteous policy of former times. Such sentence the future will pass on present wrongs. Men, measures, and all earthly interests pass away ; but Principles are Eternal. Truth, justice, and goodness partake of the omnipotence and immutableness of God, whose essence they are. In these it becomes us to place a calm, joyful trust, in the darkest hour.

LETTER ON CATHOLICISM,

TO THE

EDITOR OF THE "WESTERN MESSENGER,"

LOUISVILLE, KENTUCKY.

ON CATHOLICISM.

Boston, *June*, 1836.

My Dear Sir,

I have received your letter, expressing a very earnest desire that I would make some contribution to the pages of the "Western Messenger." Your appeal is too strong to be resisted. I feel that I must send you something, though circumstances, which I cannot control, do not allow me to engage in any elaborate discussion. I have therefore resolved to write you a letter, with the same freedom which I should use, if writing not for the public, but to a friend. Perhaps it may meet the wants, and suit the frank spirit of the West, more than a regular essay. But judge for yourself, and do what you will with my hasty thoughts.

I begin with expressing my satisfaction in your having planted yourself in the West. I am glad for your own sake, as well as for the sake of the cause you have adopted. I say, your own sake. You have chosen the good part. The first question to be asked by a young man entering into active life, is, in what situation he can find the greatest scope and excitement to his

powers and good affections ?   That sphere is the best
for a man, in which he can best unfold the faculties of a
Man, in which he can do justice to his whole nature ;
in which his intellect, heart, conscience, will be called
into the most powerful life.   I am always discouraged
when I hear a young man asking for the easiest condition, when I see him looking out for some beaten
path, in which he may move on mechanically, and with
the least expense of thought or feeling.   The young
minister sometimes desires to become a fixture in an
established congregation, which is bound to its place of
worship by obstinate ties of habit, and which can therefore be kept together with little effort of his own.   If
the congregation happens to be what is called a respectable one, that is, if it happens so far to regard the rules
of worldly decorum as never to shock him by immorali-
ties, and never to force him into any new or strenuous
exertion for its recovery, so much the better.   Such a
minister is among the most pitiable members of the community.   Happily this extreme case is rare.   But the
case is not rare of those, who, wishing to do good, still
desire to reconcile usefulness with all the comforts of
life, who shrink from the hazards, which men take in
other pursuits, who want the spirit of enterprise, who
prefer to reap where others have sowed, and to linger
round the places of their nativity.   At a time when men
of other professions pour themselves into the new parts
of the country, and are seeking, their fortunes with
buoyant spirits, and overflowing hopes, the minister
seems little inclined to seek what is better than fortune
in untried fields of labor.   Of all men, the minister
should be first to inquire, where shall I find the circumstances most fitted to wake up my whole soul, to task

all my faculties, to inspire a profound interest, to carry me out of myself? I believe *you* have asked yourself this question, and I think you have answered it wisely. You have thrown yourself into a new country, where there are admirable materials, but where a congregation is to be created by your own faithfulness and zeal. Not even a foundation is laid, on which you can build. There are no mechanical habits among the people, which the minister can use as labor-saving machines, which will do much of his work for him, which will draw people to church whether he meets their wants or not. Still more, there are no rigid rules, binding you down to specific modes of action, cramping your energies, warring with your individuality. You may preach in your own way, preach from your observation of the effects produced on a free-speaking people. Tradition does not take the place of your own reason. In addition to this, you see and feel the pressing need of religious instruction, in a region where religious institutions are in their infancy. That under such circumstances, a man who starts with the true spirit will make progress, can hardly be doubted. You have peculiar trials, but in these you find impulses, which, I trust, are to carry you forward to greater usefulness, and to a higher action of the whole soul.

Boston has sometimes been called the Paradise of ministers; and undoubtedly the respect in which the profession is held, and the intellectual helps afforded here, give some reason for the appellation. But there are disadvantages also, and one in particular, to which you are not exposed. Shall I say a word of evil of this good city of Boston? Among all its virtues it does not abound in a tolerant spirit. The yoke of opinion is a

heavy one, often crushing individuality of judgment and
action. A censorship, unfriendly to free exertion, is
exercised over the pulpit as well as over other concerns. No city in the world is governed so little by a
police, and so much by mutual inspection, and what is
called public sentiment. We stand more in awe of one
another, than most people. Opinion is less individual,
or runs more into masses, and often rules with a rod
of iron. Undoubtedly opinion, when enlightened, lofty,
pure, is a useful sovereign; but in the present imperfect state of society, it has its evils as well as benefits.
It suppresses the grosser vices, rather than favors the
higher virtues. It favors public order, rather than
originality of thought, moral energy, and spiritual life.
To prescribe its due bounds, is a very difficult problem.
Were its restraints wholly removed, the decorum of the
pulpit would be endangered; but that these restraints
are excessive in this city, and especially in our denomination, that they often weigh oppressively on the young
minister, and that they often take from ministers of all
ages the courage, confidence, and authority which their
high mission should inspire, cannot, I fear, be denied.
The minister here, on entering the pulpit, too often feels,
that he is to be judged rather than to judge; that instead of meeting sinful men, who are to be warned or
saved, he is to meet critics to be propitiated or dis-
armed. He feels, that should he trust himself to his
heart, speak without book, and consequently break some
law of speech, or be hurried into some daring hyper-
bole, he should find little mercy. Formerly Felix trem-
bled before Paul; now the successor of Paul more frequently trembles. Foreigners generally set down as
one of our distinctions, the awe in which we stand of

opinion, the want of freedom of speech, the predominance of caution and calculation over impulse. This feature of our society exempts it from some dangers; and those persons who see only ruin in the reforming spirit of the times, will prize it as our best characteristic. Be this as it may, one thing is sure, that it does not give energy to the ministry, or favor the nobler action or higher products of the mind. Your situation gives you greater freedom. You preach, I understand, wholly without notes. In this you may carry your liberty too far. Writing is one of the great means of giving precision, clearness, consistency, and energy to thought. Every other sermon, I think, should be written, if circumstances allow it. But he who only preaches from notes, will never do justice to his own powers and feelings. The deepest fountains of eloquence within him will not be unsealed. He will never know the full power given him over his fellow-creatures.

The great danger to a minister at this time is the want of life, the danger of being dead while he lives. Brought up where Christianity is established, he is in danger of receiving it as a tradition. Brought up, where a routine of duty is marked out for him, and a certain style of preaching imposed, he is in danger of preaching from tradition. Ministers are strongly tempted to say what they are expected to say. Accordingly their tones and looks too often show, that they understand but superficially what is meant by their words. You see that they are talking of that which is not *real* to them. This danger of lifelessness is great in old congregations, made up of people of steady habits and respectable characters. The minister in such a case is apt to feel as if his hearers needed no mighty change,

and as if his work were accomplished, when his tru-
isms, expressed with more or less propriety, are received with due respect. He ought to feel, that the
people may be spiritually dead with their regular habits,
as he may be with his regular preaching; that both
may need to be made alive. It is the advantage of
such a situation as you are called to fill, that you can
do nothing without life. A machine in a western pulpit
cannot produce even the show of an effect. The people may be less enlightened than we are, more irregular
in habits, more defective in character; but they must
have living men to speak to them, and must hear a
voice which, whether true or erring, still comes from
the soul, or they cannot be brought to hear. This is
no small compensation for many disadvantages.

This Life of which I speak, though easily recognised
by a congregation, cannot be easily described by them,
just as the most ignorant man can distinguish a living
from a dead body, but knows very little in what vitality
consists. A common mistake is, that Life in the minister is strong emotion. But it consists much more in
the clear perception, the deep conviction of the Reality
of religion, the *reality* of virtue, of man's spiritual nature, of God, of Immortality, of Heaven. The tone
which most proves a minister to be alive, is that of calm,
entire confidence in the *truth* of what he says, the tone
of a man who speaks of what he has seen and handled,
the peculiar tone which belongs to one who has come
fresh from what he describes, to whom the future world
is as substantial as the present, who does not echo what
others say of the human soul, but feels his own spiritual
nature as others feel their bodies, and to whom God is
as truly present as the nearest fellow-creature. Strong

emotion in the pulpit is too often a fever caught by sympathy, or a fervor worked up for the occasion, or a sensibility belonging more to the nerves than the mind, and excited by vague views which fade away before the calm reason. Hence enthusiasts often become skeptics. The great sign of life is to see and feel, that there is something real, substantial, immortal, in Christian virtue; to be conscious of the reality and nearness of your relations to God and the invisible world. This is the life, which the minister needs, and which it is his great work to communicate. My hope is, that by sending ministers into new situations, where new wants cry to them for supply, a living power may be awakened, to which a long established routine of labors is not favorable, and which may spread beyond them to their brethren.

I pass now to another subject. We hear much of the Catholic religion in the West, and of its threatening progress. There are not a few here who look upon this alarm as a pious fraud, who consider the cry of " No Popery," as set up by a particular sect to attract to itself distinction and funds; but fear is so natural, and a panic spreads so easily, that I see no necessity of resorting to so unkind an explanation. It must be confessed that Protestantism enters on the warfare with Popery under some disadvantages, and may be expected to betray some consciousness of weakness. Most Protestant sects are built on the Papal foundation. Their creeds and excommunications embody the grand idea of Infallibility, as truly as the decrees of Trent and the Vatican; and if the people must choose between different infallibilities, there is much to incline them to that of Rome. This has age, the majority of votes, more daring assumption, and bolder denunciation on its side. The popes of our different sects are certainly less imposing to the imagination than the Pope at Rome.

I trust, however, that, with these advantages, Catholicism is still not very formidable. It has something more to do, than to fight with sects; its great foe is the progress of society. The creation of dark times, it cannot stand before the light. In this country in particular, it finds no coadjutors in any circumstances, passions, or institutions. Catholicism is immovable, and movement and innovation are the order of the day. It rejects the idea of melioration, and the passion for improvement is inflaming all minds. It takes its stand in the Past, and this generation are living in the Future. It clings to forms, which the mind has outgrown. It will not modify doctrines in which the intelligence of the age cannot but recognise the stamp of former ignorance. It forbids free inquiry, and inquiry is the spirit of the age, the boldest inquiry, stopping nowhere, invading every region of thought. Catholicism wrests from the people the right to choose their own ministers, and the right of election is the very essence of our institutions. It establishes an aristocratical priesthood, and the whole people are steeped in republicanism. It withholds the Scriptures, and the age is a reading one, and reads the more what is forbidden. Catholicism cannot comprehend that the past is not the present, cannot comprehend the revolution which the art of printing and the revival of learning have effected. Its memory seems not to come down lower than the middle ages. It aims to impose restraints on thought, which were comparatively easy before the press was set in motion, and labors to shore up institutions, in utter unconscious-

ness that the state of society, and the modes of thinking on which they rested, have passed away.

The political revolutions of the times are enough to
seal the death-warrant of Catholicism, but it has to encounter a far more important spiritual revolution. Catholicism belongs to what may be called the dogmatical
age of Christianity, the age when it was thought our
religion might be distilled into a creed, which would
prove an elixir of life to whoever would swallow it.
We have now come to learn, that Christianity is not a
dogma, but a spirit, that its essence is the spirit of its
divine founder, that it is of little importance what church
a man belongs to, or what formula of doctrines he sub-
scribes, that nothing is important but the supreme love,
choice, pursuit of moral perfection, shining forth in the
life and teachings of Christ. This is the true Catholic doctrine, the creed of the true Church, gathering
into one spiritual communion all good and holy men
of all ages and regions, and destined to break down all
the earthly clay-built, gloomy barriers, which now separate the good from one another. To this great idea
of reason and revelation, of the understanding and heart,
of experience and philosophy, to this great truth of an
advanced civilization, Catholicism stands in direct hostility. How sure then is its fall!

The great foe of the Romish Church is not the theo-
logian. *He* might be imprisoned, chained, burned. It
is human nature waking up to a consciousness of its
powers, catching a glimpse of the perfection for which
it was made, beginning to respect itself, thirsting for
free action and developement, learning through a deep
consciousness that there is something diviner than forms,
or churches, or creeds, recognising in Jesus Christ its

own celestial model, and claiming kindred with all who
have caught any portion of his spiritual life and disinterested love; here, here is the great enemy of Catholicism. I look confidently to the ineradicable, ever-
unfolding principles of human nature, for the victory
over all superstitions. Reason and conscience, the
powers by which we discern the true and the right, are
immortal as their author. Oppressed for ages, they yet
live. Like the central fires of the earth, they can
heave up mountains. It is encouraging to see under
what burdens and clouds they have made their way; and
we must remember, that, by every new developement,
they are brought more into contact with the life-giving,
omnipotent truth and character of Jesus Christ. It
makes me smile, to hear immortality claimed for Catholicism or Protestantism, or for any past interpretations
of Christianity; as if the human soul had exhausted itself in its infant efforts, or as if the men of one or a
few generations could bind the energy of human thought
and affection for ever. A theology at war with the
laws of physical nature would be a battle of no doubtful issue. The laws of our spiritual nature give still
less chance of success to the system, which would
thwart or stay them. The progress of the individual
and of society, which has shaken the throne of Rome,
is not an accident, not an irregular spasmodic effort,
but the natural movement of the soul. Catholicism
must fall before it. In truth, it is very much fallen
already. It exists, and will long exist as an outward
institution. But compare the Catholicism of an intelligent man of the nineteenth century with what it was in
the tenth. The name, the letter remain, — how changed
the spirit! The silent reform spreading in the very

bosom of Catholicism, is as important as the reformation of the sixteenth century, and in truth more effectual.

Catholicism has always hoped for victory over Protestantism, on the ground of the dissensions of Protestants. But its anticipations have not approached fulfilment, and they show us how the most sagacious err,
when they attempt to read futurity. I have long since
learned to hear with composure the auguries of the
worldy wise. The truth is, that the dissensions of Protestantism go far to constitute its strength. Through
them its spirit, which is freedom, the only spirit which
Rome cannot conquer, is kept alive. Had its members been organized, and bound into a single church,
it would have become a despotism as unrelenting, and
corrupt, and hopeless as Rome. But this is not all.
Protestantism, by being broken into a great variety of
sects, has adapted itself to the various modifications of
human nature. Every sect has embodied religion in a
form suited to some large class of minds. It has met
some want, answered to some great principle of the
soul, and thus every new denomination has been a new
standard, under which to gather and hold fast a host
against Rome. One of the great arts, by which Catholicism spread and secured its dominion, was its wonderful flexibleness, its most skilful adaptation of itself
to the different tastes, passions, wants of men ; and to
this means of influence and dominion, Protestantism
could oppose nothing, but variety of sects. I do not
recollect, that I ever saw this feature of Catholicism
brought out distinctly, and yet nothing in the system has
impressed me more strongly. The Romish religion
calls itself one, but it has a singular variety of forms

and aspects. For the lover of forms and outward religion, it has a gorgeous ritual. To the mere man of
the world, it shows a pope on the throne, bishops in
palaces, and all the splendor of earthly dominion. At
the same time, for the self-denying, ascetic, mystical,
and fanatical, it has all the forms of monastic life. To
him, who would scourge himself into godliness, it offers
a whip. For him who would starve himself into spirituality, it provides the mendicant convents of St. Fran-
cis. For the anchorite, it prepares the death-like silence of La Trappe. To the passionate young woman,
it presents the raptures of St. Theresa, and the marriage of St. Catharine with her Saviour. For the restless pilgrim, whose piety needs greater variety than the
cell of the monk, it offers shrines, tombs, relics, and
other holy places in Christian lands, and above all, the
holy sepulchre near Calvary. To the generous, sym-
pathizing enthusiast, it opens some fraternity or sister-
hood of Charity. To him, who inclines to take heaven
by violence, it gives as much penance as he can ask;
and to the mass of men, who wish to reconcile the two
worlds, it promises a purgatory, so far softened down
by the masses of the priest and the prayers of the
faithful, that its fires can be anticipated without overwhelming dread. This composition of forces in the
Romish Church seems to me a wonderful monument of
skill. When, in Rome, the traveller sees by the side of
the purple, lackeyed cardinal, the begging friar; when,
under the arches of St. Peter, he sees a coarsely dressed monk holding forth to a ragged crowd; or when,
beneath a Franciscan church, adorned with the most
precious works of art, he meets a charnel-house, where
the bones of the dead brethren are built into walls, be-

tween which the living walk 'to read. their mortality ;
he is amazed, if he gives himself time for reflection,
at the infinite variety of machinery which Catholicism
has brought to bear on the human mind ; at the sagaci-
ty with which it has adapted itself to the various tastes
and propensities of human nature. Protestantism at-
tains this end by more simple, natural, and in the main
more effectual ways. All the great principles of our
nature are represented in different sects, which have
on the whole a keener passion for self-aggrandizement
than the various orders in the Romish Church, and thus
men of all varieties of mind find something congenial,
find a class to sympathize with.

And, here, I cannot but observe, that Episcopacy
renders good service to the Protestant cause. Without being thoroughly Protestant, it is especially efficient
against Catholicism ; and this good work it does by its
very proximity to Rome. From the wide diffusion and
long continuance of Catholicism, we may be sure that
it embodies some great idea, and answers some want,
which is early and powerfully developed in the progress
of civilization. There is of consequence a tendency
to Catholicism in society, though more and more restrained by higher tendencies. Happily, Episcopacy
is built on the same great idea, but expresses it in a
more limited and rational form. It is Catholicism improved, or mother church with a lower mitre and a less
royal air ; and by meeting the want which carries men
to the Romish Church, stops numbers on their way to
it. Hence, Catholicism hates Episcopacy more than
any other form of dissent. Sects are apt to hate each
other in proportion to their proximity. The old prov-
erb that two of a trade cannot agree, applies to reli-

gion as strongly as to common life. — The amount is, that Catholicism derives little aid from Protestant divisions. In an age as unimproved in Christianity as the present, these divisions are promising symptoms. They prevent men from settling down in a rude Christianity. They keep alive inquiry and zeal. They are essential to freedom and progress. Without these, Protestantism would be only a new edition of Catholicism ; and the old pope would certainly beat any new one who could be arrayed against him.

Do you ask me, how I think Catholicism may be most successfully opposed ? I know but one way. Spread just, natural, ennobling views of religion. Lift men above Catholicism, by showing them the great spiritual purpose of Christianity. Violence will avail nothing. Romanism cannot be burned down, like the convent at Charlestown. That outrage bound every Catholic faster to his church, and attracted to it the sympathies of the good. Neither is Popery to be subdued by virulence and abuse. The priest can call as hard names as the Protestant pastor. Neither do I think that any thing is to be gained by borrowing from the Catholic Church her forms, and similar means of influence. Borrowed forms are peculiarly formal. No sect will be benefited by forms which do not grow from its own spirit. A sect which has true life, will seize by instinct the emblems and rites, which are in accordance with itself; and, without life, it will only find in borrowed rites its winding-sheet. It is not uncommon to hear persons who visit Catholic countries, recommending the introduction of this or that usage of Romanism among ourselves. For example, they enter Catholic churches and see at all hours worshippers be-

fore one or another altar, and contrasting with this the
desertion of our houses of worship during the week,
doubt whether we are as pious; and wish to open the
doors of our sanctuaries, that Protestants may at all
hours approve themselves as devoted as the Papists.
Now such recommendations show a misconception of
the true foundation and spirit of Roman usages. In the
case before us, nothing is more natural than that Catholics should go to churches or public places to pray.
In the first place, in the southern countries of Europe,
where Catholicism first took its form, the people live in
public. They are an outdoor people. Their domestic
occupations go on in the outward air. That they should
perform their private devotions in public, is in harmony
with all their habits. What a violence it would be to
ours! In the next place, the Catholic believes that
the church has a peculiar sanctity. A prayer offered
from its floor finds its way to heaven more easily than
from any other spot. The pernicious superstition of
his religion carries him to do the work of his religion
in one consecrated place, and therefore he does it the
less elsewhere. Again: Catholic churches are attrac-
tive from the miraculous virtue ascribed to the images
which are worshipped there. Strange, monstrous as
the superstition is, yet nothing is more common in Catholic countries than the ascription of this or that supernatural agency to one or another shrine or statue. A
saint, worshipped at one place, or under one image, will
do more, than if worshipped elsewhere. I recollect
asking an Italian, why a certain church of rather humble appearance, in a large city, was so much frequented.
He smiled, and told me, that the Virgin, who was
adored there, was thought particularly propitious to

those who had bought tickets in the lottery. Once more, we can easily conceive why visiting the churches, for daily prayer, has been encouraged by the priesthood. The usage brought the multitude still more under priestly power, and taught them to associate their most secret aspirations of piety with the church. Who, that takes all these circumstances into consideration, can expect Protestants to imitate the Catholics in frequenting the church for secret devotion, or can wish it? Has not Jesus said, " When thou prayest, go into thy closet, and shut thy door, and pray to thy Father, who seeth in secret " ? Catholicism says, " When thou prayest, go into the public church, and pray before the multitude." Of the little efficacy of this worship we have too painful proofs. The worship of the churches of Italy is directed chiefly to the Virgin. She is worshipped as *the Virgin*. The great idea of this Catholic deity is purity, chastity; and yet, unless all travellers deceive us, the country where she is worshipped is disfigured by licentiousness, beyond all countries of the civilized world. I return to my position. We need borrow nothing from Catholicism. Episcopacy retained (did not borrow) as much of the ritual of that church as is wanted in the present age, for those among us who have Catholic propensities. Other sects, if they need forms, must originate them, and this they must do not mechanically, but from the promptings of the spiritual life, from a thirst for new modes of manifesting their religious hopes and aspirations. Woe to that church, which looks round for forms to wake it up to spiritual life. The dying man is not to be revived by a new dress, however graceful. The disease of a languid sect is too deep to be healed by ceremonies. It needs deeper modes of cure. Let it get life, and it will naturally create the emblems or rites which it needs to express and maintain its spiritual force.

The great instrument of influence and dominion in the Catholic Church, is one which we should shudder to borrow, but which may still give important hints as to the means of promoting religion. I refer to Confession. Nothing too bad can be said of this. By laying open the secrets of all hearts to the priest, it makes the priest the master of all. Still, to a good man it gives the power of doing good, a power, which, I doubt not, is often conscientiously used. It gives to the religious teacher an access to men's minds and conscience, such as the pulpit does not furnish. Instead of scattering generalities among the crowd, he can administer to each soul the very instruction, warn-, mg, encouragement it needs. In Catholic countries there is little preaching, nor is it necessary. The confessional is far more powerful than the pulpit. And what do we learn from this ? That Protestants should adopt confession ? No. But the question arises, whether the great principle of confession, that on which its power rests, viz. access to the individual mind, may not be used more than it is by Protestant teachers ; whether such access may not be gained by honorable and generous means, and so used as to be guarded against abuse. Preaching is now our chief reliance ; but preaching is an arrow which shoots over many heads, and flies wide of the hearts of more. Its aim is too vague to do much execution. It is melancholy to think how little clear knowledge on the subject of duty and religion, is communicated by the pulpit, and how often the emotion which it excites, for want of clear views, for want of wisdom, runs into morbidness or excess. - No art, no science is taught so vaguely as religion from the pulpit. No book is so read or expounded as the Bible is, that is, in minute fragments, and without those helps of method, by which all other branches are taught. Is not a freer, easier, opener communication with his pupils needed, than the minister does or can hold from the pulpit? Should not modes of teaching and intercourse be adopted, by which he can administer truth to different minds, according to their various capacities and wants. Must not he rely less on preaching, and more on more familiar communication.

This question becomes of more importance, because it is very plain that preaching is becoming less and less efficacious. Preaching is not what it was in the first age of Christianity. Then, when there was no printing, comparatively no reading, Christianity could only be spread by the living voice. Hence to preach became synonymous with teaching. It was the great means of access to the multitude. Now the press preaches incomparably more than the pulpit. Through this, all are permitted to preach. Woman, if she may not speak in the church, may speak from the printing room, and her touching expositions of religion, not learned in theological institutions, but in the schools of affection, of sorrow, of experience, of domestic change, sometimes make their way to the heart more surely than the minister's homilies. The result is, that preaching does not hold the place now, which it had in dark and unrefined ages. The minister addresses from his pulpit many as well educated as himself, and almost every parishioner has at home better sermons than he hears in public. The minister, too, has competitors in the laity, as they are called, who very wisely refuse to leave to him the monopoly of public speaking, and who are encroaching on his province more and more. In this altered condition of the world, the ministry is to undergo important changes. What they must be, I have not time now to inquire. I will only say, that the vagueness which belongs to so much religious instruction from the pulpit, must give place to a teaching which shall meet more the wants of the individual, and the wants of the present state of society. Great principles must be expounded in accommodation to different ages, capacities, stages of improvement, and an intercourse be established by which all classes may be helped to apply them to their own particular conditions. How shall Christianity be brought to bear on the individual, and on society at the present moment, in its present struggles ? This is the great question to be solved, and the reply to it will determine the form which the Christian ministry is to take. I imagine, that in seeking the solution of this problem, it will be discovered, that the ministry must have greater freedom than in past times. It will be discovered, that the individual minister must not be rigidly tied down to certain established modes of operation, that he must not be required to cast his preaching into the old mould, to circumscribe himself to the old topics, to keep in motion a machinery which others have invented, but that he will do most good if left to work according to his own nature, according to the promptings of the Holy Spirit within his own breast. I imagine it will be discovered, that, as justice may be administered without a wig, and the executive function without a crown or sceptre, so Christianity may be

24 *

administered in more natural and less formal ways than
-have prevailed, and that the minister, in growing less
technical, will find religion becoming, to himself and others, a more living reality. I imagine, that our present
religious organizations will silently melt away, and that
hierarchies will be found no more necessary for religion
than for literature, science, medicine, law, or the elegant and useful arts. But I will check these imagin-
ings. The point from which I started was, that Catholicism might teach us one element of an effectual ministry, that the Protestant teacher needs and should seek
access to the individual mind, beyond what he now
possesses; and the point at which I stop is, that this
access is to be so sought and so used, as not to in-
fringe religious liberty, the rights of private judgment,
the free action of the individual mind. Nothing but
this liberty can secure it from the terrible abuse to
which it has been exposed in the Catholic Church.

In the free remarks, which I have now made on
certain denominations of Christians, I have been in-
fluenced by no unkindness or disrespect towards the
individuals who compose them. In all sects I recognise joyfully true disciples of the common Master.
Catholicism boasts of some of the best and greatest
names in history, so does Episcopacy, so Presbyteri-
anism, &c. I exclude none. I know that Christianity
is mighty enough to accomplish its end in all. I cannot
however speak of religious, any more than of political
parties, without betraying the little respect I have for
them as parties. There is no portion of human history
more humbling than that of sects. When I meditate
on the grand moral, spiritual purpose of Christianity,
in which all its glory consists; when I consider how

plainly Christianity attaches importance to nothing but
to the moral excellence, the disinterested, divine virtue,
which was embodied in the teaching and life of its
founder ; and when from this position I look down on
the sects which have figured, and now figure in the
church ; when I see them making such a stir about
matters generally so unessential; when I see them seizing on a disputed and disputable doctrine, making it a
watch-word, a test of God's favor, a bond of communion, a ground of self-complacency, a badge of peculiar holiness, a warrant for condemning its rejectors,
however imbued with the spirit of Christ ; when I see
them overlooking the weightier matters of the law, and
laying infinite stress here on a bishop and prayer-book,
there on the quantity of water applied in baptism, and
there on some dark solution of an incomprehensible
article of faith ; when I see the mock dignity of their
exclusive claims to truth, to churchship, to the promises of God's word ; when I hear the mimic thunder-
bolts of denunciation and excommunication, which they
delight to hurl ; when I consider how their deep theology, in proportion as it is examined, evaporates into
words, how many opposite and extravagant notions are
covered by the same broad shield of mystery and tradition, and how commonly the persuasion of infallibility
is proportioned to the absurdity of the creed ; when I
consider these things, and other matters of like import,
I am lost in amazement at the amount of arrogant folly,
of self-complacent intolerance, of almost incredible blindness to the end and essence of Christianity, which the
history of sects reveals. I have indeed profound respect for individuals in all communions of Christians.
But on sects, and on the spirit of sects, I *must* be

allowed to look with grief, shame, pity, I had almost said, contempt. In passing these censures, I claim no superiority. I am sure there are thousands of all sects, who think and feel as I do in this particular, and who, far from claiming superior intelligence, are distinguished by following out the plain dictates, the natural impulses, and spontaneous judgments of conscience and common sense.

It is time for me to finish this letter, which indeed has grown under my hands beyond all reasonable bounds. But I must add a line or two in reply to your invitation to visit you. You say, that Kentucky will not exclude me for my opinions on slavery. I rejoice to hear it, not for my own sake, but for the sake of the country. I rejoice in a tolerant spirit, wherever manifested. What you say accords with what I have heard, of the frank, liberal character of Kentucky. All our accounts of the West make me desire to visit it. I desire to see nature under new aspects; but still more to see a new form of society. I hear of the defects of the West; but I learn that a man there feels himself to be a man, that he has a self-respect which is not always to be found in older communities, that he speaks his mind freely, that he acts more from generous impulses, and less from selfish calculations. These are good tidings. I rejoice that the intercourse between the East and West is increasing. Both will profit. The West may learn from us the love of order, the arts which adorn and cheer life, the institutions of education and religion, which lie at the foundation of our greatness, and may give us in return the energies and virtues which belong to and distinguish a fresher state of society. Such exchanges I regard as the most precious fruits of the Union, worth more than exchanges of products of industry, and they will do more, to bind us together as one people.

You press me to come and preach in your part of the country. I should do it cheerfully if I could. It would rejoice me to bear a testimony, however feeble, to great truths in your new settlements. I confess, however, that I fear, that my education would unfit me for great usefulness among you. I fear that the habits, rules, and criticisms, under which I have grown up, and almost grown old, have not left me the freedom and courage which are needed in the style of address best suited to the Western people. I have fought against these chains. I have labored to be a free man, but in the state of the ministry and of society here, freedom is a hard acquisition. I hope the rising generation will gain it more easily and abundantly than their fathers.

I have only to add, my young brother, my best wishes for your usefulness. I do not ask for you enjoyment. I ask for you something better and greater, something which includes it, even a spirit to live and die for a cause, which is dearer than your own enjoyment. If I were called to give you one rule, which your situation demands above all others, it would be this. Live a life of faith and hope. Believe in God's great purposes towards the human race. Believe in the mighty power of truth and love. Believe in the omnipotence of Christianity. Believe that Christ lived and died to breathe into his church and into society a diviner spirit than now exists. Believe in the capacities and greatness of human nature. Believe that the celestial virtue, re-

vealed in the life and teaching of Jesus Christ, is not
a bright vision for barren admiration, but is to become
a reality in your own and others' souls. Carry to your
work a trustful spirit. Do not waste your breath in
wailing over the times. Strive to make them better. Do
not be disheartened by evils. Feel through your whole
soul, that evil is not the mightiest power in the universe, that it is 'permitted only to call forth the energy
of love, wisdom, persuasion, and prayer for its removal. Settle it in your mind, that a minister can never
speak an effectual word without faith. Be strong in the
Lord and the power of his might. Allow me to say,
that I have a good hope of you. I learned some time
ago, from one of your dear friends, that you comprehended the grandeur of your work as a Christian minister. I learned that the pulpit, from which a divinely
moved teacher communicates everlasting truths, seemed
to you more glorious than a throne. I learned, that
you had come to understand what is the greatest power
which God gives to man, the power of acting generously on the soul of his brother; of communicating to
others a divine spirit, of awakening in others a heavenly
life, which is to outlive the stars. I then felt that you
would not labor in vain. You have indeed peculiar
trials. You are dwelling far from your brethren, but
there is a sense of God's presence more cheering than
the dearest human society. There is a consciousness
of working with God, more strengthening than all human coöperation. There is a sight, granted to the
pure mind, of the cross of Christ, which makes privations and sufferings in the cause of his truth seem
light, which makes us sometimes to rejoice in tribula-
tion, like the primitive heroes of our faith. My young

brother, I wish you these blessings. What else ought I to wish for you?

This letter, you will perceive, is written in great haste. The opinions indeed have been deliberately formed; but they probably might have been expressed with greater caution. If it will serve, in your judgment, the cause of truth, freedom, and religion, you are at liberty to insert it in your work.

Your sincere friend,

WILLIAM E. CHANNING.

EXTRACTS FROM A LETTER

ON

CREEDS.

ON CREEDS.

My aversion to human creeds as bonds of Christian union, as conditions of Christian fellowship, as means of fastening ´chains on men's minds, constantly gains strength.

My first objection to them is, that they separate us from Jesus Christ. To whom am I to go for my knowledge of the Christian religion, but to the Great Teacher, to the Son of God, to him in whom the fulness of the divinity dwelt. This is my great privilege as a Christian, that I may sit at the feet not of a human but divine master, that I may repair to him in whom truth lived and spoke without a mixture of error ; who was eminently the Wisdom of God and the light of the world. And shall man dare to interpose between me and my heavenly guide and Saviour, and prescribe to me the articles of my Christian faith ? What is the state of mind in which I shall best learn the truth ? It is that, in which I forsake all other teachers for Christ, in which my mind is brought nearest to him ; it is that in which I lay myself open most entirely to the impressions of his mind. Let me go to Jesus with a human voice sounding in my ears, and telling me what I must

hear from the Great Teacher, and how can I listen to
him in singleness of heart ?   All Protestant sects indeed tell the learner to listen to Jesus Christ ; but most
of them shout around him their own articles so vehemently and imperiously, that the voice of the heavenly
master is well nigh drowned.   He is told to listen to
Christ, but told that he will be damned, if he receives
any lessons but such as are taught in the creed.   He
is told that Christ's word is alone infallible, but that
unless it is received as interpreted by fallible men, he
will be excluded from the communion of Christians.
This is what shocks me in the creed-maker.   He inter-
poses himself between me and my Saviour.   He dares
not trust me alone with Jesus.   He dares not leave
me to the word of God.   This I cannot endure.   The
nearest possible communication with the mind of Christ,
is my great privilege as a Christian.   I must learn
Christ's truth from Christ himself, as he speaks in the
records of his life, and in the men whom he trained
up and supernaturally prepared to be his witnesses to
the world.   On what ground, I ask, do the creed-makers
demand assent to their articles as condition of church
membership or salvation ?   What has conferred on them
infallibility ?   " Show me your proofs," I say to them,
" of Christ speaking in you.   Work some miracle.
Utter some prophecy.   Show me something divine in
you, which other men do not possess.   Is it possible,
that you are unaided men, like myself, having no more
right to interpret the New Testament than myself, and
that you yet exalt your interpretations as infallible standards of truth, and the necessary conditions of salvation.   Stand out of my path.   I wish to go to the
master.   Have you words of greater power than his ?

Can you speak to the human conscience or heart in a mightier voice than he ? What is it which emboldens you to tell me what I must learn of Christ or be lost ? "

I cannot but look on human creeds with feelings approaching contempt. When I bring them into contrast with the New Testament, into what insignificance do they sink! What are they? Skeletons, freezing abstractions, metaphysical expressions of unintelligible dogmas ; and these I am to regard as the expositions of the fresh, living, infinite truth which came from Jesus ! I might with equal propriety be required to hear and receive the lispings of infancy as the expressions of wisdom. Creeds are to the Scriptures, what rush-lights are to the sun. The creed-maker defines Jesus in half a dozen lines, perhaps in metaphysical terms, and calls me to assent to this account of my Saviour. I learn less of Christ by this process, than I should learn of the sun, by being told that this glorious luminary is a circle about a foot in diameter. There is but one way of knowing Christ. We must place ourselves near him, see him, hear him, follow him from his cross to the heavens, sympathize with him and obey him, and thus catch clear and bright glimpses of his divine glory.

Christian Truth is Infinite. Who can think of shutting it up in a few lines of an abstract creed ? You might as well compress the boundless atmosphere, the fire, the all-pervading light, the free winds of the universe, into separate parcels, and weigh and label them, as break up Christianity into a few propositions. Christianity is freer, more illimitable, than the light or the winds. It is too mighty to be bound down by man's puny hands. It is a spirit rather than a rigid doctrine,

25 *

the spirit of boundless love. The Infinite cannot be defined and measured out like a human manufacture. It cannot be reduced to a system. It cannot be comprehended in a set of precise ideas. It is to be felt rather than described. The spiritual impressions which a true Christian receives from the character and teachings of Christ, and in which the chief efficacy of the religion lies, can be poorly brought out in words. Words are but brief, rude hints of a Christian's mind. His thoughts and feelings overflow them. To those who feel as he does, he can make himself known ; for such can understand the tones of the heart ; but he can no more lay down his religion in a series of abstract propositions, than he can make known in a few vague terms the expressive features and inmost soul of a much-loved friend. It has been the fault of all sects, that they have been too anxious to define their religion. They have labored to circumscribe the infinite. Christianity, as it exists in the mind of the true disciple, is not made up of fragments, of separate ideas which he can express in detached propositions. It is a vast and ever-unfolding whole, pervaded by one spirit, each precept and doctrine deriving its vitality from its union with all. When I see this generous, heavenly doctrine compressed and cramped in human creeds, I feel as I should were I to see screws and chains applied to the countenance and limbs of a noble fellow-creature, deforming and destroying one of the most beautiful works of God.

From the Infinity of Christian truth, of which I have spoken, it follows that our views of it must always be very imperfect, and ought to be continually enlarged. The wisest theologians are children who have caught but faint glimpses of the religion; who have taken but their first lessons; and whose business it is "to grow in the knowledge of Jesus Christ." Need I say how hostile to this growth is a fixed creed, beyond which we must never wander? Such a religion as Christ's demands the highest possible activity and freedom of the soul. Every new gleam of light should be welcomed with joy. Every hint should be followed out with eagerness. Every whisper of the divine voice in the soul should be heard. The love of Christian truth should be so intense, as to make us willing to part with all other things for a better comprehension of it. Who does not see that human creeds, setting bounds to thought, and telling us where all inquiry must stop, tend to repress this holy zeal, to shut our eyes on new illumination, to hem us within the beaten paths of man's construction, to arrest that perpetual progress which is the life and glory of an immortal mind.

It is another and great objection to creeds, that, wherever they acquire authority, they interfere with that simplicity and godly sincerity, on which the efficacy of religious teaching very much depends. That a minister should speak with power, it is important that he should speak from his own soul, and not studiously conform himself to modes of speaking which others have adopted. It is important that he should give out the truth in the very form in which it presents itself to his mind, in the very words which offer themselves spontaneously as the clothing of his thoughts. To express our own minds frankly, directly, fearlessly, is the way to reach other minds. Now it is the effect of creeds to check this free utterance of thought. The minister must seek words which will not clash with the consecrated articles of his church. If new ideas spring up in his mind, not altogether consonant with what the creed-monger has established, he must cover them with misty language. If he happen to doubt the standard of his church, he must strain its phraseology, must force it beyond its obvious import, that he may give his assent to it without departures from truth. All these processes must have a blighting effect on the mind and heart. They impair self-respect. They cloud the intellectual eye. They accustom men to tamper with truth. In proportion as a man dilutes his thought and suppresses his conviction, to save his orthodoxy from suspicion ; in proportion as he borrows his words from others, instead of speaking in his own tongue ; in proportion as he distorts language from its common use, that he may stand well with his party ; in that proportion he clouds and degrades his intellect, as well as undermines the manliness and integrity of his character. How deeply do I commiserate the minister, who, in the warmth and freshness of youth, is visited with glimpses of higher truth than is embodied in the creed, but who dares not be just to himself, and is made to echo what is not the simple, natural expression of his own mind ! Better were it for us to beg our bread and clothe ourselves in rags, than to part with Christian simplicity and frankness. Better for a minister to preach in barns or the open air, where he may speak the truth from the fulness of his soul, than to lift up in cathedrals, amidst pomp and wealth, a voice which is not true to his inward thoughts If they who wear the chains of creeds, once knew the happiness of breathing the air of freedom, and of moving with an unincumbered spirit, no wealth or power in the world's gift would bribe them to part with their spiritual liberty.

Another sad effect of creeds is, that they favor unbelief. It is not the object of a creed to express the simple truths of our religion, though in these its efficiency chiefly lies, but to embody and decree those mysteries about which Christians have been contending. I use the word "mysteries," not in the Scriptural but popular sense, as meaning doctrines which give a shock to the reason and seem to contradict some acknowledged truth. Such mysteries are the staples of creeds. The celestial virtues of Christ's character, these are not inserted into articles of faith. On the contrary, doctrines which from their darkness or unintelligibleness have provoked controversy, and which owe their importance very much to the circumstance of having been fought for or fought against for ages, these are thrown by the creed-makers into the foremost ranks of the religion, and made its especial representatives. Christianity as set forth in creeds is a propounder of dark sayings, of riddles, of knotty propositions, of apparent contradictions. Who, on reading these standards, would catch a glimpse of the simple, pure, benevolent, practical character of Christianity? And what is the result? Christianity becoming identified, by means of creeds, with so many dark doctrines, is looked on by many as a subject for theologians to quarrel about, but too thorny or perplexed for common minds, while it is spurned by many more as an insult on human reason, as a triumph of fanaticism over common sense.

It is a little remarkable that most creeds, whilst they abound in mysteries of human creation, have renounced the great mystery of religion. There is in religion a great mystery. I refer to the doctrine of Free-will or moral liberty. How to reconcile this with God's fore-knowledge and human dependence, is a question which has perplexed the greatest minds. It is probable that much of the obscurity arises from our applying to God the same kind of foreknowledge as men possess by their acquaintance with causes, and from our supposing the Supreme Being to bear the same relation to time as man. It is probable that juster views on these subjects will relieve the freedom of the will from some of its difficulties. Still the difficulties attending it are great. It is a mystery in the popular sense of the word. Now is it not strange that theologians who have made and swallowed so many other mysteries, have generally rejected this, and rejected it on the ground of objections less formidable than those which may be urged against their own inventions ? A large part of the Protestant world have sacrificed man's freedom of will to God's foreknowledge and sovereignty, thus virtually subverting all religion, all duty, all responsibility. They have made man a machine, and destroyed the great distinction between him and the brute. There seems a fatality attending creeds. After burdening Christianity with mysteries of which it is as innocent as the unborn child, they have generally renounced the real mystery of religion, of human nature. They have subverted the foundation of moral government, by taking from man the only capacity which makes him responsible, and in this way have fixed on the commands and threatenings of God the character of a cruel despotism. What a lesson against man's attempting to impose his wisdom on his fellow-creatures as the truth of God !

ADDRESS ON TEMPERANCE.

DELIVERED BY REQUEST OF THE

COUNCIL OF THE MASSACHUSETTS TEMPERANCE SOCIETY,

AT THE ODEON, BOSTON, FEBRUARY 28, 1837,

THE DAY APPOINTED FOR THE SIMULTANEOUS MEETING OF THE FRIENDS
OF TEMPERANCE THROUGHOUT THE WORLD.

ADDRESS ON TEMPERANCE.

I SEE before me the representatives of various societies for the promotion of temperance. It is a good and great cause, and I shall be grateful to God, if, by the service now allotted me, I can in any degree encourage them in their work, or throw new light on their path. The present occasion may well animate a Christian minister. What a noble testimony does this meeting bear to the spirit and influences of the Christian faith! Why is this multitude brought together? Not for selfish gratification, not for any worldly end, but for the purpose of arresting a great moral and social evil, of promoting the virtue, dignity, well-being of men. And whence comes this sympathy with the fallen, the guilty, the miserable? Have we derived it from the schools of ancient philosophy, or from the temples of Greece and Rome? No. We inherit it from Jesus Christ. We have caught it from his lips, his life, his cross. This meeting, were we to trace its origin, would carry us back to Bethlehem and Calvary. The impulse which Christ

gave to the human soul, having endured for ages, is now
manifesting itself more and more, in new and increasing
efforts of philanthropy for the redemption of the world
from every form of evil. Within these walls the authority of Christ has sometimes been questioned, his character traduced. To the blasphemer of that holy name,
what a reply is furnished by the crowd which these walls
now contain ! A religion, which thus brings and knits
men together, for the help, comfort, salvation of their
erring, lost fellow-creatures, bears on its front a broad,
bright, unambiguous stamp of Divinity. Let us be grateful that we were born under its light, and more grateful
still if we have been, in any measure, baptized into its
disinterested and divine love.

I cannot hope, in the present stage of the temperance
effort, to render any important aid to your cause by nov-
elty of suggestion. Its friends have thoroughly explored
the ground over which I am to travel. Still every man,
who is accustomed to think for himself, is naturally attracted to particular views or points in the most familiar
subject ; and, by concentrating his thoughts on these, he
sometimes succeeds in giving them a new prominence,
in vindicating their just rank, and in securing to them an
attention which they may not have received, but which
is their due.

On the subject of intemperance, I have sometimes
thought, perhaps without foundation, that its chief, essential evil was not brought out as thoroughly and frequently as its secondary evils, and that there was not a sufficient conviction of the depth of its causes and of the
remedies which it demands. With these impressions,
I invite your attention to the following topics : — the
great essential evil of intemperance, — the extent of its

temptations, — its causes, — the means of its prevention or cure.

I. I begin with asking, what is the great, essential evil of intemperance ? The reply is given, when I say, that intemperance is the *voluntary extinction of reason.* The great evil is inward or spiritual. The intemperate man divests himself, for a time, of his rational and moral nature, casts from himself self-consciousness and self-command, brings on phrensy, and, by repetition of this insanity, prostrates more and more his rational and moral powers. He sins immediately and directly against the rational nature, that divine principle, which distinguishes between truth and falsehood, between right and wrong action, which distinguishes man from the brute. This is the essence of the vice, what constitutes its peculiar guilt and woe, and what should particularly impress and awaken those who are laboring for its suppression. All the other evils of intemperance are light compared with this, and almost all flow from this ; and it is right, it is to be desired, that all other evils should be joined with and follow this. It is to be desired, when a man lifts a suicidal arm against his highest life, when he quenches reason and conscience, that he and all others should receive solemn, startling warning of the greatness of his guilt ; that terrible outward calamities should bear witness to the inward ruin which he is working ; that the hand-writing of judgment and woe on his countenance, form, and whole condition, should declare what a fearful thing it is for a man, God's rational offsprmg, to renounce his reason and become a brute. It is common for those who argue against intemperance, to describe the bloated countenance of the drunkard, now flushed and now deadly pale. They describe his trembling,

palsied limbs. They describe his waning prosperity,
his poverty, his despair. They describe his desolate,
cheerless home, his cold hearth, his scanty board, his
heart-broken wife, the squalidness of his children ; and
we groan in spirit over the sad recital. But it is right,
that all this should be. It is right, that he, who, fore-
warned, puts out the lights of understanding and conscience within him, who abandons his rank among
God's rational creatures, and takes his place among
brutes, should stand a monument of wrath among his
fellows, should be a teacher wherever he is seen, a
teacher, in every look and motion, of the awful guilt of
destroying reason. Were we so constituted, that reason
could be extinguished, and the countenance retain its
freshness, the form its grace, the body its vigor, the
outward condition its prosperity, and no striking change
be seen in one's home, so far from being gainers, we
should lose some testimonies of God's parental care.
His care and goodness, as well as his justice, are manifested in the fearful mark he has set on the drunkard, in
the blight which falls on all the drunkard's joys. These
outward evils, dreadful as they seem, are but faint types
of the ruin within. We should see in them God's respect to his own image in the soul, his parental warnings
against the crime of quenching the intellectual and
moral life.

We are too apt to fix our thoughts on the consequences or punishments of crime, and to overlook the
crime itself. This is not turning punishment to its highest use. Punishment is an outward sign of inward evil.
It is meant to reveal something more terrible than itself.
The greatness of punishment is a mode of embodying,
making visible, the magnitude of the crime to which it

is attached. The miseries of intemperance, its loath-
someness, ghastliness, and pains, are not seen aright,
if they do not represent to us the more fearful desolation wrought by this sin in the soul.

Among the evils of intemperance, much importance
is given to the poverty of which it is the cause. But
this evil, great as it is, is yet light in comparison with
the essential evil of intemperance, which I am so anxious to place distinctly before you. What matters it
that a man be poor, if he carry into his poverty the
spirit, energy, reason, and virtues of a Man? What
matters it that a man must, for a few years, live on
bread and water? How many of the richest are redue-
ed by disease to a worse condition than this? Honest,
virtuous, noble-minded poverty is a comparatively light
evil. The ancient philosopher chose it as the condition of virtue. It has been the lot of many a Christian.
The poverty of the intemperate man owes its great
misery to its cause. He who makes himself a beggar,
by having made himself a brute, is miserable indeed.
He who has no solace, who has only agonizing recollections and harrowing remorse, as he looks on his cold
hearth, his scanty table, his ragged children, has indeed
to bear a crushing weight of woe. That he suffers, is
a light thing. That he has brought on himself this suffering by the voluntary extinction of his reason, this is
the terrible thought, the intolerable curse.

We are told, that we must keep this or that man from
drunkenness, to save him from " coming on the town,"
from being a burden to the city. The motive is not to
be overlooked; but I cannot keep my thoughts fixed
for a moment on the few hundred or thousand dollars,
which the intemperate cost. When I go to the poor-

26 *

house, and see tne degradation, the spiritual weakness, the abjectness, the half-idiot imbecility written on the drunkard's countenance, I see a ruin which makes the cost of his support a grain of dust in the scale. I am not sorry that society is taxed for the drunkard. I would it were taxed more. I would the burden of sustaining him were so heavy, that we should be compelled to wake up, and ask how he may be saved from ruin. It is intended, wisely intended by God, that sin shall spread its miseries beyond itself, that no human being shall suffer alone, that the man who falls shall draw others with him, if not into his guilt, at least into a portion of his woe. If one member of the social body suffer, others must suffer too ; and this is well. This is one of the dependencies, by which we become interested in one another's moral safety, and are summoned to labor for the rescue of the fallen.

Intemperance is to be pitied and abhorred for its own sake, much more than for its outward consequences. These consequences owe their chief bitterness to their criminal source. We speak of the miseries which the drunkard carries into his family. But take away his own brutality, and how lightened would be these miseries. We talk of his wife and children in rags. Let the rags continue ; but suppose them to be the effects of an innocent cause. Suppose the drunkard to have been a virtuous husband, and an affectionate father, and that sickness, not vice, has brought his family thus low. Suppose his wife and children bound to him by a strong love, which a life of labor for their support, and of unwearied kindness has awakened ; suppose them to know that his toils for their welfare had broken down his frame ; suppose him able to say, " We are poor in this

world's goods, but rich in affection and religious trust.
I am going from you; but I leave you to the Father
of the fatherless and to the widow's God." Suppose
this, and how changed these rags! How changed the
cold, naked room! The heart's warmth can do much
to withstand the winter's cold; and there is hope, there
is honor in this virtuous indigence. What breaks the
heart of the drunkard's wife? It is not that he is poor,
but that he is a drunkard. Instead of that bloated face,
now distorted with passion, now robbed of every gleam
of intelligence, if the wife could look on an affectionate
countenance, which had for years been the interpreter
of a well principled mind and faithful heart, what an
overwhelming load would be lifted from her. It is a
husband, whose touch is polluting, whose infirmities are
the witnesses of his guilt, who has blighted all her hopes,
who has proved false to the vow which made her his;
it is such a husband who makes home a hell, not one
whom toil and disease and providence have cast on the
care of wife and children.

We look too much at the consequences of vice, too
little at the vice itself. It is vice, which is the chief
weight of what we call its consequence, vice which is
the bitterness in the cup of human woe.

II. I proceed now to offer some remarks on the
extent of temptations to this vice. And on this point,
I shall not avail myself of the statistics of intemperance. I shall not attempt to number its victims. I
wish to awaken universal vigilance, by showing that the
temptations to this excess are spread through all classes
of society. We are apt to speak as if the laborious,
uneducated, unimproved, were alone in danger, and as

if we ourselves had no interest in this cause, except as
others are concerned.   But-it is not so ; multitudes in
all classes are in danger.   In truth, when we recall the
sad histories of not a few in every circle, who once
stood among the firmest and then yielded to temptation,
we are taught, that none of us should dismiss fear, that
we too may be walking on the edge of the abyss.   The
young are exposed to intemperance, for youth wants
forethought, loves excitement, is apt to place happiness
in gayety, is prone to convivial pleasure, and too often
finds or makes this the path to hell; nor are the old
secure, for age unnerves the mind as well as the body,
and silently steals away the power of self-control.   The
idle are in scarcely less peril than the over-worked
laborer ; for uneasy cravings spring up in the vacant
mind, and the excitement of intoxicating draughts is
greedily sought as an escape from the intolerable weariness of having nothing to do.   Men of a coarse, unrefined character fall easily into intemperance, because
they see little in its brutality to disgust them.   It is a
sadder thought, that men of genius and sensibility are
hardly less exposed.   Strong action of the mind is
even more exhausting than the toil of the hands.   It
uses up, if I may so say, the finer spirits, and leaves
either a sinking of the system which craves for tonics,
or a restlessness which seeks relief in deceitful seda-
tives.   Besides, it is natural for minds of great energy,
to hunger for strong excitement ; and this, when not
found in innocent occupation and amusement, is too
often sought in criminal indulgence.   These remarks
apply peculiarly to men whose genius is poetical, imagi-
native, allied with, and quickened by, peculiar sensibility.   Such men, living in worlds of their own creation,

kindling themselves with ideal beauty and joy, and too
often losing themselves in reveries, in which imagination ministers to appetite, and the sensual triumphs over
the spiritual nature, are peculiarly in danger of losing
the balance of the mind, of losing calm thought, clear
judgment, and moral strength of will, become children
of impulse, learn to despise simple and common pleasures, and are hurried to ruin by a feverish thirst of high-
wrought, delirious gratification.   In such men, these
mental causes of excess are often aggravated by peculiar irritableness of the nervous system.   Hence the
records of literature are so sad.   Hence the brightest
lights of the intellectual world have so often undergone
disastrous eclipse ; and the inspired voice of genius, so
thrilling, so exalting, has died away in the brutal or idiot
cries of intemperance.   I have now been speaking of
the highest order of intellectual men ; but it may be
said of men of education in general, that they must not
feel themselves beyond peril.   It is said, that as large
a proportion of intemperate men can be found among
those, who have gone through our colleges, as among
an equal number of men in the same sphere of life,
who have not enjoyed the same culture.   It must not,
however, be inferred, that the cultivation of the intellect affords no moral aids.   The truth is, that its good
tendencies are thwarted.   Educated men fall victims to
temptation as often as other men, not because education
is inoperative, but because our public seminaries give
a partial training, being directed almost wholly to the
developement of the intellect, and very little to moral
culture, and still less to the invigoration of the physical
system.   Another cause of the evil is probably this,
that young men, liberally educated, enter on professions

which give at first little or no occupation, which expose them, perhaps for years, to the temptations of leisure, the most perilous in an age of inexperience and passion. Accordingly, the ranks of intemperance are recruited from that class which forms the chief hope of society. And I would I could stop here. But there is another prey on which intemperance seizes, still more to be deplored, and that is Woman. I know no sight on earth more sad, than woman's countenance, which once knew no suffusion but the glow of exquisite feeling, or the blush of hallowed modesty, crimsoned, deformed by intemperance. Even woman is not safe. The delicacy of her physical organization exposes her to inequalities of feeling, which tempt to the seductive relief given by cordials. Man with his iron nerves little knows what the sensitive frame of woman suffers, how many desponding imaginations throng on her in her solitudes, how often she is exhausted by unremitting cares, and how much the power of self-control is impaired by repeated derangements of her frail system. The truth should be told. In all our families, no matter what their condition, there are endangered individuals, and fear and watchfulness in regard to intemperance belong to all.

Do not say, that I exaggerate your exposure to intemperance. Let no man say, when he thinks of the drunkard, broken in health and spoiled of intellect, "I can never so fall." He thought as little of falling in his earlier years. The promise of his youth was as bright as yours; and even after he began his downward course, he was as unsuspicious as the firmest around him, and would have repelled as indignantly the admonition to beware of intemperance. The danger of this vice lies in its almost imperceptible approach. Few who perish by it know its first accesses. Youth does not see or suspect drunkenness in the sparkling beverage, which quickens all its susceptibilities of joy. The invalid does not see it in the cordial, which his physician prescribes, and which gives new tone to his debilitated organs. The man of thought and genius detects no palsying poison in the draught, which seems a spring of inspiration to intellect and imagination. The lover of social pleasure little dreams, that the glass, which animates conversation, will ever be drunk in solitude, and will sink him too low for the intercourse in which he now delights. Intemperance comes with noiseless step, and binds its first cords with a touch too light to be felt. This truth of mournful experience should be treasured up by us all, and should influence the habits and arrangements of domestic and social life in every class of the community.

Such is the extent of the temptations of this vice. It is true, however, that whilst its ravages may be traced through all conditions, they are chiefly to be found in the poorer and laboring portions of society. Here its crimes and woes swell to an amount which startles and appalls us. Here the evil is to be chiefly withstood. I shall, therefore, in my following remarks, confine myself very much to the causes and remedies of intemperance in this class of the community.

III. Among the causes of intemperance in the class of which I have spoken, not a few are to be found in the present state of society, which every man does something to confirm, and which brings to most of us many privileges. On these I shall now insist, because

they show our obligation to do what we can to remove
the evil.   It is just, that they who receive good, should
aid those who receive harm from our present social
organization.   Undoubtedly, the primary cause of intemperance is in the intemperate themselves, in their
moral weakness and irresolution, in the voluntary surrender of themselves to temptation.   Still, society, by
increasing temptation and diminishing men's power to
resist, becomes responsible for all wide-spread vices,
and is bound to put forth all its energy for their suppression.   This leads me to consider some of the causes
of intemperance, which have their foundation in our
social state.

One cause of the commonness of intemperance in
the present state of things, is the heavy burden of care
and toil which is laid on a large multitude of men.
Multitudes, to earn subsistence for themselves and their
families, are often compelled to undergo a degree of
labor exhausting to the spirits and injurious to health.
Of consequence, relief is sought in stimulants.   We do
not find that civilization lightens men's toils; as yet it
has increased them; and in this effect, I see the sign
of a deep defect in what we call the progress of society.
It cannot be the design of the Creator, that the whole
of life. should be spent in drudgery for the supply of
animal wants.   That civilization is very imperfect, in
which the mass of men can redeem no time from bodily
labor, for intellectual, moral, and social culture.   It
is melancholy to witness the degradation of multitudes
to the condition of beasts of burden.   Exhausting toils
unfit the mind to withstand temptation.   The man,
spent with labor, and cut off by his condition from
higher pleasures, is impelled to seek a deceitful solace

in sensual excess. How the condition of society shall be so changed as to prevent excessive pressure on any class, is undoubtedly a hard question. One thing seems plain, that there is no tendency in our present institutions and habits to bring relief. On the contrary, rich and poor seem to be more and more oppressed with incessant toil, exhausting forethought, anxious struggles, feverish competitions. Some look to legislation to lighten the burden of the laboring class. But equal laws and civil liberty have no power to remove the shocking contrast of condition which all civilized communities present. Inward, spiritual improvement, I believe, is the only sure remedy for social evils. What we need is a new diffusion of Christian, fraternal love, to stir up the powerful and prosperous to succour liberally and encourage the unfortunate or weak, and a new diffusion of intellectual and moral force, to make the multitude efficient for their own support, to form them to self-control, and to breathe a spirit of independence, which will seorn to ask or receive unnecessary relief.

Another cause, intimately connected with the last, is the intellectual depression and the ignorance to which many are subjected. They who toil from morning to night, without seasons of thought and mental improvement, are of course exceedingly narrowed in their faculties, views, and sources of gratification. The present moment, and the body, engross their thoughts. The pleasures of intellect, of imagination, of taste, of reading, of cultivated society, are almost entirely denied them. What pleasures but those of the senses remain? Unused to reflection and forethought, how dim must be their perceptions of religion and duty, and how little fitted are they to cope with temptation! Undoubtedly

in this country, this cause of intemperance is less operative than in others. There is less brutal ignorance
here than elsewhere ; but, on the other hand, the facilities of excess are incomparably greater, so that for
the uneducated, the temptation to vice may be stronger
in this than in less enlightened lands. Our outward
prosperity, unaccompanied with proportionate moral and
mental improvement, becomes a mighty impulse to intemperance, and this impulse the prosperous are bound
to withstand.

I proceed to another cause of intemperance among
the poor and laboring classes, and that is the general
sensuality and earthliness of the community. There is
indeed much virtue, much spirituality, in the prosperous
classes, but it is generally unseen. There is a vastly
greater amount in these classes of worldiness, of devotion to the senses, and this stands out in bold relief.
The majority live unduly for the body. Where there is
little intemperance in the common acceptation of that
term, there is yet a great amount of excess. Thousands, who are never drunk, place their chief happiness
in pleasures of the table. How much of the intellect
of this community is palsied, how much of the expression of the countenance blotted out, how much of the
spirit buried, through unwise indulgence ! What is the
great lesson, which the more prosperous classes teach to
the poorer ? Not self-denial, not spirituality, not the
great Christian truth, that human happiness lies in the
triumphs of the mind over the body, in inward force
and life. The poorer are taught by the richer, that the
greatest good is ease, indulgence. The voice which
descends from the prosperous, contradicts the lessons
of Christ and of sound philosophy. It is the sensuality,

the earthliness of those who give the tone to public sentiment, which is chargeable with a vast amount of the intemperance of the poor. How is the poor man to resist intemperance ? Only by a moral force, an energy of will, a principle of self-denial in his soul. And where is this taught him ? Does a higher morality come to him from those whose condition makes them his superiors ? The great inquiry which he hears among the better educated is, What shall we eat and drink, and wherewithal shall we be clothed ? Unceasing struggles for outward, earthly, sensual good, constitute the chief activity which he sees around him. To suppose that the poorer classes should receive lessons of luxury and self-indulgence from the more prosperous, and should yet resist the most urgent temptations to excess, is to expect from them a moral force, in which we feel ourselves to be sadly wanting. In their hard conflicts, how little of life-giving truth, of elevating thought, of heavenly aspiration, do they receive from those above them in worldly condition !

Another cause of intemperance, is the want of self-respect which the present state of society induces among the poor and laborious. Just as far as wealth is the object of worship, the measure of men's importance, the badge of distinction, so far there will be a tendency to self-contempt and self-abandonment among those whose lot gives them no chance of its acquisition. Such naturally feel as if the great good of life were denied them. They see themselves neglected. Their condition cuts them off from communication with the improved. They think they have little stake in the general weal. They do not feel as if they had a character to lose. Nothing reminds them of the greatness of their nature. Nothing teaches them, that in their obscure lot they may secure the highest good on earth. Catching from the general tone of society the ruinous notion, that wealth is honor as well as happiness, they see in their narrow lot nothing to inspire self-respect. In this delusion, they are not more degraded than the prosperous ; they but echo the voice of society ; but to them the delusion brings a deeper, immediate ruin. By sinking them in their own eyes, it robs them of a powerful protection against low vices.. It prepares them for coarse manners, for gross pleasures, for descent to brutal degradation. Of all classes of society, the poor should be treated with peculiar deference, as the means of counteracting their chief peril ; I mean, the loss of self-respect. But to all their other evil is added peculiar neglect. Can we then wonder that they fall ?

I might name other causes in our social constitution favoring intemperance ; but I must pass them, and will suggest one characteristic of our times, which increases all the tendencies to this vice. Our times are distinguished by what is called a love of excitement ; in other words, by a love of strong stimulants. To be stimulated, excited, is the universal want. The calmness, sobriety, plodding industry of our fathers, have been succeeded by a feverish restlessness. The books that are read are not the great, standard, immortal works of genius, which require calm thought, and inspire deep feeling ; but ephemeral works, which are run through with a railroad rapidity, and which give a pleasure not unlike that produced by exhilarating draughts. Business is become a race, and is hurried on by the excitement of great risks, and the hope of great profits. Even religion partakes the general restlessness. In some places, extravagant measures, which storm the nervous system, and drive the more sensitive to the borders of insanity, are resorted to for its promotion. Everywhere people go to church to be excited rather than improved. This thirst for stimulants cannot be shut up in certain spheres. It spreads through and characterizes the community. It pervades those classes, who, unhappily, can afford themselves but one strong stimulus, intoxicating liquor ; and among these, the spirit of the age breaks out in intemperance.

IV. I have now set before you some of the causes of intemperance in our present social state ; and this I have done that you may feel that society, in all its ranks, especially in the highest, is bound in justice to resist the evil ; and not only justice, but benevolence pleads with us to spare no efforts for its prevention or cure. The thought that in the bosom of our society, are multitudes standing on the brink of perdition, multitudes who are strongly tempted to debase and destroy their rational nature, to sink into brutal excess, to seal their ruin in this world and in the world to come, ought to weigh on us as a burden, ought to inspire deeper concern than the visitation of pestilence, ought to rouse every man who has escaped this degradation, to do what he may to rescue the fallen, and still more, to save the falling.

The question now comes, how shall we arrest, how suppress, this great evil ? Such is our last inquiry, and to this I answer, there are two modes of action. To rescue men, we must act on them inwardly or outwardly. We must either give them strength within to withstand the temptations to intemperance, or we must remove these temptations without. We must increase the power of resistance, or diminish the pressure which is to be resisted. Both modes of influence are useful, but the first incalculably the most important. No man is safe against this foe, but he who is armed with moral force, with strength in his own soul, with the might of principle, and a virtuous will. The great means, then, of repressing intemperance in those portions of society which are most exposed to it, is to communicate to them, or awaken in them, moral strength, the power of self-denial, a nobler and more vigorous action of conscience and religious principle. In other words, to save the laboring and poor from intemperance, we must set in action amongst them, the means of intellectual, moral, and religious improvement. We must strive to elevate them as rational and moral beings, to unfold their highest nature. It is idle to think, that, whilst these classes remain the same in other respects, they can be cured of intemperance. Intemperance does not stand alone in their condition and character. It is a part or sign of general degradation. It can only be effectually removed by exalting their whole character and condition. To heal a diseased limb or organ, you must relieve and strengthen the whole body. So it is with the mind. We cannot, if we would, remove those vices from the poor, which are annoying to ourselves, and leave them, in other respects, as corrupt as before. Nothing but a general improvement of their nature, can fortify them against the crimes which make them scourges alike to themselves and to their race.

And how may moral strength, force of principle, be communicated to the less prosperous classes of society? I answer first, the surest means is, to increase it among the more favored. All classes of a community have connexions, sympathies. Let selfishness and sensuality reign among the prosperous and educated, and the poor and uneducated will reflect these vices in grosser forms. That man is the best friend to temperance among high and low, whose character and life express clearly and strongly moral energy, self-denial, superiority to the body, superiority to wealth, elevation of sentiment and principle. The greatest benefactor to society is not he who serves it by single acts, but whose general character is the manifestation of a higher life and spirit than pervades the mass. Such men are the salt of the earth. The might of individual virtue surpasses all other powers. The multiplication of individuals of true force and dignity of mind, would be the surest of all omens of the suppression of intemperance in every condition of society.

Another means is, the cultivation of a more fraternal intercourse than now exists between the more and less improved portions of the community. Our present social barriers and distinctions, in so far as they restrict sympathy, and substitute the spirit of caste, the bigotry of rank, for the spirit of humanity, for reverence of our common nature, ought to be reprobated as gross violations of the Christian law. Those classes of society which have light, strength, and virtue, are bound to communicate these to such as want them. The weak, ignorant, falling and fallen, ought not to be cut off from their more favored brethren, ought not to be left to act continually and exclusively on one another, and thus to propagate their crimes and woes without end. The good should form a holy conspiracy against evil, should assail it by separate and joint exertion, should approach it, study it, weep and pray over it, and throw all their souls into efforts for its removal. My friends, you whom God has prospered, whom he has enlightened, in whose hearts he has awakened a reverence for himself, what are you doing for the fallen, the falling, the miserable of your race ? When an improved Christian thinks of the mass of unpited, unfriended guilt in this city, must he not be shocked at the hardness of all our hearts ? Are we not all of one blood, one nature, one heavenly descent ; and are outward distinctions, which to-morrow are to be buried for ever in the tomb, to divide us from one another, to cut off the communications of brotherly sympathy and aid ? In a Christian community, not one human being should be left to fall, without counsel, remonstrance, sympathy, encouragement, from others more enlightened and virtuous than himself. Say not this cannot be done. I know it cannot be done without great changes in our habits, views, feelings ; but these changes must be made. A new bond must unite the scattered portions of men. A new sense of responsibility must stir up the enlightened, the prosperous, the virtuous. Christianity demands this. The progress of society demands it. I see blessed omens of this, and they are among the brightest features of our times.

Again, to elevate and strengthen the more exposed classes of society, it is indispensable that a Higher Education should be afforded them. We boast of the means of education afforded to the poorest here. It may be said with truth, in regard to both rich and poor, that these means are very deficient. As to moral education, hardly any provisions are made for it in our public schools. To educate is something more than to teach those elements of knowledge which are needed to get a subsistence. It is to exercise and call out the higher faculties and affections of a human being. Education is not the authoritative, compulsory, mechanical training of passive pupils, but the influence of gifted and quickening minds on the spirits of the young. Such education is, as yet, sparingly enjoyed, and cannot be too fervently desired. Of what use, let me ask, is the wealth of this community, but to train up a better generation than ourselves ? Of what use, I ask, is freedom, except to call forth the best powers of all classes and of every individual ? What, but human improvement, is the great end of society ? Why ought we to sustain so anxiously republican institutions, if they do not tend to form a nobler race of men, and to spread nobleness through all conditions of social life ? It is a melancholy and prevalent error among us, that persons in the laboring classes are denied by their conditions any considerable intellectual improvement. They must live, it is thought, to work, not to fulfil the great end of a human being, which is to unfold his divinest powers and affections. But it is not so. The poorest child might, and ought to have liberal means of self-improvement; and were there a true reverence among us for human nature and for Christianity, he would find them. In a letter, recently received from a most intelligent traveller in Germany, I am informed, that in certain parts of that country, there is found, in the most depressed classes, a degree of intellectual culture, not generally supposed to consist with their lot ; that a sense of the beautiful in nature and art produces much happiness in a portion of society, which among us is thought to be disqualified for this innocent and elevated pleasure ; that the teaching in Sunday schools is in some places more various than

here, and that a collection of books, and a degree of
scientific knowledge may be met in cottages far inferior
to the dwellings of our husbandmen. " In short," my
friend adds, " I have seen abundant proof, that intellectual culture, as found here, spreads its light and comfort through a class, that hardly exists at all with us, or,
where it does exist, is generally supposed to labor under
a degree of physical wretchedness inconsistent with such
culture." Information of this kind should breathe new
hope into philanthropic labors for the intellectual and
moral life of every class in society. How much may
be done in this city to spread knowledge, vigor of
thought, the sense of beauty, the pleasures of the imagination and the fine arts, and, above all, the influences of
religion, through our whole community! Were the
prosperous and educated to learn, that, after providing
for their families, they cannot better employ their possessions and influence, than in forwarding the improvement and elevation of society, how soon would this city
be regenerated! How many generous spirits might be
enlisted here by a wise bounty in the work of training
their fellow-creatures! Wealth cannot be better used,
than in rescuing men of vigorous and disinterested minds
from worldly toils and cares, in giving them time and
opportunity for generous self-culture, and in enabling
them to devote their whole strength and being to a like
culture of their race. The surest mark of a true civilization is, that the arts which minister to sensuality decrease, and spiritual employments are multiplied, or that
more and more of the highest ability in the state is
withdrawn from labors for the animal life, and consecrated to the work of calling forth the intellect, the
imagination, the conscience, the pure affections, the

moral energy of the community at large, and especially of the young. What is now wasted among us in private show and luxury, if conscientiously and wisely devoted to the furnishing of means of generous culture to all classes among us, would render this city the wonder and joy of the whole earth. What is thus wasted might supply not only the means of education in the sciences, but in the refined arts. Music might here be spread as freely as in Germany, and be made a lightener of toil, a cheerer of society, a relief of loneliness, a solace in the poorest dwellings. Still more, what we now waste would furnish this city, in a course of years, with the chief attractions of Paris, with another Louvre, and with a Garden of Plants, where the gifted of all classes might have opportunity to cultivate the love of nature and art. Happily, the cause of a higher education begins to find friends here. Thanks to that enlightened and noble-minded son of Boston, whose ashes now slumber on a foreign shore, but who has left to his birthplace a testimony of filial love, in his munificent bequest for the diffusion of liberal instruction through this metropolis. Honored be the name of Lowell, the intellectual benefactor of his native city! A community, directing its energies chiefly to a higher education of its rising members, to a generous developement of human nature, would achieve what as yet has not entered human thought; and it is for this end, that we ought to labor. Our show, and our luxury, how contemptible in comparison with the improvement of our families, neighbourhood, and race!

Allow me here to express an earnest desire, that our legislators, provoked to jealousy by the spirit of improvement in other states, and moved by zeal for the ancient honor of this Commonwealth, may adopt some strong measures for the advancement of education among us. We need an institution for the formation of better teachers ; and, until this step is taken, we can make no important progress. The most crying want in this Commonwealth is the want of accomplished teachers. We boast of our schools ; but our schools do comparatively little, for want of educated instructors. Without good teaching, a school is but a name. An institution for training men to train the young, would be a fountain of living waters, sending forth streams to refresh present and future ages. As yet, our legislators have denied to the poor and laboring classes this principal means of their elevation. We trust they will not always prove blind to the highest interest of the state.

We want better teachers and more teachers for all classes of society, for rich and poor, for children and adults. We want that the resources of the community should be directed to the procuring of better instructors, as its highest concern. One of the surest signs of the regeneration of society will be, the elevation of the art of teaching to the highest rank in the community. When a people shall learn, that its greatest benefactors and most important members are men devoted to the liberal instruction of all its classes, to the work of raising to life its buried intellect, it will have opened to itself the path of true glory. This truth is making its way. Socrates is now regarded as the greatest man in an age of great men. The name of King has grown dim before that of Apostle. To teach, whether by word or action, is the highest function on earth. It is commonly supposed, that instructors are needed only in the earlier years of life. But ought the education of a human being ever to cease? And may it not always be forwarded by good instruction? Some of us, indeed, can dispense with all teachers save the silent book. But to the great majority, the voice of living teachers is an indispensable means of cultivation. The discovery and supply of this want would give a new aspect to a community. Nothing is more needed, than that men of superior gifts and of benevolent spirit, should devote themselves to the instruction of the less enlightened classes in the great end of life, in the dignity of their nature, in their rights and duties, in the history, laws, and institutions of their country, in the philosophy of their employments, in the laws, barmonies, and productions of outward nature, and especially, in the art of bringing up children in health of body, and in vigor and purity of mind. We need a new profession or vocation, the object of which shall be to wake up the intellect in those spheres where it is now buried in habitual slumber. We honor, and cannot too much honor the philanthropist, who endows permanent institutions for the relief of human suffering; but not less good, I apprehend, would be accomplished by inquiring for and seizing on men of superior ability and disinterestedness, and by sending them forth to act immediately on society. A philanthropist, who should liberally afford to one such man the means of devoting himself to the cultivation of the poorer classes of society, would confer invaluable good. One gifted man, with his heart in the work, who should live among the uneducated, to spread useful knowledge and quickening truth, by conversation and books, by frank and friendly intercourse, by encouraging meetings for improvement, by forming the more teachable into classes, and giving to these the animation of his presence and guidance, by bringing parents to an acquaintance with the principles of physical, intellectual, and moral education, by instructing families in the means and conditions of health, by using, in a word, all the methods which an active, generous mind would discover or invent for awakening intelligence and moral life ; one gifted man, so devoted, might impart a new tone and spirit to a considerable circle ; and what would be the result, were such men to be multiplied and combined, so that a community might be pervaded by their influence ? We owe much to the writings of men of genius, piety, science, and exalted virtue. But most of these remain shut up in narrow spheres. We want a class of liberal instructors, whose vocation it shall be to place the views of the most enlightened minds within the reach of a more and more extensive portion of their fellow-creatures. The wealth of a community should flow out like water for the preparation and employment of such teachers, for enlisting powerful and generous minds in the work of giving impulse to their race. Jesus Christ in instituting the ministry, laid the foundation of the intellectual and moral agency which I now urge. On this foundation we ought to build more and more, until a life-giving influence shall penetrate all classes of society. What a painful thought is it, that such an immense amount of intellectual and moral power, of godlike energy, is this very moment lying dead among us ! Can we do nothing for its resurrection ? Until this be done, we may lop off the branches of intemperance ; but its root will live ; and happy shall we be if its poisonous shade do not again darken our land. — Let it not be said that the laborious can find no time for such instruction as is now proposed. More or less leisure, if sought, can be found in almost every life. Nor let it be said that men, able and disposed to carry on this work, must not be looked for in such a world as ours. Christianity, which has wrought so many miracles of beneficence, which has sent forth so many apostles and martyrs, so many Howards and Clarksons, can raise up laborers for this harvest also. Nothing is needed but a new pouring out of the spirit of Christian love, nothing but a new comprehension of the brotherhood of the human race, to call forth efforts which seem impossibilities in a self-seeking and self-indulging age.

I will add but one more means of giving moral power and general improvement to those portions of the community, in which intemperance finds its chief victims. We must not only promote education in general, but especially send among them Christian instruction, Christian teachers, who shall be wholly devoted to their spiritual welfare. And here, I cannot but express my joy at the efforts made for establishing a ministry among the poor in this and other cities. Though not sustained as it should be, it yet subsists in sufficient vigor to show what it can accomplish. I regard this institution, as among the happiest omens of our times. It shows, that the spirit of him who came to seek and to save that which was lost, is not dead among us. Christianity is the mighty power before which intemperance is to fall. Christianity, faithfully preached, assails and withstands this vice, by appealing, as nothing else can, to men's hopes and fears, by speaking to the conscience in the name of the Almighty Judge, by speaking to the heart in the name of the Merciful Father, by proffering strength to human weakness and pardon to human guilt, by revealing to men an immortal nature within, and an eternal state before them, by spreading over this life a brightness borrowed from the life to come, by awakening geneious affections, and binding man by new ties to God and his race. But Christianity, to fulfil this part of its mission, to reach those who are most exposed to intemperance, must not only speak in the churches, where these are seldom found, but must enter their dwellings in the persons of its ministers, must commune with them in the language of friendship, must take their children under its guardianship and control. The ministry for the poor, sustained by men worthy of the function, will prove one of the most powerful barriers ever raised against intemperance.

The means of suppressing this vice, on which I have hitherto insisted, have for their object to strengthen and elevate the whole character of the classes most exposed to intemperance. I would now suggest a few means fitted to accomplish the same end, by diminishing or removing the temptations to this vice.

The first means, which I shall suggest of placing a people beyond the temptations to intemperance, is to furnish them with the means of innocent pleasure. This topic, I apprehend, has not been sufficiently insisted on. I feel its importance and propose to enlarge upon it, though some of the topics which I may introduce may seem to some hardly consistent with the gravity of this occasion. We ought not, however, to respect the claims of that gravity which prevents a faithful exposition of what may serve and improve our fellow-creatures.

I have said, a people should be guarded against temptation to unlawful pleasures, by furnishing the means of innocent ones. By innocent pleasures I mean such as excite moderately; such as produce a cheerful frame of mind, not boisterous mirth ; such as refresh, instead of exhausting, the system ; such as occur frequently, rather than continue long ; such as send us back to our daily duties, invigorated in body and in spirit ; such as we can partake in the presence and society of respectable friends ; such as consist with, and are favorable to, a grateful piety ; such as are chastened by self-respect, and are accompanied with the consciousness that life has a higher end than to be amused. In every community there *must* be pleasures, relaxations, and means of agreeable excitement ; and if innocent ones are not furnished, resort will be had to criminal. Man was made to enjoy, as well as to labor ; and the state of society should be adapted to this principle of human nature. France, especially before the revolution, has been represented as a singularly temperate country ; a fact to be explained, at least in part, by the constitutional cheerfulness of that people, and by the prevalence of simple and innocent gratifications, especially among the peasantry. Men drink to excess very often to shake off depression, or to satisfy the restless thirst for agreeable excitement, and these motives are excluded in a cheerful community. A gloomy state of society, in which there are few innocent recreations, may be expected to abound in drunkenness, if opportunities are afforded. The savage drinks to excess, because his hours of sobriety are - dull and unvaried, because, in losing the consciousness of his condition and his existence, he loses little which he wishes to retain. The laboring classes are most exposed to intemperance, because they have at present few other pleasurable excitements. A

28 *

man, who, after toil, has resources of blameless recreation is less tempted than other men to seek self-oblivion. He has too many of the pleasures of a man, to take up with those of a brute. Thus, the encouragement of simple, innocent enjoyments is an important means of temperance.

These remarks show the importance of encouraging the efforts, which have commenced among us, for spreading the accomplishment of Music through our whole community. It is now proposed that this shall be made a regular branch in our schools; and every friend of the people must wish success to the experiment. I am not now called to speak of all the good influences of music, particularly of the strength which it may and ought to give to the religious sentiment, and to all pure and generous emotions. Regarded merely as a refined pleasure, it has a favorable bearing on public morals. Let taste and skill in this beautiful art be spread among us, and every family will have a new resource. Home will gain a new attraction. Social intercourse will be more cheerful, and an innocent public amusement will be furnished to the community. Public amusements, bringing multitudes together to kindle with one emotion, to share the same innocent joy, have a humanizing influence; and among these bonds of society, perhaps no one produces so much unmixed good as music. What a fulness of enjoyment has our Creator placed within our reach, by surrounding us with an atmosphere which may be shaped into sweet sounds? And yet this goodness is almost lost upon us, through want of culture of the organ by which this provision is to be enjoyed.

Dancing is an amusement, which has been discour-

aged in our country by many of the best people, and
not without reason. Dancing is associated in their
minds with balls ; and this is one of the worst forms of
social pleasure. The time consumed in preparation for
a ball, the waste of thought upon it, the extravagance
of dress, the late hours, the exhaustion of strength, the
exposure of health, and the languor of the succeeding
day,—these and other evils, connected with this amusement, are strong reasons for banishing it from the community. But dancing ought not therefore to be proscribed. On the contrary, balls should be discouraged
for this among other reasons, that dancing, instead of
being a rare pleasure, requiring elaborate preparation,
may become an every-day amusement, and may mix
with our common intercourse. This exercise is among
the most healthful. The body as well as the mind
feels its gladdening influence. No amusement seems
more to have a foundation in our nature. The animation
of youth overflows spontaneously in harmonious movements. The true idea of dancing entitles it to favor. Its
end is, to realize perfect grace in motion ; and who does
not know, that a sense of the graceful is one of the
higher faculties of our nature ? It is to be desired,
that dancing should become too common among us to
be made the object of special preparation as in the ball ;
that members of the same family, when confined by
unfavorable weather, should recur to it for exercise and
exhilaration ; that branches of the same family should
enliven in this way their occasional meetings ; that it
should fill up an hour in all the assemblages for relaxation, in which the young form a part. It is to be desired, that this accomplishment should be extended to
the laboring classes of society, not only as an inno-

cent pleasure, but as a means of improving the manners. Why shall not gracefulness be spread through the whole community ? From the French nation, we learn, that a degree of grace and refinement of manners may pervade all classes. The philanthropist and Christian must desire to break down the partition-walls between human beings in different conditions ; and one means of doing this is, to remove the conscious awkwardness, which confinement to laborious occupations is apt to induce. An accomplishment, giving free and graceful movement, though a far weaker bond than intellectual or moral culture, still does something to bring those who partake it, near each other.

I approach another subject, on which a greater variety of opinion exists than on the last, and that is the Theatre. In its present state, the theatre deserves no encouragement. It is an accumulation of immoral influences. It has nourished intemperance and all vice. In saying this, I do not say that the amusement is radically, essential evil. I can conceive of a theatre, which would be the noblest of all amusements, and would take a high rank among the means of refining the taste and elevating the character of a people. The deep woes, the mighty and terrible passions, and the sublime emotions of genuine tragedy, are fitted to thrill us with human sympathies, with profound interest in our nature, with a consciousness of what man can do and dare and suffer, with an awed feeling of the fearful mysteries of life. The soul of the spectator is stirred from its depths ; and the lethargy, in which so many live, is roused, at least for a time, to some intenseness of thought and sensibility. The drama answers a high purpose, when it places us in the presence of the most

solemn and striking events of human history, and lays
bare to us the human heart in its most powerful, ap-
palling, glorious workings. But how little does the
theatre accomplish its end? How often is it disgraced
by monstrous distortions of human nature, and still
more disgraced by profaneness, coarseness, indelicacy,
low wit, such as no woman, worthy of the name, can
hear without a blush, and no man can take pleasure in
without self-degradation. Is it possible, that a Christian and a refined people can resort to theatres, where
exhibitions of dancing are given fit only for brothels,
and where the most licentious class in the community
throng unconcealed to tempt and destroy? That the
theatre should be suffered to exist in its present degradation is a reproach to the community. Were it to fall,
a better drama might spring up in its place. In the
mean time, is there not an amusement, having an affinity with the drama, which might be usefully introduced
among us? I mean, Recitation. A work of genius,
recited by a man of fine taste, enthusiasm, and powers
of elocution, is a very pure and high gratification.
Were this art cultivated and encouraged, great numbers, now insensible to the most beautiful compositions,
might be waked up to their excellence and power. It
is not easy to conceive of a more effectual way of
spreading a refined taste through a community. The
drama, undoubtedly, appeals more strongly to the passions than recitation; but the latter brings out the meaning of the author more. Shakspeare, worthily recited,
would be better understood than on the stage. Then,
in recitation, we escape the weariness of listening to
poor performers, who, after all, fill up most of the time
at the theatre. Recitation, sufficiently varied, so as to

include pieces of chaste wit, as well as of pathos, beauty, and sublimity, is adapted to our present intellectual progress, as much as the drama falls below it. Should this exhibition be introduced among us successfully, the result would be, that the power of recitation would be extensively called forth, and this would be added to our social and domestic pleasures.

I have spoken in this discourse of intellectual culture, as a defence against intemperance, by giving force and elevation to the mind. It also does great good as a source of amusement; and on this ground should be spread through the community. A cultivated mind may be said to have infinite stores of innocent gratification. Every thing may be made interesting to it, by becoming a subject of thought or inquiry. Books, regarded merely as a gratification, are worth more than all the luxuries on earth. A taste for literature secures cheerful occupation for the unemployed and languid hours of life; and how many persons, in these hours, for want of innocent resources, are now impelled to coarse and brutal pleasures. How many young men can be found in this city, who, unaccustomed to find a companion in a book, and strangers to intellectual activity, are almost driven, in the long, dull evenings of winter, to haunts of intemperance, and depraving society. It is one of the good signs of the times, that lectures on literature and science are taking their place among our public amusements, and attract even more than theatres. This is one of the first fruits of our present intellectual culture. What a harvest may we hope for from its wider diffusion !

In these remarks, I have insisted on the importance of increasing innocent gratifications in a community.

Let us become a more cheerful, and we shall become a more temperate people. To increase our susceptibility of innocent pleasure, and to remove many of the sufferings which tempt to evil habits, it would be well if physical, as well as moral education were to receive greater attention. There is a puny, half-healthy, half-diseased state of the body, too common among us, which, by producing melancholy and restlessness, and by weakening the energy of the will, is a strong incitement to the use of hurtful stimulants. Many a case of intemperance has had its origin in bodily infirmity. Physical vigor is not only valuable for its own sake, but it favors temperance, by opening the mind to cheerful impressions, and by removing those indescribable feelings of sinking, disquiet, depression, which experience alone can enable you to understand. I have pleaded for mental culture ; but nothing is gained by sacrificing the body to the mind. Let not intellectual education be sought at the expense of health. Let not our children in their early years be instructed, as is too common, in close, unventilated rooms, where they breathe for hours a tainted air. Our whole nature must be cared for. We must become a more cheerful, animated people ; and for this end we must propose, in our systems of education, the invigoration of both body and mind.

I am aware, that the views now expressed may not find unmixed favor with all the friends of temperance. To some, perhaps to many, religion and amusement seem mutually hostile, and he, who pleads for the one, may fall under suspicion of unfaithfulness to the other. But to fight against our nature, is not to serve the cause of piety or sound morals. God, who gave us our nature, who has constituted body and mind incapable of continued effort, who has implanted a strong desire for recreation after labor, who has made us for smiles much more than for tears, who has made laughter the most contagious of all sounds, whose Son hallowed a marriage feast by his presence and sympathy, who has sent the child fresh from his creating hand to develope its nature by active sports, and who has endowed both young and old with a keen susceptibility of enjoyment from wit and humor, — He, who has thus formed us, cannot have intended us for a dull, monotonous life, and cannot frown on pleasures which solace our fatigue and refresh our spirits for coming toils. It is not only possible to reconcile amusement with duty, but to make it the means of more animated exertion, more faithful attachments, more grateful piety. True religion is at once authoritative and benign. It calls us to suffer, to die, rather than to swerve a hair's breadth from what God enjoins as right and good; but it teaches us, that it is right and good, in ordinary circumstances, to unite relaxation with toil, to accept God's gifts with cheerfulness, and to lighten the heart, in the intervals of exertion, by social pleasures. A religion, giving dark views of God, and infusing superstitious fear of innocent enjoyment, instead of aiding sober habits, will, by making men abject and sad, impair their moral force, and prepare them for intemperance as a refuge from depression or despair.

Two other means remain to be mentioned, for re moving the temptations to intemperance, and these are, the discouragement of the use and the discouragement of the sale of ardent spirits in the community.

First, we should discourage the use of ardent spirits in the community. It is very plain, too plain to be insisted on, that to remove what intoxicates, is to remove intoxication. In proportion as ardent spirits are banished from our houses, our tables, our hospitalities, in proportion as those who have influence and authority in the community, abstain themselves, and lead their dependents to abstain from their use, in that proportion, the occasions of excess must be diminished, the temptations to it must disappear. It is objected, I know, that, if we begin to give up what others will abuse, we must give up every thing, because there is nothing which men will not abuse. I grant, that it is not easy to define the limits at which concessions are to stop. Were we called on to relinquish an important comfort of life, because others were perverting it into an instrument of crime and woe, we should be bound to pause and deliberate before we act. But no such plea can be set up in the case before us. Ardent spirits are not an important comfort, and in no degree a comfort. They give no strength; they contribute nothing to health; they can be abandoned without the slightest evil. They aid men neither to bear the burden nor to discharge the duties of life; and in saying this, I stop short of the truth. It is not enough to say, that they never do good; they generally injure. In their moderate use, they act, in general, unfavorably on body and mind. According to respectable physicians, they are not digested like food, but circulate unchanged like a poison through the system. Like other poisons, they may occasionally benefit as medicines; but when made a beverage by the healthy, they never do good; they generally are pernicious. They are no more intended by Providence for drink, than opium is designed for food. Consider next, that ardent spirits are not only without benefit, when

moderately used, but that they instigate to immoderate
use ; that they beget a craving, a feverish thirst, which
multitudes want power to resist ; that in some classes
of society, great numbers become their victims, are bereft by them of reason, are destroyed in body and soul,
destroyed here and hereafter ; that families are thus
made desolate, parents hurried to a premature grave,
and children trained up to crime and shame. Consider
all this, and then judge, as in the sight of God, whether
you are not bound to use your whole influence in banishing the use of spirits, as one of the most pernicious
habits, from the community. If you were to see, as
a consequence of this beverage, a loathsome and mor-
tal disease breaking out occasionally in all ranks, and
sweeping away crowds in the most depressed portion
of society, would you not lift up your voices against it ;
and is not an evil more terrible than pestilence, the actual, frequent result of the use of spirituous liquors ?
That use you are bound to discourage ; and how ? By
abstaining wholly yourselves, by excluding ardent spirits
wholly from your tables, by giving your whole weight
and authority to abstinence. This practical, solemn
testimony, borne by the good and respectable, cannot
but spread a healthful public sentiment through the whole
community. This is especially our duty at the present
moment, when a great combined effort of religious and
philanthropic men is directed against this evil, and when
an impression has been made on the community, sur-
passing the most sanguine hopes. At the present moment, he who uses ardent spirits, or introduces them
into his hospitalities, virtually arrays himself against the
cause of temperance and humanity. He not merely
gives an example to his children and his domestics,

which he may one day bitterly rue ; he withstands the good in their struggles for the virtue and happiness of mankind. He forsakes the standard of social reform, and throws himself into the ranks of its foes.

After these remarks, it will follow, that we should discourage the sale of ardent spirits. What ought not to be used as a beverage, ought not to be sold as such. What the good of the community requires us to expel, no man has a moral right to supply. That intemperance is dreadfully multiplied by the number of licensed shops for the retailing of spirits, we all know. That these should be shut, every good man desires. Law, however, cannot shut them except in a limited extent, or only in a few favored parts of the country. Law is here the will of the people, and the legislature can do little, unless sustained by the public voice. To form, then, an enlightened and vigorous public sentiment, which will demand the suppression of these licensed nurseries of intemperance, is a duty to which every good man is bound, and a service in which each may take a share. And not only should the vending of spirits in these impure haunts be discouraged ; the vending of them by respectable men should be regarded as a great public evil. The retailer takes shelter under the wholesale dealer, from whom he purchases the pernicious draught ; and has he not a right so to do ? Can we expect that he should shrink from spreading on a small scale, what others spread largely without rebuke ? Can we expect his conscience to be sensitive, when he treads in the steps of men of reputation ? Of the character of those who vend spirits, I do not judge. They grew up in the belief of the innocence of the traffic, and this conviction they may sincerely retain. But error, though sincere, is error still. Right and wrong do not depend on human judgment or human will. Truth and duty may be hidden for ages ; but they remain unshaken as God's throne ; and when, in the course of his providence, they are made known to one or a few, they must be proclaimed, whoever may be opposed. Truth, truth, is the hope of the world. Let it be spoken in kindness, but with power.

Some of the means of withstanding intemperance have now been stated. Other topics, were there time, I should be glad to offer to your attention. But I must pause. —I will only add, that every lover of his race has strong encouragement to exert himself for the prevention of intemperance. The striking success of societies instituted for this end should give animation and hope. But even had these associations and these efforts failed, I should not despair. From the very terribleness of the evil, we may derive incitement and hope in our labors for its suppression. It cannot be, that God has created moral beings to become brutes, or placed them in circumstances irresistibly impelling them to this utter renunciation of the proper good of their nature. There are, there must be, means of prevention or cure for this deadliest moral disease. The unhappiness is, that too many of us, who call ourselves the friends of temperance, have not virtue and love enough to use powerfully the weapons of the spirit, for the succour of the tempted and fallen. We are ourselves too sensual, to rescue others from sensuality. The difference between us and the intemperate man is too small, to fit us for his deliverance. But that there are means of withstanding intemperance ; that it is the design and tendency of Christianity to raise up men fit and worthy to wield these means ; and that there are always some, who are prepared to lead the way in this holy work, I cannot doubt. I see, indeed, a terrible energy in human appetites and passions. But I do not faint. Truth is mightier than error ; virtue, than vice ; God, than the evil man. In contending earnestly against intemperance, we have the help and friendship of Him who is Almighty. We have allies in all that is pure, rational, divine in the human soul, in the progressive intelligence of the age, in whatever elevates public sentiment, in religion, in legislation, in philosophy, in the yearnings of the parent, in the prayers of the Christian, in the teachings of God's house, in the influences of God's Spirit. With these allies, friends, helpers, let good men not despair, but be strong in the faith, that, in due time, they shall reap, if they faint not.

29 *

NOTES.

I have spoken of the causes of intemperance which are found in our state of society. I should wrong, however, the community to which I belong, were I to leave the impression, that our social condition offers nothing but incitements to this vice. It presents obstacles as well as affords facilities to it. And this ought to be understood, as an encouragement to the efforts, which, according to the preceding remarks, we are bound to make for its suppression. The growth of intelligence among us, is a powerful antagonist to intemperance. In proportion as we awaken and invigorate men's faculties, we help them to rise above a brutal life; we take them out of the power of the present moment, enlarge their foresight, give them the means of success in life, open to them sources of innocent pleasure, and prepare them to bear part in respectable society. It is true, that intelligence or knowledge is not virtue. It may not overcome selfishness; but it makes our self-love wiser and more reflecting, gives us a better understanding of our own interests, teaches prudence if not generosity, and, in this way, is a powerful guardian against ruinous excess. We have another defence against intemperance, in our freedom. Freedom nourishes self-respect, and, by removing all obstructions to exertion, by opening to men the means of bettering their lot, favors an animated, hopeful industry, thus rescuing a people from depression, despondence, and languor, which are among the chief temptations to brutalizing excess. It is indeed said, that freedom generates all forms of licentiousness, and, consequently, intemperance But it is, I believe, a well established fact, that this vice has decreased since our struggle for independence. The habits and manners of the last generation were more perilous to temperance than our own. Social intercourse was more deformed by excess. Men in mature life visited taverns, and the young could not meet, without the danger of drowning reason in wine. It is a false notion, that we are wholly indebted for our present reform in this particular to temperance societies. These have done great good, and deserve great praise ; but the influence which is now carrying us on preceded them. They are its effects, not causes. An important change of habits had commenced before their institution, and this seems to me an important view, and one of the chief encouragements to joint and individual exertion for the suppression of this vice. Did I believe, that our present social condition offered nothing but materials to intemperance, that it excluded all contrary influences, and that our whole hope for stemming this evil rested on the temperance societies, I should be tempted to despond. Such societies can avail little, except when they act in concurrence with causes in the condition of society. Such causes exist, and one great use of temperance societies is to bring them into more energetic and extensive action.

I have not insisted on one of the means of temperance on which great stress has been laid, that is, the influence of Public Opinion. To bring this to bear against intemperance, has been regarded by not a few as the chief method of subduing the evil. Too much, I think, is hoped from it. One obvious remark is, that the classes most exposed to intemperance are removed very much from the power of public opinion. But, passing over this, I think we generally look to this influence for more than it can accomplish. We lay upon it a greater weight than it can bear. Public opinion may even work against the cause which it is meant to support, when made a substitute for individual exertion. A man, temperate because public opinion exacts it, has not the virtue of temperance, nor a stable ground of temperate habits. The remark is especially applicable to these times. Opinion, in former days, was more permanent than at present. There were few or no causes in operation to unsettle general convictions. Society was cast into fixed forms. Ages passed away, and slight changes were seen in manners and in modes of thinking. But the present is a revolutionary age. Society, breaking from its old moorings, is tossed on a restless and ever-stormy ocean. Opinion no longer affords that steady guidance, which in former times supplied the place of private judgment and individual principle. There is no truth which sophistry does not now assail, no falsehood which may not become a party bond. The great work to which religion and benevolence are now called, is not to sweep away multitudes by storm, not to lay on men the temporary, brittle chains of opinion, but to fix deep, rational conviction in individuals, to awaken the reason to eternal truth and the conscience to immutable duty. We are apt to labor to secure to virtue the power of fashion. We must secure to it the power of conviction. It is the essence of fashion to change. Nothing is sure but truth. No other foundation can sustain a permanent reform. The temperance, which rests on other men's opinions and practice, is not a man's own virtue, but a reflection of what exists around him. It lies on the surface. It has not penetrated the soul.

That opinion may exert a great and useful influence, is not denied ; but it must be enlightened opinion, appealing to the reason and the conscience of the individual ; not to passion, interest, or fear, nor proscribing all who differ. We want public opinion to bear on temperance, but to act rationally, generously, nor passionately, tyrannically, and with the spirit of persecution. Men cannot be driven into temperance. Let the temperate become a party, and breathe the violence of party, and they will raise up a party as violent as their own. The friends of truth must not call passion to their aid, for the erroneous and vicious have a greater stock of passion than they, and can wield this weapon to more effect. It is not by numbers or a louder cry, that good men are to triumph over the bad. Their goodness, their consciousness of truth, and universal love, must be manifested in clear, strong, benevolent appeals to the reason and heart. They must speak in the tone of the friend of their race. This will do infinitely more than the clamor of hosts.

It seems to me an important remark, that public opinion cannot do for virtue what it does for vice. It is the essence of virtue to look above opinion. Vice is consistent with, and very often strengthened by, entire subserviency to it. It is a motive to be cautiously used, because the mind, which passively yields to it, will find it a debilitating, rather than an invigorating influence. The moral independence which can withstand public sentiment, is men's only safety. Whenever public sentiment shall be enlightened enough to promote this superiority to itself, it will be a noble spring. In proportion as it wars against this self-subsistence, it subverts the only foundation of substantial, enduring reform.

It is sometimes very hazardous to attempt to extirpate a common vice by making it disgraceful, and passing on it a sentence of outlawry. If, indeed, the vice be confined to the poor and obscure, the brand of infamy may easily be fixed on it ; but when it spreads higher, and is taken under the protection of fashion, it can not only parry the weapon of disgrace in the hand of its adversaries, but turn this against them. Fashion is singularly expert in the use of ridicule. What it wants in reason, it can supply in sneers and laughter. Sometimes it puts on indifference as a coat of mail. It has especially the art of attaching the idea of vulgarity to a good cause ; and what virtue has courage to encounter this most dreaded form of opinion ?

SELF-CULTURE.

AN ADDRESS

INTRODUCTORY TO THE FRANKLIN LECTURES,

Delivered at Boston, Sept., 1838.

THIS Address was intended to make two lectures; but the author was led to abridge it and deliver it as one, partly by the apprehension, that some passages were too abstract for a popular address, partly to secure the advantages of presenting the whole subject at once and in close connexion, and for other reasons which need not be named. Most of the passages which were omitted, are now published. The author respectfully submits the discourse to those for whom it was particularly intended, and to the public, in the hope, that it will at least bring a great subject before the minds of some, who may not as yet have given to it the attention it deserves.

ADDRESS ON SELF-CULTURE.

My respected Friends :

By the invitation of the committee of arrangements for the Franklin Lectures, I now appear before you to offer some remarks introductory to this course. My principal inducement for doing so is my deep interest in those of my fellow-citizens, for whom these lectures are principally designed. I understood that they were to be attended chiefly by those who are occupied by manual labor ; and, hearing this, I did not feel myself at liberty to decline the service to which I had been invited. I wished by compliance to express my sympathy with this large portion of my race. I wished to express my sense of obligation to those, from whose industry and skill I derive almost all the comforts of life. I wished still more to express my joy in the efforts they are making for their own improvement, and my firm faith in their success. These motives will give a particular character and bearing to some of my remarks. I shall speak occasionally as among those who live by the labor of their hands. But I shall not speak as one separated

from them. I belong rightfully to the great fraternity
of working men. Happily in this community we all are
bred and born to work ; and this honorable mark, set on
us all, should bind together the various portions of the
community.

I have expressed my strong interest in the mass of
the people ; and this is founded, not on their usefulness
to the community, so much as on what they are in themselves. Their condition is indeed obscure ; but their
importance is not on this account a whit the less. The
multitude of men cannot, from the nature of the case, be
distinguished ; for the very idea of distinction is, that a
man stands out from the multitude. They make little
noise and draw little notice in their narrow spheres of
action ; but still they have their full proportion of personal worth and even of greatness. Indeed every man,
in every condition, is great. It is only our own diseased sight which makes him little. A man is great as
a man, be he where or what he may. The grandeur of
his nature turns to insignificance all outward distinctions.
His powers of intellect, of conscience, of love, of
knowing God, of perceiving the beautiful, of acting on
his own mind, on outward nature, and on his fellow-
creatures, these are glorious prerogatives. Through the
vulgar error of undervaluing what is common, we are
apt indeed to pass these by as of little worth. But as in
the outward creation, so in the soul, the common is the
most precious. Science and art may invent splendid
modes of illuminating the apartments of the opulent ;
but these are all poor and worthless, compared with the
common light which the sun sends into all our windows,
which he pours freely, impartially over hill and valley,
which kindles daily the eastern and western sky ; and so

the common lights of reason, and conscience, and love, are of more worth and dignity than the rare endowments which give celebrity to a few. Let us not disparage that nature which is common to all men ; for no thought can measure its grandeur. It is the image of God, the image even of his infinity, for no limits can be set to its unfolding. He who possesses the divine powers of the soul is a great being, be his place what it may. You may clothe him with rags, may immure him in a dungeon, may chain him to slavish tasks. But he is still great. You may shut him out of your houses ; but God opens to him heavenly mansions. He makes no show indeed in the streets of a splendid city ; but a clear thought, a pure affection, a resolute act of a virtuous will, have a dignity of quite another kind and far higher than accumulations of brick and granite and plaster and stucco, however cunningly put together, or though stretching far beyond our sight. Nor is this all. If we pass over this grandeur of our common nature, and turn our thoughts to that comparative greatness, which draws chief attention, and which consists in the decided superiority of the individual to the general standard of power and character, we shall find this as free and frequent a growth among the obscure and unnoticed as in more conspicuous walks of life. The truly great are to be found everywhere, nor is it easy to say, in what condition they spring up most plentifully. Real greatness has nothing to do with a man's sphere. It does not lie in the magnitude of his outward agency, in the extent of the effects which he produces. The greatest men may do comparatively little abroad. Perhaps the greatest in our city at this moment are buried in obscurity. Grandeur of character lies wholly in force of soul, that is, in the force of thought, moral principle, and love, and this may be found in the humblest condition of life. A man brought up to an obscure trade, and hemmed in by the wants of a growing family, may, in his narrow sphere, perceive more clearly, discriminate more keenly, weigh evidence more wisely, seize on the right means more decisively, and have more presence of mind in difficulty, than another who has accumulated vast stores of knowledge by laborious study; and he has more of intellectual greatness. Many a man, who has gone but a few miles from home, understands human nature better, detects motives and weighs character more sagaciously, than another, who has travelled over the known world, and made a name by his reports of different countries. It is force of thought which measures intellectual, and so it is force of principle which measures moral greatness, that highest of human endowments, that brightest manifestation of the Divinity. The greatest man is he who chooses the Right with invincible resolution, who resists the sorest temptations from within and without, who bears the heaviest burdens cheerfully, who is calmest in storms and most fearless under menace and frowns, whose reliance on truth, on virtue, on God, is most unfaltering; and is this a greatness, which is apt to make a show, or which is most likely to abound in conspicuous station? The solemn conflicts of reason with passion; the victories of moral and religious principle over urgent and almost irresistible solicitations to self-indulgence; the hardest sacrifices of duty, those of deep-seated affection and of the heart's fondest hopes; the consolations, hopes, joys, and peace, of disappointed, persecuted, scorned, deserted virtue; these are of course unseen;

so that the true greatness of human life is almost wholly out of sight. Perhaps in our presence, the most heroic deed on earth is done in some silent spirit, the loftiest purpose cherished, the most generous sacrifice made, and we do not suspect it. I believe this greatness to be most common among the multitude, whose names are never heard. Among common people will be found more of hardship borne manfully, more of unvarnished truth, more of religious trust, more of that generosity which gives what the giver needs himself, and more of a wise estimate of life and death, than among the more prosperous. — And even in regard to influence over other beings, which is thought the peculiar prerogative of distinguished station, I believe, that the difference between the conspicuous and the obscure does not amount to much. Influence is to be measured, not by the extent of surface it covers, but by its *kind*. A man may spread his mind, his feelings, and opinions, through a great extent ; but if his mind be a low one, he manifests no greatness. A wretched artist may fill a city with daubs, and by a false, showy style achieve a reputation ; but the man of genius, who leaves behind him one grand picture, in which immortal beauty is embodied, and which is silently to spread a true taste in his art, exerts an incomparably higher influence. Now the noblest influence on earth is that exerted on character ; and he who puts forth this, does a great work, no matter how narrow or obscure his sphere. The father and mother of an unnoticed family, who, in their seclusion, awaken the mind of one child to the idea and love of perfect goodness, who awaken in him a strength of will to repel all temptation, and who send him out prepared to profit by the conflicts of life, surpass in influence a

Napolean breaking the world to his sway. And not only is their work higher in kind ; who knows, but that they are doing a greater work even as to extent or surface than the conqueror ? Who knows, but that the being, whom they inspire with holy and disinterested principles, may communicate himself to others ; and that, by a spreading agency, of which they were the silent origin, improvements may spread through a nation, through the world ? In these remarks you will see why I feel and express a deep interest in the obscure, in the mass of men. The distinctions of society vanish before the light of these truths. I attach myself to the multitude, not because they are voters and have political power ; but because they are men, and have within their reach the most glorious prizes of humanity.

In this country the mass of the people are distinguished by possessing means of improvement, of self-culture, possessed nowhere else. To incite them to the use of these, is to render them the best service they can receive. Accordingly I have chosen for the subject of this lecture, Self-culture, or the care which every man owes to himself, to the unfolding and perfecting of his nature. I consider this topic as particularly appropriate to the introduction of a course of lectures, in consequence of a common disposition to regard these and other like means of instruction, as able of themselves to carry forward the hearer. Lectures have their use. They stir up many, who, but for such outward appeals, might have slumbered to the end of life. But let it be remembered, that little is to be gained simply by coming to this place once a-week, and giving up the mind for an hour to be wrought upon by a teacher. Unless we are roused to act upon ourselves, unless we engage in the

work of self-improvement, unless we purpose strenuously to form and elevate our own minds, unless what
we hear is made a part of ourselves by conscientious
reflection, very little permanent good is received.

Self-culture, I am aware, is a topic too extensive for
a single discourse, and I shall be able to present but a
few views which seem to me most important. My aim
will be, to give first the Idea of self-culture, next its
Means, and then to consider some objections to the
leading views which I am now to lay before you.

Before entering on the discussion, let me offer one
remark. Self-culture is something possible. It is not
a dream. It has foundations in our nature. Without this conviction, the speaker will but declaim, and
the hearer listen without profit. There are two powers
of the human soul which make self-culture possible, the
self-searching and the self-forming power. We have
first the faculty of turning the mind on itself; of recalling its past, and watching its present operations ; of
learning its various capacities and susceptibilities, what
it can do and bear, what it can enjoy and suffer ; and of
thus learning in general what our nature is, and what
it was made for. It is worthy of observation, that we
are able to discern not only what we already are, but
what we may become, to see in ourselves germs and
promises of a growth to which no bounds can be set,
to dart beyond what we have actually gained to the
idea of Perfection as the end of our being. It is by this
self-comprehending power that we are distinguished from
the brutes, which give no signs of looking into themselves. Without this there would be no self-culture,
for we should not know the work to be done ; and one
reason why self-culture is so little proposed is, that so

few penetrate into their own nature. To most men, their own spirits are shadowy, unreal, compared with what is outward. When they happen to cast a glance inward, they see there only a dark, vague chaos. They distinguish perhaps some violent passion, which has driven them to injurious excess; but their highest powers hardly attract a thought; and thus multitudes live and die as truly strangers to themselves, as to countries of which they have heard the name, but which human foot has never trodden.

But self-culture is possible, not only because we can enter into and search ourselves. We have a still nobler power, that of acting on, determining and forming ourselves. This is a fearful as well as glorious endowment, for it is the ground of human responsibility. We have the power not only of tracing our powers, but of guiding and impelling them; not only of watching our passions, but of controlling them; not only of seeing our faculties grow, but of applying to them means and influences to aid their growth. We can stay or change the current of thought. We can concentrate the intellect on objects which we wish to comprehend. We can fix our eyes on perfection, and make almost everything speed us towards it. This is indeed a noble prerogative of our nature. Possessing this, it matters little what or where we are now, for we can conquer a better lot, and even be happier for starting from the lowest point. Of all the discoveries which men need to make, the most important at the present moment, is that of the self-forming power treasured up in themselves. They little suspect its extent, as little as the savage apprehends the energy which the mind is created to exert on the material world. It transcends in importance all our power over outward nature. There is more of divinity in it, than in the force which impels the outward universe; and yet how little we comprehend it! How it slumbers in most men unsuspected, unused! This makes self-culture possible, and binds it on us as a solemn duty.

I. I am first to unfold the idea of self-culture; and this, in its most general form, may easily be seized. To cultivate any thing, be it a plant, an animal, a mind, is to make grow. Growth, expansion is the end. Nothing admits culture, but that which has a principle of life, capable of being expanded. He, therefore, who does what he can to unfold all his powers and capacities, especially his nobler ones, so as to become a well proportioned, vigorous, excellent, happy being, practises self-culture.

This culture, of course, has various branches corresponding to the different capacities of human nature; but, though various, they are intimately united and make progress together. The soul, which our philosophy divides into various capacities, is still one essence, one life; and it exerts at the same moment, and blends in the same act, its various energies of thought, feeling, and volition. Accordingly, in a wise self-culture, all the principles of our nature grow at once by joint, harmonious action, just as all parts of the plant are unfolded together. When therefore you hear of different branches of self-improvement, you will not think of them as distinct processes going on independently of each other, and requiring each its own separate means. Still a distinct consideration of these is needed to a full comprehension of the subject, and these I shall proceed to unfold.

First, self-culture is Moral, a branch of singular importance. When a man looks into himself, he discovers two distinct orders or kinds of principles, which it behoves him especially to comprehend. He discovers desires, appetites, passions, which terminate in himself, which crave and seek his own interest, gratification, distinction ; and he discovers another principle, an antagonist to these, which is Impartial, Disinterested, Universal, enjoining on him a regard to the rights and happiness of other beings, and laying on him obligations which *must* be discharged, cost what they may, or however they may clash with his particular pleasure or gain. No man, however narrowed to his own interest, however hardened by selfishness, can deny, that there springs up within him a great idea in opposition to interest, the idea of Duty, that an inward voice calls him more or less distinctly, to revere and exercise Impartial Justice, and Universal Good-will. This disinterested principle in human nature we call sometimes reason, sometimes conscience, sometimes the moral sense or faculty. But, be its name what it may, it is a real principle in each of us, and it is the supreme power within us, to be cultivated above all others, for on its culture the right developement of all others depends. The passions indeed may be stronger than the conscience, may lift up a louder voice ; but their clamor differs wholly from the tone of command in which the conscience speaks. They are not clothed with its authority, its binding power. In their very triumphs they are rebuked by the moral principle, and often cower before its still, deep, menacing voice. No part of self-knowledge is more important than to discern clearly these two great principles, the self-seeking and the disinterested; and the most important part of self-culture is to depress the former, and to exalt the latter, or to enthrone the sense of duty within us. There are no limits to the growth of this moral force in man, if he will cherish it faithfully. There have been men, whom no power in the universe could turn from the Right, by whom death in its most dreadful forms has been less dreaded, than transgression of the inward law of universal justice and love.

In the next place, self-culture is Religious. When we look into ourselves, we discover powers, which link us with this outward, visible, finite, ever-changing world. We have sight and other senses to discern, and limbs and various faculties to secure and appropriate the material creation. And we have, too, a power, which cannot stop at what we see and handle, at what exists within the bounds of space and time, which seeks for the Infinite, Uncreated Cause, which cannot rest till it ascend to the Eternal, All-comprehending Mind. This we call the religious principle, and its grandeur cannot be exaggerated by human language; for it marks out a being destined for higher communion than with the visible universe. To develope this, is eminently to educate ourselves. The true idea of God, unfolded clearly and livingly within us, and moving us to adore and obey him, and to aspire after likeness to him, is the noblest growth in human, and, I may add, in celestial natures. The religious principle, and the moral, are intimately connected, and grow together. The former is indeed the perfection and highest manifestation of the latter. They are both disinterested. It is the essence of true religion to recognise and adore in God the attributes of Impartial Justice and Universal Love, and to hear him commanding us in the conscience to become what we adore.

Again. Self-culture is Intellectual. We cannot look into ourselves without discovering the intellectual principle, the power which thinks, reasons, and judges, the power of seeking and acquiring truth. This, indeed, we are in no danger of overlooking. The intellect being the great instrument by which men compass their wishes, it draws more attention than any of our other powers. When we speak to men of improving themselves, the first thought which occurs to them is, that they must cultivate their understanding, and get knowledge and skill. By education, men mean almost exclusively intellectual training. For this, schools and colleges are instituted, and to this the moral and religious discipline of the young is sacrificed. Now I reverence, as much as any man, the intellect; but let us never exalt it above the moral principle. With this it is most intimately connected. In this its culture is founded, and to exalt this is its highest aim. Whoever desires that his intellect may grow up to soundness, to healthy vigor, must begin with moral discipline. Reading and study are not enough to perfect the power of thought. One thing above all is needful, and that is, the Disinterestedness which is the very soul of virtue. To gain truth, which is the great object of the understanding, I must seek it disinterestedly. Here is the first and grand condition of intellectual progress. I must choose to receive the truth, no matter how it bears on myself. I must follow it, no matter where it leads, what interests it opposes, to what persecution or loss it lays me open, from what party it severs me, or to what party it allies. Without this fairness of mind, which is only another phrase for disinterested love of truth, great native powers of understanding are perverted and led astray ; genius runs wild ; " the light within us becomes darkness." The subtilest reasoners, for want of this, cheat themselves as well as others, and become entangled in the web of their own sophistry. It is a fact well known in the history of science and philosophy, that men, gifted by nature with singular intelligence, have broached the grossest errors, and even sought to undermine the grand primitive truths on which human virtue, dignity, and hope depend. And, on the other hand, I have known instances of men of naturally moderate powers of mind, who, by a disinterested love of truth and their fellow-creatures, have gradually risen to no small force and enlargement of thought. Some of the most useful teachers in the pulpit and in schools, have owed their power of enlightening others, not so much to any natural superiority, as to the simplicity, impartiality, and disinterestedness of their minds, to their readiness to live and die for the truth. A man, who rises above himself, looks from an eminence on nature and providence, on society and life. Thought expands, as by a natural elasticity, when the pressure of selfishness is removed. The moral and religious principles of the soul, generously cultivated, fertilize the intellect. Duty, faithfully performed, opens the mind to truth, both being of one family, alike immutable, universal, and everlasting.

I have enlarged on this subject, because the connexion between moral and intellectual culture is often overlooked, and because the former is often sacrificed to the latter. The exaltation of talent, as it is called, above virtue and religion, is the curse of the age. Education is now chiefly a stimulus to learning, and thus men acquire power without the principles which alone make it a good. Talent is worshipped ; but, if divorced from rectitude, it will prove more of a demon than a god.

Intellectual culture consists, not chiefly, as many are apt to think, in accumulating information, though this is important, but in building up a force of thought which may be turned at will on any subjects, on which we are called to pass judgment. This force is manifested in the concentration of the attention, in accurate, penetrating observation, in reducing complex subjects to their elements, in diving beneath the effect to the cause, in detecting the more subtile differences and resemblances of things, in reading the future in the present, and especially in rising from particular facts to general laws or universal truths. This last exertion of the intellect, its rising to broad views and great principles, constitutes what is called the philosophical mind, and is especially worthy of culture. What it means, your own observation must have taught you. You must have taken note of two classes of men, the one always employed on details, on particular facts, and the other using these facts as foundations of higher, wider truths. The latter are philosophers. For example, men had for ages seen pieces of wood, stones, metals falling to the ground. Newton seized on these particular facts, and rose to the idea, that all matter tends, or is attracted, towards all matter, and then defined the law according to which this attraction or force acts at different distances, thus giving us a grand principle, which, we have reason to think, extends to and controls the whole outward creation. One man reads a history, and can tell you all its events, and there stops. Another combines these events, brings them under one view, and learns the great causes which are at work on this or another nation, and what are its great tendencies, whether to freedom or despotism, to one or another form of civilization. So, one man talks continually about the particular actions of this or another neighbour ; whilst another looks beyond the acts to the inward principle from which they spring, and gathers from them larger views of human nature. In a word, one man sees all things apart and in fragments, whilst another strives to discover the harmony, connexion, unity of all. One of the great evils of society is, that men, occupied perpetually with petty details, want general truths, want broad and fixed principles. Hence many, not wicked, are unstable, habitually · inconsistent, as if they were overgrown children rather than men. To build up that strength of mind, which apprehends and cleaves to great universal truths, is the highest intellectual self-culture ; and here I wish you to observe how entirely this culture agrees with that of the moral and the religious principles of our nature, of which I have previously spoken. In each of these, the improvement of the soul consists in raising it above what is narrow, particular, individual, selfish, to the universal and unconfined. To improve a man, is to liberalize, enlarge him in thought, feeling, and purpose Narrowness of intellect and heart, this is the degradation from which all culture aims to rescue the human being.

Again. Self-culture is social, or one of its great offices is to unfold and purify the affections, which spring

up instinctively in the human breast, which bind together husband and wife, parent and child, brother and sister; which bind a man to friends and neighbours, to his
country, and to the suffering who fall under his eye,
wherever they belong. The culture of these is an important part of our work, and it consists in converting
them from instincts into principles, from natural into
spiritual attachments, in giving them a rational, moral,
and holy character. For example, our affection for our
children is at first instinctive; and if it continue such,
it rises little above the brute's attachment to its young.
But when a parent infuses into his natural love for his
offspring, moral and religious principle, when he comes
to regard his child as an intelligent, spiritual, immortal
being, and honors him as such, and desires first of all
to make him disinterested, noble, a worthy child of
God and the friend of his race, then the instinct rises
into a generous and holy sentiment. It resembles God's
paternal love for his spiritual family. A like purity
and dignity we must aim to give to all our affections.

Again. Self-culture is Practical, or it proposes, as
one of its chief ends, to fit us for action, to make us
efficient in whatever we undertake, to train us to firmness of purpose and to fruitfulness of resource in common life, and especially in emergencies, in times of
difficulty, danger, and trial. But passing over this and
other topics for which I have no time, I shall confine
myself to two branches of self-culture which have been
almost wholly overlooked in the education of the people, and which ought not to be so slighted.

In looking at our nature, we discover, among its admirable endowments, the sense or perception of Beauty.
We see the germ of this in every human being, and

there is no power which admits greater cultivation ; and why should it not be cherished in all ? It deserves remark, that the provision for this principle is infinite in the universe. There is but a very minute portion of the creation which we can turn into food and clothes, or gratification for the body ; but the whole creation may be used to minister to the sense of beauty. Beauty is an all-pervading presence. It unfolds in the number-less flowers of the spring. It waves in the branches of the trees and the green blades of grass. It haunts the depths of the earth and sea, and gleams out in the hues of the shell and the precious stone. And not only these minute objects, but the ocean, the mountains, the clouds, the heavens, the stars, the rising and setting sun, all overflow with beauty. The universe is its temple ; and those men, who are alive to it, cannot lift their eyes without feeling themselves encompassed with it on every side. Now this beauty is so precious, the enjoy-ments it gives are so refined and pure, so congenial with our tenderest and noble feelings, and so akin to wor-ship, that it is painful to think of the multitude of men as living in the midst of it, and living almost as blind to it, as if, instead of this fair earth and glorious sky, they were tenants of a dungeon. An infinite joy is lost to the world by the want of culture of this spiritual en-dowment. Suppose that I were to visit a cottage, and to see its walls lined with the choicest pictures of Ra-phael, and every spare nook filled with statues of the most exquisite workmanship, and that I were to learn, that neither man, woman, nor child ever cast an eye at these miracles of art, how should I feel their priva-tion ; how should I want to open their eyes, and to help them to comprehend and feel the loveliness and

31*

grandeur which in vain courted their notice! But every husbandman is living in sight of the works of a diviner Artist; and how much would his existence be elevated, could he see the glory which shines forth in their forms, hues, proportions, and moral expression! I have spoken only of the beauty of nature, but how much of this mysterious charm is found in the elegant arts, and especially in literature? The best books have most beauty. The greatest truths are wronged if not linked with beauty, and they win, their way most surely and deeply into the soul when arrayed in this their natural and fit attire. Now no man receives the true culture of a man, in whom the sensibility to the beautiful is not cherished; and I know of no condition in life from which it should be excluded. Of all luxuries, this is the cheapest and most at hand; and it seems to me to be most important to those conditions, where coarse labor tends to give a grossness to the mind. From the diffusion of the sense of beauty in ancient Greece, and of the taste for music in modern Germany, we learn that the people at large may partake of refined gratifications, which have hitherto been thought to be necessarily restricted to a few.

What beauty is, is a question which the most penetrating minds have not satisfactorily answered; nor, were I able, is this the place for discussing it. But one thing I would say; the beauty of the outward creation is intimately related to the lovely, grand, interesting attributes of the soul. It is the emblem or expression of these. Matter becomes beautiful to us, when it seems to lose its material aspect, its inertness, finiteness, and grossness, and by the etherial lightness of its forms and motions seems to approach spirit; when it images to us pure and gentle affections ; when it spreads out into a vastness which is a shadow of the Infinite; or when in more awful shapes and movements it speaks of the Omnipotent. Thus outward beauty is akin to something deeper and unseen, is the reflection of spiritual attributes ; and of consequence the way to see and feel it more and more keenly, is to cultivate those moral, re- ligious, intellectual, and social principles of which I have already spoken, and which are the glory of the spiritual nature ; and I name this, that you may see, what I am anxious to show, the harmony which subsists among all branches of human culture, or how each forwards and is aided by all.

There is another power, which each man should cul- tivate according to his ability, but which is very much neglected in the mass of the people, and that is, the power of Utterance. A man was not made to shut up his mind in itself ; but to give it voice and to exchange it for other minds. Speech is one of our grand distinc- tions from the brute. Our power over others lies not so much in the amount of thought within us, as in the power of bringing it out. A man, of more than ordi- nary intellectual vigor, may, for want of expression, be a cipher, without significance, in society. And not only does a man influence others, but he greatly aids his own intellect, by giving distinct and forcible utterance to his thoughts. We understand ourselves better, our con- ceptions grow clearer, by the very effort to make them clear to another. Our social rank, too, depends a good deal on our power of utterance. The principal dis- tinction between what are called gentlemen and the vulgar lies in this, that the latter are awkward in man- ners, and are especially wanting in propriety, clearness,

grace, and force of utterance. A man who cannot
open his lips without breaking a rule of grammar, without showing in his dialect or brogue or uncouth tones his
want of cultivation, or without darkening his meaning
by a confused, unskilful mode of communication, cannot take the place to which, perhaps, his native good
sense entitles him. To have intercourse with respectable people, we must speak their language. On this
account, I am glad that grammar and a correct pronun-
ciation are taught in the common schools of this city.
These are not trifles ; nor are they superfluous to any
class of people. They give a man access to social
advantages, on which his improvement very much depends. The power of utterance should be included by
all in their plans of self-culture.

I have now given a few views of the culture, the
improvement, which every man should propose to himself. I have all along gone on the principle, that a man
has within him capacities of growth, which deserve and
will reward intense, unrelaxing toil. I do not look on
a human being as a machine, made to be kept in action
by a foreign force, to accomplish an unvarying succession of motions, to do a fixed amount of work, and then
to fall to pieces at death, but as a being of free spiritual
powers ; and I place little value on any culture, but
that which aims to bring out these and to give them
perpetual impulse and expansion. I am aware, that
this view is far from being universal. The common
notion has been, that the mass of the people need no
other culture than is necessary to fit them for their
various trades ; and, though this error is passing away,
it is far from being exploded. But the ground of a

man's culture lies in his nature, not in his calling. His powers are to be unfolded on account of their inherent dignity, not their outward direction. He is to be educated, because he is a man, not because he is to make shoes, nails, or pins. A trade is plainly not the great end of his being, for his mind cannot be shut up in it ; his force of thought cannot be exhausted on it. He has faculties to which it gives no action, and deep wants it cannot answer. Poems, and systems of theology and philosophy, which have made some noise in the world, have been wrought at the work-bench and amidst the toils of the field. How often, when the arms are mechanically plying a trade, does the mind, lost in reverie or day-dreams, escape to the ends of the earth ! How often does the pious heart of woman mingle the greatest of all thoughts, that of God, with household drudgery ! Undoubtedly a man is to perfect himself in his trade, for by it he is to earn his bread and to serve the community. But bread or subsistence is not his highest good ; for, if it were, his lot would be harder than that of the inferior animals, for whom nature spreads a table and weaves a wardrobe, without a care of their own. Nor was he made chiefly to minister to the wants of the community. A rational, moral being cannot, without infinite wrong, be converted into a mere instrument of others' gratification. He is necessarily an end, not a means. A mind, in which are sown the seeds of wisdom, disinterestedness, firmness of purpose, and piety, is worth more than all the outward material interests of a world. It exists for itself, for its own perfection, and must not be enslaved to its own or others' animal wants. You tell me, that a liberal culture is needed for men who are to fill high stations, but not for such as are doomed to vulgar labor. I answer, that Man is a greater name than President or King. Truth and goodness are equally precious, in whatever sphere they are found. Besides, men of all conditions sustain equally the relations, which give birth to the highest virtues and demand the highest powers. The laborer is not a mere laborer. He has close, tender, responsible connections with God and his fellow-creatures. He is a son, husband, father, friend, and Christian. He belongs to a home, a country, a church, a race ; and is such a man to be cultivated only for a trade ? Was he not sent into the world for a great work ? To educate a child perfectly requires profounder thought, greater wisdom, than to govern a state ; and for this plain reason, that the interests and wants of the latter are more superficial, coarser, and more obvious, than the spiritual capacities, the growth of thought and feeling, and the subtile laws of the mind, which must all be studied and comprehended, before the work of education can be thoroughly performed ; and yet to all conditions this greatest work on earth is equally committed by God. What plainer proof do we need that a higher culture, than has yet been dreamed of, is needed by our whole race ?

II. I now proceed to inquire into the Means, by which the self-culture, just described, may be promoted ; and here I know not where to begin. The subject is so extensive, as well as important, that I feel myself unable to do any justice to it, especially in the limits to which I am confined. I beg you to consider me as presenting but hints, and such as have offered themselves with very little research to my own mind.

And, first, the great means of self-culture, that which includes all the rest, is to fasten on this culture as our Great End, to determine deliberately and solemnly, that we will make the most and the best of the powers which God has given us. Without this resolute purpose, the best means are worth little, and with it the poorest become mighty. You may see thousands, with every opportunity of improvement which wealth can gather, with teachers, libraries, and apparatus, bringing nothing to pass, and others, with few helps, doing wonders ; and simply because the latter are in earnest, and the former not. A man in earnest finds means, or, if he cannot find, creates them. A vigorous purpose makes much out of little, breathes power into weak instruments, disarms difficulties, and even turns them into assistances. Every condition has means of progress, if we have spirit enough to use them. Some volumes have recently been published, giving examples or histories of " knowledge acquired under difficulties " ; and it is most animating to see in these what a resolute man can do for himself. A great idea, like this of Self-culture, if seized on clearly and vigorously, burns like a living coal in the soul. He who deliberately adopts a great end, has, by this act, half accomplished it, has scaled the chief barrier to success.

One thing is essential to the strong purpose of self-culture now insisted on, namely, faith in the practicableness of this culture. A great object, to awaken resolute choice, must be seen to be within our reach. The truth, that progress is the very end of our being, must not be received as a tradition, but comprehended and felt as a reality. Our minds are apt to pine and starve, by being imprisoned within what we have already attained. A true faith, looking up to something better, catching glimpses of a distant perfection, prophesying to ourselves improvements proportioned to our conscientious labors, gives energy of purpose, gives wings to the soul ; and this faith will continually grow, by acquainting ourselves with our own nature, and with the promises of Divine help and immortal life which abound in Revelation.

Some are discouraged from proposing to themselves improvement, by the false notion, that the study of books, which their situation denies them, is the all-important, and only sufficient means. Let such consider, that the grand volumes, of which all our books are transcripts, I mean nature, revelation, the human soul, and human life, are freely unfolded to every eye. The great sources of wisdom are experience and observation ; and these are denied to none. To open and fix our eyes upon what passes without and within us, is the most fruitful study. Books are chiefly useful, as they help us to interpret what we see and experience. When they absorb men, as they sometimes do, and turn them from observation of nature and life, they generate a learned folly, for which the plain sense of the laborer could not be exchanged but at great loss. It deserves attention that the greatest men have been formed without the studies, which at present are thought by many most needful to improvement. Homer, Plato, Demosthenes, never heard the name of chemistry, and knew less of the solar system than a boy in our common schools. Not that these sciences are unimportant ; but the lesson is, that human improvement never wants the means, where the purpose of it is deep, and earnest in the soul.

The purpose of self-culture, this is the life and strength of all the methods we use for our own elevation. I reiterate this principle on account of its great importance; and I would add a remark to prevent its misapprehension. When I speak of the purpose of self-culture, I mean, that it should be sincere. In other words, we must make self-culture really and truly our end, or choose it for its own sake, and not merely as a means or instrument of something else. And here I touch a common and very pernicious error. Not a few persons desire to improve themselves only to get property and to rise in the world; but such do not properly choose improvement, but something outward and foreign to themselves; and so low an impulse can produce only a stinted, partial, uncertain growth. A man, as I have said, is to cultivate himself because he is a man. He is to start with the conviction, that there is something greater within him than in the whole material creation, than in all the worlds which press on the eye and ear; and that inward improvements have a worth and dignity in themselves, quite distinct from the power they give over outward things. Undoubtedly a man is to labor to better his condition, but first to better himself. If he knows no higher use of his mind than to invent and drudge for his body, his case is desperate as far as culture is concerned.

In these remarks, I do not mean to recommend to the laborer indifference to his outward lot. I hold it important, that every man in every class should possess the means of comfort, of health, of neatness in food and apparel, and of occasional retirement and leisure. These are good in themselves, to be sought for their own sakes, and still more, they are important means of the self-culture for which I am pleading. A clean, comfortable dwelling, with wholesome meals, is no small aid to intellectual and moral progress. A man living in a damp cellar or a garret open to rain and snow, breathing the foul air of a filthy room, and striving without success to appease hunger on scanty or unsavory food, is in danger of abandoning himself to a desperate, selfish recklessness. Improve then your lot. Multiply comforts, and still more get wealth if you can by honorable means, and if it do not cost too much. A true cultivation of the mind is fitted to forward you in your worldly concerns, and you ought to use it for this end. Only, beware, lest this end master you ; lest your motives sink as your condition improves; lest you fall victims to the miserable passion of vying with those around you in show, luxury, and expense. Cherish a true respect for yourselves. Feel that your nature is worth more than every thing which is foreign to you. He who has not caught a glimpse of his own rational and spiritual being, of something within himself superior to the world and allied to the divinity, wants the true spring of that purpose of self-culture, on which I have insisted as the first of all the means of improvement.

I proceed to another important means of self-culture, and this is the control of the animal appetites. To raise the moral and intellectual nature, we must put down the animal. Sensuality is the abyss in which very many souls are plunged and lost. Among the most prosperous classes, what a vast amount of intellectual life is drowned in luxurious excesses ! It is one great curse of wealth, that it is used to pamper the senses ; and among the poorer classes, though luxury is wanting, yet a gross feeding often prevails, under which the spirit is whelmed. It is a sad sight to walk through our streets, and to see how many countenances bear marks of a lethargy and a brutal coarseness, induced by unrestrained indulgence. Whoever would cultivate the soul, must restrain the appetites. I am not an advocate for the doctrine, that animal food was not meant for man ; but that this is used among us to excess, that as a people we should gain much in cheerfulness, activity, and buoyancy of mind, by less gross and stimulating food, I am strongly inclined to believe. Above all, let me urge on those, who would bring out and elevate their higher nature, to abstain from the use of spirituous liquors. This bad habit is distinguished from all others by the ravages it makes on the reason, the intellect ; and this effect is produced to a mournful extent, even when drunkenness is escaped. Not a few men, called temperate, and who have thought themselves such, have learned, on abstaining from the use of ardent spirits, that for years their minds had been clouded, impaired by moderate drinking, without their suspecting the injury. Multitudes in this city are bereft of half their intellectual energy, by a degree of indulgence which passes for innocent. Of all the foes of the working class, this is the deadliest. Nothing has done more to keep down this class, to destroy their self-respect, to rob them of their just influence in the community, to render profitless the means of improvement within their reach, than the use of ardent spirits as a drink. They are called on to withstand this practice, as they regard their honor, and would take their just place in society. They are under solemn obligations to give their sanction to every effort for its suppression.

They ought to regard as their worst enemies (though unintentionally such), as the enemies of their rights, dignity, and influence, the men who desire to flood city and country with distilled poison. I lately visited a flourishing village, and on expressing to one of the respected inhabitants the pleasure I felt in witnessing 'so many signs of progress, he replied, that one of the causes of the prosperity I witnessed, was the disuse of ardent spirits by the people. And this reformation we may be assured wrought something higher than outward prosperity. In almost every family so improved, we cannot doubt that the capacities of the parent for intellectual and moral improvement were enlarged, and the means of education made more 'effectual to the child. I call on working men to take hold of the cause of temperance as peculiarly *their* cause. These remarks are the more needed, in consequence of the efforts made far and wide, to annul at the present moment a recent law for the suppression of the sale of ardent spirits in such quantities as favor intemperance. I know, that there are intelligent and good men, who believe, that, in enacting this law, government transcended its limits, left its true path, and established a precedent for legislative interference with all our pursuits and pleasures. No one here looks more jealously on government than myself. But I maintain, that this is a case which stands by itself, which can be confounded with no other, and on which government from its very nature and end is peculiarly bound to act. Let it never be forgotten, that the great end of government, its highest function, is, not to make roads, grant charters, originate improvements, but to prevent or repress Crimes against individual rights and social order. For this end it ordains a .penal code, erects prisons, and inflicts fearful punishments. Now if it be true, that a vast proportion of the crimes, which government is instituted to prevent and repress, have their origin in the use of ardent spirits ; if our poor-houses, work-houses, jails, and penitentiaries, are tenanted in a great degree by those whose first and chief impulse to crime came from the distillery and dram-shop ; if murder and theft, the most fearful outrages on property and life, are most frequently the issues' and consummation of intemperance, is not government bound to restrain by legislation the vending of the stimulus to these terrible social wrongs ? Is government never to act as a parent, never to remove the causes or occasions of wrong-doing ? Has it but one instrument for repressing crime, namely, public, infamous punishment, an evil only inferior to crime ? Is government a usurper, does it wander beyond its sphere, by imposing restraints on an article, which does no imaginable good, which can plead no benefit conferred on body or mind, which unfits the citizen for the discharge of his duty to his country, and which, above all, stirs up men to the perpetration of most of the crimes, from which it is the highest and most solemn office of government to protect society ?

I come now to another important measure of self-culture, and this is, intercourse with superior minds. I have insisted on our own activity as essential to our progress; but we were not made to live or advance alone. Society is as needful to us as air or food. A child doomed to utter loneliness, growing up without sight or sound of human beings, would not put forth equal power with many brutes ; and a man, never brought

32 *

into contact with minds superior to his own, will probably run one and the same dull round of thought and action to the end of life.

It is chiefly through books that we enjoy intercourse with superior minds, and these invaluable means of communication are in the reach of all. In the best books, great men talk to us, give us their most precious thoughts, and pour their souls into ours. God be thanked for books. They are the voices of the distant and the dead, and make us heirs of the spiritual life of past ages. Books are the true levellers. They give to all, who will faithfully use them, the society, the spiritual presence, of the best and greatest of our race. No matter how poor I am. No matter though the prosperous of my own time will not enter my obscure dwelling. If the Sacred Writers will enter and take up their abode under my roof, if Milton will cross my threshold to sing to me of Paradise, and Shakspeare to open to me the worlds of imagination and the workings of the human heart, and Franklin to enrich me with his practical wisdom, I shall not pine for want of intellectual companionship, and I may become a cultivated man though excluded from what is called the best society in the place where I live.

To make this means of culture effectual, a man must select good books, such as have been written by right-minded and strong-minded men, real thinkers, who instead of diluting by repetition what others say, have something to say for themselves, and write to give relief to full, earnest souls; and these works must not be skimmed over for amusement, but read with fixed attention and a reverential love of truth. In selecting books, we may be aided much by those who have studied more than ourselves. But, after all, it is best to be determined in this particular a good deal by our own tastes. The best books for a man are not always those which the wise recommend, but oftener those which meet the peculiar wants, the natural thirst of his mind, and therefore awaken interest and rivet thought. And here it may be well to observe, not only in regard to books but in other respects, that self-culture must vary with the individual. All means do not equally suit us all. A man must unfold himself freely, and should respect the peculiar gifts or biases by which nature has distinguished him from others. Self-culture does not demand the sacrifice of individuality. It does not regularly apply an established machinery, for the sake of torturing every man into one rigid shape, called perfection. As the human countenance, with the same features in us all, is diversified without end in the race, and is never the same in any two individuals, so the human soul, with the same grand powers and laws, expands into an infinite variety of forms, and would be wofully stinted by modes of culture requiring all men to learn the same lesson or to bend to the same rules.

I know how hard it is to some men, especially to those who spend much time in manual labor, to fix attention on books. Let them strive to overcome the difficulty, by choosing subjects of deep interest, or by reading in company with those whom they love. Nothing can supply the place of books. They are cheering or soothing companions in solitude, illness, affliction. The wealth of both continents would not compensate for the good they impart. Let every man, if possible, gather some good books under his roof, and obtain access for himself and family to some social library. Almost any luxury should be sacrificed to this.

One of the very interesting features of our times, is the multiplication of books, and their distribution through all conditions of society. At a small expense, a man can now possess himself of the most precious treasures of English literature. Books, once confined to a few by their costliness, are now accessible to the multitude ; and in this way a change of habits is going on in society, highly favorable to the culture of the people. Instead of depending on casual rumor and loose conversation for most of their knowledge and objects of thought ; instead of forming their judgments in crowds, and receiving their chief excitement from the voice of neighbours, men are now learning to study and reflect alone, to follow out subjects continuously, to determine for themselves what shall engage their minds, and to call to their aid the knowledge, original views, and reasonings of men of all countries and ages ; and the results must be, a deliberateness and independence of judgment, and a thoroughness and extent of information, unknown in former times. The diffusion of these silent teachers, books, through the whole community, is to work greater effects than artillery, machinery, and legislation. Its peaceful agency is to supersede stormy revolutions. The culture, which it is to spread, whilst an unspeakable good to the individual, is also to become the stability of nations.

Another important means of self-culture, is to free ourselves from the power of human opinion and example, except as far as this is sanctioned by our own deliberate judgment. We are all prone to keep the level of those we live with, to repeat their words, and dress our minds as well as bodies after their fashion ; and hence the spiritless tameness of our characters and lives. Our greatest danger, is not from the grossly wicked around us, but from the worldly, unreflecting multitude, who are borne along as a stream by foreign impulse, and bear us along with them. Even the influence of superior minds may harm us, by bowing us to servile acquiescence and damping our spiritual activity. The great use of intercourse with other minds, is to stir up our own, to whet our appetite for truth, to carry our thoughts beyond their old tracks. We need connexions with great thinkers to make us thinkers too. One of the chief arts of self-culture, is to unite the childlike teachableness, which gratefully welcomes light from every human being who can give it, with manly resistance of opinions however current, of influences however generally revered, which do not approve themselves to our deliberate judgment. You ought indeed patiently and conscientiously to strengthen your reason by other men's intelligence, but you must not prostrate it before them. Especially if there springs up within you any view of God's word or universe, any sentiment or aspiration which seems to you of a higher order than what you meet abroad, give reverent heed to it; inquire into it earnestly, solemnly. Do not trust it blindly, for it may be an illusion; but it may be the Divinity moving within you, a new revelation, not supernatural but still most precious, of truth or duty; and if, after inquiry, it so appear, then let no clamor, or scorn, or desertion turn you from it. Be true to your own highest convictions. Intimations from our own souls of something more perfect than others teach, if faithfully followed, give us a consciousness of spiritual force and progress, never experienced by the vulgar of high life or low life, who march, as they are drilled, to the step of their times.

Some, I know, will wonder, that I should think the mass of the people capable of such intimations and glimpses of truth, as I have just supposed. These are commonly thought to be the prerogative of men of genius, who seem to be born to give law to the minds of the multitude. Undoubtedly nature has her nobility, and sends forth a few to be eminently "lights of the world." But it is also true that a portion of the same divine fire is given to all; for the many could not receive with a loving reverence the quickening influences of the few, were there not essentially the same spiritual life in both. The minds of the multitude are not masses of passive matter, created to receive impressions unresistingly from abroad. They are not wholly shaped by foreign instruction; but have a native force, a spring of thought in themselves. Even the child's mind outruns its lessons, and overflows in questionings which bring the wisest to a stand. Even the child starts the great problems, which philosophy has labored to solve for ages. But on this subject I cannot now enlarge. Let me only say, that the power of original thought is particularly manifested in those who thirst for progress, who are bent on unfolding their whole nature. A man who wakes up to the consciousness of having been created for progress and perfection, looks with new eyes on himself and on the world in which he lives. This great truth stirs the soul from its depths, breaks up old associations of ideas, and establishes new ones, just as a mighty agent of chemistry, brought into contact with natural substances, dissolves the old affinities which had bound their particles together, and arranges them anew. This truth particularly aids us to penetrate the mysteries of human life. By revealing to us the end of our being, it helps us to comprehend more and more the wonderful, the infinite system, to which we belong. A man in the common walks of life, who has faith in perfection, in the unfolding of the human spirit, as the great purpose of God, possesses more the secret of the universe, perceives more the harmonies or mutual adaptations of the world without and the world within him, is a wiser interpreter of Providence, and reads nobler lessons of duty in the events which pass before him, than the profoundest philosopher who wants this grand central truth. Thus illuminations, inward suggestions, are not confined to a favored few, but visit all who devote themselves. to a generous self-culture.

Another means of self-culture may be found by every man in his Condition or Occupation, be it what it may. Had I time, I might go through all conditions of life, from the most conspicuous to the most obscure, and might show how each furnishes continual aids to improvement. But I will take one example, and that is, of a man living by manual labor. This may be made the means of self-culture. For instance, in almost all labor, a man exchanges his strength for an equivalent in the form of wages, purchase-money, or some other product. In other words, labor is a system of contracts, bargains, imposing mutual obligations. Now the man, who, in working, no matter in what way, strives perpetually to fulfil his obligations thoroughly, to do his whole work faithfully, to be honest not because honesty is the best policy, but for the sake of justice, and that he may render to every man his due, such a laborer is continually building up in himself one of the greatest principles of morality and religion. Every blow on the anvil, on the earth, or whatever material he works upon, contributes something to the perfection of his nature.

Nor is this all. Labor is a school of benevolence as well as justice. A man to support himself must serve others. He must do or produce something for their comfort or gratification. This is one of the beautiful ordinations of Providence, that, to get a living, a man must be useful. Now this usefulness ought to be an end in his labor as truly as to earn his living. He ought to think of the benefit of those he works for, as well as of his own ; and in so doing, in desiring amidst his sweat and toil to serve others as well as himself, he is exercising and growing in benevolence, as truly as if he were distributing bounty with a large hand to the poor. Such a motive hallows and dignifies the commonest pursuit. It is strange, that laboring men do not think more of the vast usefulness of their toils, and take a benevolent pleasure in them on this account. This beautiful city, with its houses, furniture, markets, public walks, and numberless accommodations, has grown up under the hands of artisans and other laborers, and ought they not to take a disinterested joy in their work ? One would think, that a carpenter or mason, on passing a house which he had reared, would say to himself, " This work of mine is giving comfort and enjoyment every day and hour to a family, and will continue to be a kindly shelter, a domestic gathering-place, an abode of affection, for a century or more after I sleep in the dust ; " and ought not a generous satisfaction to spring up at the thought ? It is by thus interweaving goodness with common labors, that we give it strength and make it a habit of the soul.

Again. Labor may be so performed as to be a high impulse to the mind. Be a man's vocation what it may, his rule should be to do its duties perfectly, to do the best he can, and thus to make perpetual progress in his art. In other words, Perfection should be proposed; and this I urge not only for its usefulness to society, nor for the sincere pleasure which a man takes in seeing a work well done. This is an important means of self-culture. In this way the idea of Perfection takes root in the mind, and spreads far beyond the man's trade. He gets a tendency towards completeness in whatever he undertakes. Slack, slovenly performance in any department of life is more apt to offend him. His standard of action rises, and every thing is better done for his thoroughness in his common vocation.

There is one circumstance attending all conditions of life, which may and ought to be turned to the use of self-culture. Every condition, be it what it may, has hardships, hazards, pains. We try to escape them; we pine for a sheltered lot, for a smooth path, for cheering friends, and unbroken success. But Providence ordains storms, disasters, hostilities, sufferings; and the great question, whether we shall live to any purpose or not, whether we shall grow strong in mind and heart, or be weak and pitiable, depends on nothing so much as on our use of these adverse circumstances. Outward evils are designed to school our passions, and to rouse our faculties and virtues into intenser action. Sometimes they seem to create new powers. Difficulty is the element, and resistance the true work of a man. Self-culture never goes on so fast, as when embarrassed circumstances, the opposition of men or the elements, unexpected changes of the times, or other forms of suffering, instead of disheartening, throw us on our inward resources, turn us for strength to God, clear up to us the great purpose of life, and inspire calm resolution. No greatness or goodness is worth much, unless tried in these fires. Hardships are not on this account to be sought for. They come fast enough of themselves, and we are in more danger of sinking under, than of needing them. But when God sends them, they are noble means of self-culture, and as such, let us meet and bear them cheerfully. Thus all parts of our condition may be pressed into the service of self-improvement.

I have time to consider but one more means of self-culture. We find it in our Free Government, in our Political relations and duties. It is a great benefit of free institutions, that they do much to awaken and keep in action a nation's mind. We are told, that the education of the multitude is necessary to the support of a republic; but it is equally true, that a republic is a powerful means of educating the multitude. It is the people's University. In a free state, solemn responsibilities are imposed on every citizen; great subjects are to be discussed; great interests to be decided. The individual is called to determine measures affecting the well-being of millions and the destinies of posterity. He must consider not only the internal relations of his native land, but its connexion with foreign states, and judge of a policy which touches the whole civilized world. He is called by his participation in the national sovereignty, to cherish public spirit, a regard to the general weal. A man who purposes to discharge faithfully these obligations, is carrying on a generous self-culture. The great public questions, which divide opinion around him and provoke earnest discussion, of necessity invigorate his intellect, and accustom him to look beyond himself. He grows up to a robustness, force, enlargement of mind, unknown under despotic rule.

It may be said that I am describing what free institutions ought to do for the character of the individual, not their actual effects ; and the objection, I must own, is too true. Our institutions do not cultivate us, as they might and should ; and the chief cause of the failure is plain. It is the strength of party-spirit ; and so blighting is its influence, so fatal to self-culture, that I feel myself bound to warn every man against it, who has any desire of improvement. I do not tell you it will destroy your country. It wages a worse war against yourselves. Truth, justice, candor, fair dealing, sound judgment, self-control, and kind affections, are its natural and perpetual prey.

I do not say, that you must take no side in politics. The parties which prevail around you differ in character, principles, and spirit, though far less than the exaggeration of passion affirms ; and, as far as conscience allows, a man should support that which he thinks best. In one respect, however, all parties agree. They all foster that pestilent spirit, which I now condemn. In all of them, party-spirit rages. Associate men together for a common cause, be it good or bad, and array against them a body resolutely pledged to an opposite interest, and a new passion, quite distinct from the original sentiment which brought them together, a fierce, fiery zeal, consisting chiefly of aversion to those who differ from them, is roused within them into fearful activity. Human nature seems incapable of a stronger, more unrelenting passion. It is hard enough for an individual, when contending all alone for an interest or an opinion, to keep down his pride, wilfulness, love of victory, anger, and other personal feelings. But let him join a multitude in the same warfare, and, without singular self-control, he receives into his single breast, the vehemence, obstinacy, and vindictiveness of all. The triumph of his party becomes immeasurably dearer to him than the principle, true or false, which was the original ground of division. The conflict becomes a struggle, not for principle, but for power, for victory; and the desperateness, the wickedness of such struggles, is the great burden of history. In truth, it matters little what men divide about, whether it be a foot of land or precedence in a procession. Let them but begin to fight for it, and self-will, ill-will, the rage for victory, the dread of mortification and defeat, make the trifle as weighty as a matter of life and death. The Greek or Eastern empire was shaken to its foundation by parties, which differed only about the merits of charioteers at the amphitheatre. Party spirit is singularly hostile to moral independence. A man, in proportion as he drinks into it, sees, hears, judges by the senses and understandings of his party. He surrenders the freedom of a man, the right of using and speaking his own mind, and echoes the applauses or maledictions, with which the leaders or passionate partisans see fit that the country should ring. On all points, parties are to be distrusted; but on no one so much as on the character of opponeuts. These, if you may trust what you hear, are always men without principle and truth, devoured by selfishness, and thirsting for their own elevation, though on their country's ruin. When I was young, I was accustomed to hear pronounced with abhorrence, almost with execration, the names of men, who are now hailed by their former foes as the champions of grand principles, and as worthy of the highest public trusts. This lesson of early experience, which later years have corroborated, will never be forgotten.

Of our present political divisions I have of course nothing to say. But among the current topics of party, there are certain accusations and recriminations, grounded on differences of social condition, which seem to me so unfriendly to the improvement of individuals and the community, that I ask the privilege of giving them a moment's notice. On one side we are told, that the rich are disposed to trample on the poor ; and on the other, that the poor look with evil eye and hostile purpose on the possessions of the rich. These outcries seem to me alike devoid of truth and alike demoralizing. As for the rich, who constitute but a handful of our population, who possess not one peculiar privilege, and, what is more, who possess comparatively little of the property of the country, it is wonderful, that they should be objects of alarm. The vast and ever-growing property of this country, where is it ? Locked up in a few hands ? hoarded in a few strong boxes ? It is diffused like the atmosphere, and almost as variable, changing hands with the seasons, shifting from rich to poor, not by the violence but by the industry and skill of the latter class. The wealth of the rich is as a drop in the ocean ; and it is a well-known fact, that those men among us, who are noted for their opulence, exert hardly any political power on the community. That the rich do their whole duty ; that they adopt, as they should, the great object of the social state, which is the elevation of the people in intelligence, character, and condition, cannot be pretended ; but that they feel for the physical sufferings of their brethren, that they stretch out liberal hands for the succour of the poor, and for the support of useful public institutions, cannot be denied. Among them are admirable specimens of humanity. There is no warrant for holding them up to suspicion as the people's foes.

Nor do I regard as less calumnious the outcry against the working classes, as if they were aiming at the subversion of property. When we think of the general condition and character of this part of our population, when we recollect, that they were born and have lived amidst schools and churches, that they have been brought up to profitable industry, that they enjoy many of the accommodations of life, that most of them hold a measure of property and are hoping for more, that they possess unprecedented means of bettering their lot, that they are bound to comfortable homes by strong domestic affections, that they are able to give their children an education which places within their reach the prizes of the social state, that they are trained to the habits, and familiarized to the advantages of a high civilization; when we recollect these things, can we imagine that they are so insanely blind to their interests, so deaf to the claims of justice and religion, so profligately thoughtless of the peace and safety of their families, as to be prepared to make a wreck of social order, for the sake of dividing among themselves the spoils of the rich, which would not support the community for a month? Undoubtedly there is insecurity in all stages of society, and so there must be, until communities shall be regenerated by a higher culture, reaching and quickening all classes of the people; but there is not, I believe, a spot on earth, where property is safer than here, because, nowhere else is it so equally and righteously diffused. In aristocracies, where wealth exists in enormous masses, which have been entailed for ages by a partial legislation on a favored few, and where the multitude, after the sleep of ages, are waking up to intelligence, to self-respect, and to a knowledge of their rights, property is exposed to shocks which are not to be dreaded among ourselves. Here indeed as elsewhere, among the less prosperous members of the community, there are disappointed, desperate men, ripe for tumult and civil strife; but it is also true, that the most striking and honorable distinction of this country is to be found in the intelligence, character, and condition of the great working class. To me it seems, that the great danger to property here is not from the laborer, but from those who are making haste to be rich. For example, in this commonwealth, no act has been thought by the alarmists or the conservatives so subversive of the rights of property, as a recent law, authorizing a company to construct a free bridge, in the immediate neighbourhood of another, which had been chartered by a former legislature, and which had been erected in the expectation of an exclusive right. And with whom did this alleged assault on property originate ? With levellers ? with needy laborers ? with men bent on the prostration of the rich ? No ; but with men of business, who are anxious to push a more lucrative trade. Again, what occurrence among us has been so suited to destroy confidence, and to stir up the people against the moneyed class, as the late criminal mismanagement of some of our banking institutions ? And whence came this ? from the rich, or the poor ? From the agrarian, or the man of business ? Who, let me ask, carry on the work of spoliation most extensively in society ? Is not more property wrested from its owners by rash or dishonest failures, than by professed highwaymen and thieves? Have not a few unprincipled speculators sometimes inflicted wider wrongs and sufferings, than all the tenants of a state prison? Thus property is in more danger from those who are aspiring after wealth, than from those who live by the sweat of their brow. I do not believe, however, that the institution is in serious danger from either. All the advances of society in industry, useful arts, commerce, knowledge, jurisprudence, fraternal union, and practical Christianity, are so many hedges around honestly acquired wealth, so many barriers against revolutionary violence and rapacity. Let us not torture ourselves with idle alarms, and still more, let us not inflame ourselves against one another by mutual calumnies. Let not class array itself against class, where all have a common interest. One way of provoking men to crime, is to suspect them of criminal designs. We do not secure our property against the poor, by accusing them of schemes of universal robbery; nor render the rich better friends of the community, by fixing on them the brand of hostility to the people. Of all parties, those founded on different social conditions are the most pernicious; and in no country on earth are they so groundless as in our own.

Among the best people, especially among the more religious, there are some, who, through disgust with the violence and frauds of parties, withdraw themselves from all political action. Such, I conceive, do wrong. God has placed them in the relations, and imposed on them the duties of citizens; and they are no more authorized to shrink from these duties than from those of sons, husbands, or fathers. They owe a great debt to their country, and must discharge it by giving support to what they deem the best men and the best measures. Nor let them say, that they can do nothing. Every good man, if faithful to his convictions, benefits his country. All parties are kept in check by the spirit of the better portion of people whom they contain. Leaders are always compelled to ask what their party will bear, and to modify their measures, so as not to shock the men of principle within their ranks. A good man, not tamely subservient to the body with which he acts, but judging it impartially, criticizing it freely, bearing testimony against its evils, and withholding his support from wrong, does good to those around him, and is cultivating generously his own mind.

I respectfully counsel those whom I address, to take part in the politics of their country. These are the true discipline of a people, and do much for their education. I counsel you to labor for a clear understanding of the subjects which agitate the community, to make them your study, instead of wasting your leisure in vague, passionate talk about them. The time thrown away by the mass of the people on the rumors of the day, might, if better spent, give them a good acquaintance with the constitution, laws, history, and interests of their country, and thus establish them in those great principles by which particular measures are to be determined. In proportion as the people thus improve themselves, they will cease to be the tools of designing politicians. Their intelligence, not their passions and jealousies, will be addressed by those who seek their votes. They will exert, not a nominal, but a real influence on the government and the destinies of the country, and at the same time will forward their own growth in truth and virtue.

I ought not to quit this subject of politics, considered as a means of self-culture, without speaking of newspapers; because these form the chief reading of the bulk of the people. They are the literature of multitudes. Unhappily, their importance is not understood; their bearing on the intellectual and moral cultivation of the community little thought of. A newspaper ought to be conducted by one of our most gifted men, and its income should be such as to enable him to secure the contributions of men as gifted as himself. But we must take newspapers as they are; and a man, anxious for self-culture, may turn them to account, if he will select the best within his reach. He should exclude from his house such as are venomous or scurrilous, as he would a pestilence. He should be swayed in his choice, not merely by the ability with which a paper is conducted, but still more by its spirit, by its justice, fairness, and steady adherence to great principles. Especially, if he would know the truth, let him hear both sides. Let him read the defence as well as the attack. Let him not give his ear to one party exclusively. We condemn ourselves, when we listen to reproaches thrown on an individual and turn away from his exculpation; and is it just to read continual, unsparing invective against large masses of men, and refuse them the opportunity of justifying themselves?

A new class of daily papers has sprung up in our country, sometimes called cent papers, and designed for circulation among those who cannot afford costlier publications. My interest in the working class induced me some time ago to take one of these, and I was gratified to find it not wanting in useful matter. Two things however gave me pain. The advertising columns were devoted very much to patent medicines; and when I considered that a laboring man's whole fortune is his health, I could not but lament, that so much was done to seduce him to the use of articles, more fitted, I fear, to undermine than to restore his constitution. I was also shocked by accounts of trials in the police court. These were written in a style adapted to the most uncultivated minds, and intended to turn into matters of sport the most painful and humiliating events of life. Were the newspapers of the rich to attempt to extract amusement from the vices and miseries of the poor, a cry would be raised against them, and very justly. But is it not something worse, that the poorer classes themselves should seek occasions of laughter and merriment in the degradation, the crimes, the woes, the punishments of their brethren, of those who are doomed to bear like themselves the heaviest burdens of life, and who have sunk under the temptations of poverty? Better go to the hospital, and laugh over the wounds and writhings of the sick or the ravings of the insane, than amuse ourselves with brutal excesses and infernal passions, which not only expose the criminal to the crushing penalties of human laws, but incur the displeasure of Heaven, and, if not repented of, will be followed by the fearful retribution of the life to come.

One important topic remains. That great means of self-improvement, Christianity, is yet untouched, and its greatness forbids me now to approach it. I will only say, that if you study Christianity in its original records, and not in human creeds; if you consider its clear revelations of God, its life-giving promises of pardon and spiritual strength, its correspondence to man's reason, conscience, and best affections, and its adaptation to his wants, sorrows, anxieties, and fears ; if you consider the strength of its proofs, the purity of its precepts, the divine greatness of the character of its author, and the immortality which it opens before us, you will feel yourselves bound to welcome it joyfully, gratefully, as affording aids and incitements to self-culture, which would vainly be sought in all other means.

I have thus presented a few of the means of self-culture. The topics, now discussed, will I hope suggest others to those who have honored me with their attention, and create an interest which will extend beyond the present hour. I owe it however to truth to make one remark. I wish to raise no unreasonable hopes. I must say, then, that the means now recommended to you, though they will richly reward every man of every age who will faithfully use them, will yet not produce their full and happiest effect, except in cases where early education has prepared the mind for future improvement. They, whose childhood has been neglected, though they may make progress in future life, can hardly repair the loss of their first years ; and I say this, that we may all be excited to save our children from this loss, that we may prepare them, to the extent of our power, for an effectual use of all the means of self-culture, which adult age may bring with it. With these views, I ask you to look with favor on the recent exertions of our legislature and of private citizens, in behalf of our public schools, the chief hope of our country. The legislature has of late appointed a board of education, with a secretary, who is to devote his whole time to the improvement of public schools. An individual more fitted to this responsible office, than the gentleman who now fills it,* cannot, I believe, be found in our community ; and if his labors shall be crowned with success, he will earn a title to the gratitude of the good people of this State, unsurpassed by that of any other living citizen. Let me also recall to your minds a munificent individual, † who, by a generous donation, has encouraged the legislature to resolve on the establishment of one or more institutions called Normal Schools, the object of which is, to prepare accomplished teachers of youth, a work, on which the progress of education depends more than on any other measure. The efficient friends of education are the true benefactors of their country, and their names deserve to be handed down to that posterity, for whose highest wants they are generously providing.

There is another mode of advancing education m our whole country, to which I ask your particular attention. You are aware of the vast extent and value of the public lands of the Union. By annual sales of these, large amounts of money are brought into the national treasury, which are applied to the current expenses of the Government. For this application there is no need. In truth, the country has received detriment from the excess of its revenues. Now, I ask, why shall not the public lands be consecrated (in whole or in part, as the case may require) to the education of the people ? This measure would secure at once what the country most needs, that is, able, accomplished, quickening teachers of the whole rising generation. The present poor remuneration of instructors is a dark omen, and the only real obstacle which the cause of education has to

* Horace Mann, Esq.   † Edmund Dwight, Esq.

contend with. We need for our schools gifted men and women, worthy, by their intelligence and their moral power, to be intrusted with a nation's youth ; and, to gain these, we must pay them liberally, as well as afford other proofs of the consideration in which we hold them. In the present state of the country, when so many paths of wealth and promotion are opened, superior men cannot be won to an office so responsible and laborious as that of teaching, without stronger inducements than are now offered, except in some of our large cities. The office of instructor ought to rank and be recompensed as one of the most honorable in society ; and I see not how this is to be done, at least in our day, without appropriating to it the public domain. This is the people's property, and the only part of their property which is likely to be soon devoted to the support of a high order of institutions for public education. This object, interesting to all classes of society, has peculiar claims on those whose means of improvement are restricted by narrow circumstances. The mass of the people should devote themselves to it as one man, should toil for it with one soul. Mechanics, Farmers, Laborers ! let the country echo with your united cry, " The Public Lands for Education." Send to the public councils men who will plead this cause with power. No party triumphs, no trades-unions, no associations, can so contribute to elevate you as the measure now proposed. Nothing but a higher education can raise you in influence and true dignity. The resources of the public domain, wisely applied for successive generations to the culture of society and of the individual, would create a new people, would awaken through this community intellectual and moral energies, such as the records of no country display, and as would command the respect and emulation of the civilized world. In this grand object, the working men of all parties, and in all divisions of the land, should join with an enthusiasm not to be withstood. They should separate it from all narrow and local strifes. They should not suffer it to be mixed up with the schemes of politicians. In it, they and their children have an infinite stake. May they be true to themselves, to posterity, to their country, to freedom, to the cause of mankind.

III. I am aware, that the whole doctrine of this discourse will meet with opposition. There are not a few who will say to me, " What you tell us sounds well.; but it is impracticable. Men, who dream in their closets, spin beautiful theories ; but actual life scatters them, as the wind snaps the cobweb. You would have all men to be cultivated ; but necessity wills that most men shall work ; and which of the two is likely to prevail ? A weak sentimentality may shrink from the truth ; still it *is* true, that most men were made, not for self-culture, but for toil."

I have put the objection into strong language, that we may all look it fairly in the face. For one I deny its validity. Reason, as well as sentiment, rises up against it. The presumption is certainly very strong, that the All-wise Father, who has given to every human being reason and conscience and affection, intended that these should be unfolded ; and it is hard to believe, that He, who, by conferring this nature on all men, has made all his children, has destined the great majority to wear out a life of drudgery and unimproving toil, for the benefit of a few. God cannot have made spiritual beings to be dwarfed. In the body we see no organs created to shrivel by disuse ; much less are the powers of the soul given to be locked up in perpetual lethargy.

Perhaps it will be replied, that the purpose of the Creator is to be gathered, not from theory, but from facts ; and that it is a plain fact, that the order and prosperity of society, which God must be supposed to intend, require from the multitude the action of their hands, and not the improvement of their minds. I reply, that a social order, demanding the sacrifice of the mind, is very suspicious, that it cannot indeed be sanctioned by the Creator. Were I, on visiting a strange country, to see the vast majority of the people maimed, crippled, and bereft of sight, and were I told that social order required this mutilation, I should say, Perish this order. Who would not think his understanding as well as best feelings insulted, by hearing this spoken of as the intention of God ? Nor ought we to look with less aversion on a social system, which can only be upheld by crippling and blinding the Minds of the people.

But to come nearer to the point. Are labor and self-culture irreconcilable to each other ? In the first place, we have seen that a man, in the midst of labor, may and ought to give himself to the most important improvements, that he may cultivate his sense of justice, his benevolence, and the desire of perfection. Toil is the school for these high principles ; and we have here a strong presumption, that, in other respects, it does not necessarily blight the soul. Next we have seen, that the most fruitful sources of truth and wisdom are not books, precious as they are, but experience and observation ; and these belong to all conditions. It is another important consideration, that almost all labor demands intellectual activity, and is best carried on by those who invigorate their minds ; so that the two interests, toil and self-culture, are friends to each other. It is Mind, after all, which does the work of the world, so that the more there is of mind, the more work will be accomplished. A man, in proportion as he is intelligent, makes a given force accomplish a greater task, makes skill take the place of muscles, and, with less labor, gives a better product. Make men intelligent, and they become inventive. They find shorter processes. Their knowledge of nature helps them to turn its laws to account, to understand the substances on which they work, and to seize on useful hints, which experience continually furnishes. It is among workmen, that some of the most useful machines have been contrived. Spread education, and, as the history of this country shows, there will be no bounds to useful inventions. You think, that a man without culture will do all the better what you call the drudgery of life. Go then to the Southern plantation. There the slave is brought up to be a mere drudge. He is robbed of the rights of a man, his whole spiritual nature is starved, that he may work, and do nothing but work ; and in that slovenly agriculture, in that worn-out soil, in the rude state of the mechanic arts, you may find a comment on your doctrine, that, by degrading men, you make them more productive laborers.

But it is said, that any considerable education lifts men above their work, makes them look with disgust on their trades as mean and low, makes drudgery intolerable. I reply, that a man becomes interested in labor, just in proportion as the mind works with the hands. An enlightened farmer, who understands agricultural

chemistry, the laws of vegetation, the structure of plants,
the properties of manures, the influences of climate,
who looks intelligently on his work, and brings his knowledge to bear on exigencies, is a much more cheerful, as
well as more dignified laborer, than the peasant, whose
mind is akin to the clod on which he treads, and whose
whole life is the same dull, unthinking, unimproving toil.
But this is not all. Why is it, I ask, that we call manual
labor low, that we associate with it the idea of meanness,
and think that an intelligent people must scorn it? The
great reason is, that, in most countries, so few intelligent
people have been engaged in it. Once let cultivated
men plough, and dig, and follow the commonest labors,
and ploughing, digging, and trades, will cease to be
mean. It is the man who determines the dignity of the
occupation, not the occupation which measures the dignity of the man. Physicians and surgeons perform
operations less cleanly than fall to the lot of most mechanics. I have seen a distinguished chemist covered
with dust like a laborer. Still these men were not degraded. Their intelligence gave dignity to their work,
and so our laborers, once educated, will give dignity to
their toils. — Let me add, that I see little difference in
point of dignity, between the various vocations of men.
When I see a clerk, spending his days in adding figures,
perhaps merely copying, or a teller of a bank counting
money, or a merchant selling shoes and hides, I cannot
see in these occupations greater respectableness than in
making leather, shoes, or furniture. I do not see in
them greater intellectual activity than in several trades.
A man in the fields seems to have more chances of improvement in his work, than a man behind the counter,
or a man driving the quill. It is the sign of a narrow

mind, to imagine, as many seem to do, that there is a repugnance between the plain, coarse exterior of a laborer, and méntal culture, especially the more refining culture. The laborer, under his dust and sweat, carries the grand elements of humanity, and he may put forth ts highest powers. I doubt not, there is as genuine enthusiasm in the contemplation of nature, and in the perusal of works of genius, under a homespun garb as under finery. We have heard of a distinguished author, who never wrote so well, as when he was full dressed for company. But profound thought, and poetical inspiration, have most generally visited men, when, from narrow circumstances or negligent habits, the rent coat and shaggy face have made them quite unfit for polished saloons. A man may see truth, and may be thrilled with beauty, in one costume or dwelling as well as another ; and he should respect himself the more, for the hardships under which his intellectual force has been developed.

But it will be asked, how can the laboring classes find time for self-culture ? I answer, as I have already intimated, that an earnest purpose finds time or makes time. It seizes on spare moments, and turns larger fragments of leisure to golden account. A man, who follows his calling with industry and spirit, and uses his earnings economically, will always have some portion of the day at command ; and it is astonishing, how fruitful of improvement a short season becomes, when eagerly seized and faithfully used. It has often been observed, that they, who have most time at their disposal, profit by it least. A single hour in the day, steadily given to the study of an interesting subject, brings unexpected accumulations of knowledge. The improvements made by well-disposed pupils, in many of our country schools, which are open but three months in the year, and in our Sunday-schools, which are kept but one or two hours in the week, show what can be brought to pass by slender means. The affections, it is said, sometimes crowd years into moments, and the intellect has something of the same power. Volumes have not only been read, but written, in flying journeys. I have known a man of vigorous intellect, who had enjoyed few advantages of early education, and whose mind was almost engrossed by the details of an extensive business, but who composed a book of much original thought, in steam-boats and on horseback, while visiting distant customers. The succession of the seasons gives to many of the working class opportunities for intellectual improvement. The winter brings leisure to the husbandman, and winter evenings to many laborers in the city. Above all, in Christian countries, the seventh day is released from toil. The seventh part of the year, no small portion of existence, may be given by almost every one to intellectual and moral culture. Why is it that Sunday is not made a more effectual means of improvement? Undoubtedly the seventh day is to have a religious character; but religion connects itself with all the great subjects of human thought, and leads to and aids the study of all. God is in nature. God is in history. Instruction in the works of the Creator, so as to reveal his perfection in their harmony, beneficence, and grandeur; instruction in the histories of the church and the world, so as to show in all events his moral government, and to bring out the great moral lessons in which human life abounds; instruction in the lives of philanthropists, of saints, of men eminent for piety and virtue; all these branches of teaching enter into religion, and are appropriate to Sunday; and, through these, a vast amount of knowledge may be given to the people. Sunday ought not to remain the dull and fruitless season that it now is to multitudes. It may be clothed with a new interest and a new sanctity. It may give a new impulse to the nation's soul. — I have thus shown, that time may be found for improvement; and the fact is, that, among our most improved people, a considerable part consists of persons, who pass the greatest portion of every day at the desk, in the counting-room, or in some other sphere, chained to tasks which have very little tendency to expand the mind. In the progress of society, with the increase of machinery, and with other aids which intelligence and philanthropy will multiply, we may expect that more and more time will be redeemed from manual labor, for intellectual and social occupations.

But some will say, "Be it granted that the working classes may find some leisure; should they not be allowed to spend it in relaxation? Is it not cruel, to summon them from toils of the hand to toils of the mind? They have earned pleasure by the day's toil, and ought to partake it." Yes, let them have pleasure. Far be it from me to dry up the fountains, to blight the spots of verdure, where they refresh themselves after life's labors. But I maintain, that self-culture multiplies and increases their pleasures, that it creates new capacities of enjoyment, that it saves their leisure from being, what it too often is, dull and wearisome, that it saves them from rushing for excitement to indulgences destructive to body and soul. It is one of the great benefits of self-improvement, that it raises a people above the gratifications of the brute, and gives them pleasures

worthy of men. In consequence of the present intellectual culture of our country, imperfect as it is, a vast
amount of enjoyment is communicated to men, women,
and children, of all conditions, by books, an enjoyment
unknown to ruder times. At this moment, a number
of gifted writers are employed in multiplying entertain-
ing works. Walter Scott, a name conspicuous among
the brightest of his day, poured out his inexhaustible
mind in fictions, at once so sportive and thrilling, that
they have taken their place among the delights of all civilized nations. How many millions have been chained to
his pages! How many melancholy spirits has he steeped
in forgtfulness of their cares and sorrows! What multitudes, wearied by their day's work, have owed some
bright evening hours and balmier sleep to his magical
creations! And not only do fictions give pleasure. In
proportion as the mind is cultivated, it takes delight in
history and biography, in descriptions of nature, in trav-
els, in poetry, and even graver works. Is the laborer
then defrauded of pleasure by improvement? There
is another class of gratifications to which self-culture
introduces the mass of the people. I refer to lectures,
discussions, meetings of associations for benevolent and
literary purposes, and to other like methods of passing
the evening, which every year is multiplying among us.
A popular address from an enlightened man, who has
the tact to reach the minds of the people, is a high
gratification, as well as a source of knowledge. The
profound silence in our public halls, where these lectures
are delivered to crowds, shows that cultivation is no foe
to enjoyment. — I have a strong hope, that by the progress of intelligence, taste, and morals among all portions of society, a class of public amusements will grow

up among us, bearing some resemblance to the theatre,
but purified from the gross evils which degrade our
present stage, and which, I trust, will seal its ruin.
Dramatic performances and recitations are means of
bringing the mass of the people into a quicker sympathy
with a writer of genius, to a profounder comprehension
of his grand, beautiful, touching conceptions, than can
be effected by the reading of the closet. No commen-
tary throws such a light on a great poem or any im-
passioned work of literature, as the voice of a reader
or speaker, who brings to the task a deep feeling of his
author and rich and various powers of expression. A
crowd, electrified by a sublime thought, or softened into
a humanizing sorrow, under such a voice, partake a
pleasure at once exquisite and refined ; and I cannot but
believe, that this and other amusements, at which the
delicacy of woman and the purity of the Christian can
take no offence, are to grow up under a higher social
culture. — Let me only add, that, in proportion as culture spreads among a people, the cheapest and commonest of all pleasures, conversation, increases in delight. This, after all, is the great amusement of life,
cheering us round our hearths, often cheering our work,
stirring our hearts gently, acting on us like the balmy
air or the bright light of heaven, so silently and continually, that we hardly think of its influence. This
source of happiness is too often lost to men of all classes,
for want of knowledge, mental activity, and refinement
of feeling ; and do we defraud the laborer of his pleasure, by recommending to him improvements which will
place the daily, hourly, blessings of conversation within
his reach ?

I have thus considered some of the common objections which start up when the culture of the mass of men is insisted on, as the great end of society. For myself, these objections seem worthy little notice. The doctrine is too shocking to need refutation, that the great majority of human beings, endowed as they are with rational and immortal powers, are placed on earth, simply to toil for their own animal subsistence, and to minister to the luxury and elevation of the few. It is monstrous, it approaches impiety, to suppose that God has placed insuperable barriers to the expansion of the free, illimitable soul. True, there are obstructions in the way of improvement. But in this country, the chief obstructions lie, not in our lot, but in ourselves, not in outward hardships, but in our worldly and sensual propensities; and one proof of this is, that a true self-culture is as little thought of on exchange as in the workshop, as little among the prosperous as among those of narrower conditions. The path to perfection is difficult to men in every lot; there is no royal road for rich or poor. But difficulties are meant to rouse, not discourage. The human spirit is to grow strong by conflict. And how much has it already overcome! Under what burdens of oppression has it made its way for ages! What mountains of difficulty has it cleared! And with all this experience, shall we say, that the progress of the mass of men is to be despaired of, that the chains of bodily necessity are too strong and ponderous to be broken by the mind, that servile, unimproving drudgery is the unalterable condition of the multitude of the human race?

I conclude with recalling to you the happiest feature of our age, and that is, the progress of the mass of the people in intelligence, self-respect, and all the comforts of life. What a contrast does the present form with past times ! Not many ages ago, the nation was the property of one man, and all its interests were staked in perpetual games of war, for no end but to build up his family, or to bring new territories under his yoke. Society was divided into two classes, the high-born and the vulgar, separated from one another by a great gulf, as impassable as that between the saved and the lost. The people had no significance as individuals, but formed a mass, a machine, to be wielded at pleasure by their lords. In war, which was the great sport of the times, those brave knights, of whose prowess we hear, cased themselves and their horses in armour, so as to be almost invulnerable, whilst the common people on foot were left, without protection, to be hewn in pieces or trampled down by their betters. Who, that compares the condition of Europe a few years ago, with the present state of the world, but must bless God for the change. The grand distinction of modern times is, the emerging of the people from brutal degradation, the gradual recognition of their rights, the gradual diffusion among them of the means of improvement and happi ness, the creation of a new power in the state, the power of the people. And it is worthy remark, that this revolution is due in a great degree to religion, which, in the hands of the crafty and aspiring, had bowed the multitude to the dust, but which, in the ful ness of time, began to fulfil its mission of freedom. It was religion, which by teaching men their near rela tion to God, awakened in them the consciousness of their importance as individuals. It was the struggle for religious rights, which opened men's eyes to all their rights. It was resistance to religious usurpation, which led men to withstand political oppression. It was religious discussion, which roused the minds of all classes to free and vigorous thought. It was religion which armed the martyr and patriot in England against arbitrary power, which braced the spirits of our fathers against the perils of the ocean and wilderness, and sent them to found here the freest and most equal state on earth.

Let us thank God for what has been gained. But let us not think every thing gained. Let the people feel that they have only started in the race. How much remains to be done! What a vast amount of ignorance, intemperance, coarseness, sensuality, may still be found in our community! What a vast amount of mind is palsied and lost! When we think, that every house might be cheered by intelligence, disinterestedness, and refinement, and then remember, in how many houses the higher powers and affections of human nature are buried as in tombs, what a darkness gathers over society! And how few of us are moved by this moral desolation? How few understand, that to raise the depressed, by a wise culture, to the dignity of men, is the highest end of the social state? Shame on us, that the worth of a fellow-creature is so little felt.

I would, that I could speak with an awakening voice to the people, of their wants, their privileges, their responsibilities. I would say to them, You cannot, without guilt and disgrace, stop where you are. The past and the present call on you to advance. Let what you have gained be an impulse to something higher. Your nature is too great to be crushed. You were not created what you are, merely to toil, eat, drink, and sleep, like the inferior animals. If you will, you can rise.

No power in society, no hardship in your condition can depress you, keep you down, in knowledge, power, virtue, influence, but by your own consent. Do not be lulled to sleep by the flatteries which you hear, as if your participation in the national sovereignty made you equal to the noblest of your race. You have many and great deficiencies to be remedied; and the remedy lies, not in the ballot-box, not in the exercise of your political powers, but in the faithful education of yourselves and your children. These truths you have often heard and slept over. Awake! Resolve earnestly on Self-culture. Make yourselves worthy of your free institutions, and strengthen and perpetuate them by your intelligence and your virtues.

END OF VOL. II.